GEOGRAPHY to GCSE

Tim Bayliss

Oxford University Press

Oxford University Press, Great Clarendon Street, Oxford OX2 6DP

Oxford New York
Athens Auckland Bangkok Bogota Buenos Aires
Calcutta Cape Town Chennai Dar es Salaam
Delhi Florence Hong Kong Istanbul
Karachi Kuala Lumpur Madrid Melbourne Mexico City
Mumbai Nairobi Paris São Paulo Singapore
Taipei Tokyo Toronto Warsaw
and associated companies in Berlin Ibadan

Oxford is a trade mark of Oxford University Press

© Tim Bayliss 1998

ISBN 0 19 913397 2

First published 1998

Dedicated to Robert A. Bayliss

All rights reserved. No part of this publication may be reproduced, stored in a retrieval system, or transmitted, in any form or by any means, without the prior permission in writing of Oxford University Press. Within the UK, exceptions are allowed in respect of any fair dealing for the purpose of research or private study, or criticism or review, as permitted under the Copyright, Designs and Patents Act, 1988, or in the case of reprographic reproduction in accordance with the terms of licences issued by the Copyright Licensing Agency. Enquiries concerning reproduction outside those terms and in other countries should be sent to the Rights Department, Oxford University Press, at the address above.

Editorial and design by Hart McLeod, Cambridge

Typeset in Perpetua and Ocean

Printed in Spain by Gráficas Estella, S.A.

Acknowledgements

The author would like to thank Lucy Toffolo for commenting on the first draft and Rona Stewart for help with the index.

The publisher and authors would like to thank the following for permission to reproduce photographs and other copyright material:

Front cover image of lone euphorbia tree on savanna from Britstock-IFA.

J. Allan Cash Photo Library pages 17, 20, 23, 30, 32 (top & middle), 33 (bottom), 55 (right), 65, 72 (bottom), 91 (left), 96, 105 (left & right), 137.

Bruce Coleman pages 14, 15 (bottom), 16, 46 (top), 47, 62, 64, 72 (top & middle), 80 (top & bottom), 81, 82, 98, 99 (top), 131, 157 (left & right).

Popperfoto (Reuters) pages 19 Peter Kujundzic, 135, 138, 141, 142 Mohammad Shahidullah, 145, 155 Kimimasa Mayama.

STILL Pictures pages 7 Martin Wright; 15 (top) Nigel Dickinson; 15 (middle), 45, 88 (top) Jorgen Schytte; 43, 68, 88 (bottom) Mark Edwards; 46 (bottom) Mikkel Ostergaard; 51 André Maslennikov; 69 (top) Dylan Garcia; 89 (left & right), 91 (top right) Hartmut Schwarzbach; 90 Ron Giling; 91 (bottom right), 129 John Maier.

Telegraph Colour Library pages 27, 29, 32 (bottom), 33 (top, 2nd & 3rd from top), 37, 42, 44, 55 (left), 57, 63 (top & bottom), 66, 69 (bottom), 99 (bottom), 100 (top & bottom), 101 (left & right), 107, 116, 133 (top & bottom), 147, 150, 159.

Charlie Gray page 87.

Mark Snyder, Sygma page 139.

The Ordnance Survey map extracts on pages 84 and 85 are reproduced with the permission of the Controller of Her Majesty's Stationery Office © Crown Copyright.

Illustrations by Sheila Betts
Computer-generated layout by Keely Gilchrist

Every effort has been made to trace and contact copyright holders of material reproduced in this book. Any omissions will be rectified in subsequent printings if notice is given to the publisher.

Introduction

The challenge and relevance of Geography is undeniable. Indeed, it increases daily as our world becomes ever more complex. Geography makes the outside world make sense: it opens eyes and widens horizons. Furthermore, its importance is enhanced by its popularity at examination level where numbers opting to study the subject speak for themselves.

Key coverage of topics and issues examined by competing Examination Boards is intended – in a cost-effective format designed to reinforce study of class notes. Double page spreads normally start with key points to understand – effectively summarising the topics and issues covered and end with question sections. Test yourself questions include comprehension questions covering basic knowledge and understanding, such as key definitions, plus practice in examination skills. Stretch yourself challenges, to extend students aiming for higher grades, are also included, along with occasional examination advice. (Outline answers to these test and stretch yourself questions at the end of the book, are a revision source in themselves.)

Finally, illustrative material throughout – whether maps, diagrams, photographs or case studies – is intended to both reinforce and enhance the basic text.

Contents

HUMAN THEMES

Population
World population distribution	2
Factors discouraging and encouraging settlement	3
World population growth	4
Population distribution and growth: Egypt	6
Facts about Egypt	6
Overpopulation	7
Reasons for population change	8
The demographic transition model	9
Population structure	10
Can we expect to live to 130?	11
Cycles of misery	12
Problems facing farming in ELDCs	12
Diets and diseases	13
• Primary health care	14

Migration
Types of migration	16
West Indian immigration into Britain	17
• Migration in the European Union	18

Settlement
What is a settlement?	20
Settlement origin, growth, development and change: Kingston upon Hull	21
Settlement hierarchy, spacing, and service provision	22
Urbanisation and urban growth	24
Millionaire and super cities	25
Urban problems – and solutions – in ELDCs	26
Rural to urban migration	26
• Calcutta: a super city under pressure	28
Urban land-use zones and models	30
• Distinctive urban land-use zones in Britain	32

Planning
Organised urban change	34
Copenhagen: a planning example for all?	34
• London Docklands redevelopment	36

Transport
Transport and urban traffic management	38
Traffic management in Kingston upon Hull	39

ECONOMIC THEMES

Farming
Farming as a system	40
ELDC extensive farming systems	42
Pastoral nomadism: the Fulani of West Africa	42
Shifting cultivation: the Amerindians of Amazonia, Brazil	43
ELDC intensive farming systems	44
Plantation agriculture: rubber in Malaysia	44
Intensive subsistence rice cultivation: Ganges Valley, India and Bangladesh	45
• The Green Revolution	46
Farming in Britain	48
The European Union	50
The Common Agricultural Policy (CAP)	51
An EU problem region: southern Italy	52
Farming and public awareness	54
Soil erosion and management: Loch Leven, Scotland	55
A multi-purpose river project: the Aswan High Dam, Egypt	56

Energy
Sources of energy	58
Coal in Britain	60
Selby: a future for deep coalmining?	61
Oil and natural gas	62
North Sea oil and gas	63
Hydroelectric power	64
HEP location requirements	64
Nuclear power	66
Nuclear power location factors	66
The nuclear debate	67
ELDC energy: a case for alternatives?	68
Renewable sources of energy	69
Energy and the environment	70
Energy production: the effects on the environment	71

Industry
Employment structure	72
The sectors of industry	72
Industrial systems and location factors	74
Industrial location factors	75

Industrial location at global, national and local scales	76	Multinational companies in EMDCs and ELDCs	90
The reasons for industrial decentralisation	77	**Development**	
● *Two nations?*	78	World development characteristics	92
Industrial activity and pollution	80	W. W. Rostow's model of economic growth	92
The Lower Swansea Valley	81	World development measures	94
The iron and steel industry: development and change	82	Types of correlation	94
Historical background	82	**Trade**	
Steel making in Scunthorpe	83	World trade	96
● *OS map skills*	84	GATT and WTO	97
The micro-electronics industry: Silicon Glen and science parks	86	**Tourism**	
Manufacturing industry in ELDCs	88	Tourism	98
Reasons for the lack of industrial development in ELDCs	88	The seasonal nature of tourism	99
Examples of industries likely to develop in ELDCs	89	● *Tourism in an EMDC – Switzerland … and an ELDC – Kenya*	100
Multinational companies and aid	90		

ENVIRONMENTAL THEMES

Recreation		Savanna grasslands	130
National Parks	102	Fire!	131
● *Malham – a typical honeypot location*	104	Deserts	132
Landforms		***Hazards***	
Limestone landforms	106	Natural hazards and disasters	134
Glacial landforms of erosion	108	Tropical revolving storms	136
Glacial landforms of deposition	110	Disaster prevention and mitigation	137
Coastal landforms of erosion	112	● *Hurricane Gilbert*	138
Coastal landforms of deposition	114	Floods	140
Coastal management	115	Flooding in Bangladesh	142
River landforms	116	The Flood Action Plan	143
Water		Tsunamis	143
Drainage basins and storm hydrographs	118	Mass movements	144
The hydrological (water) cycle	118	Frost shattering	144
Weather		● *Avalanches*	146
Weather recording	120	The unstable earth: plate tectonics	148
Temperature and rainfall	122	Volcanoes	150
Depressions and anticyclones	124	Mount Etna	151
Wind	125	Earthquakes	152
Climate		Measuring 'quakes	152
World climates	126	● *The Kobe earthquake, Japan*	154
Environments		Drought	156
Tropical rainforests	128	Desertification	158
		Global warming: the greenhouse effect	160
		Greenhouse gases	161

ANSWERS TO TEST AND STRETCH YOURSELF QUESTIONS	162
INDEX	171

World population distribution

Key points

▶ World population is spread unevenly – dense in some areas, sparse in others.

▶ Both physical and human factors affect world population distribution.

Relief, drainage and climate vary around the world. So does the distribution of population. This unit will investigate whether these two facts are related.

- A **population distribution** map shows us where people live and where they do not.

- A **population density** map shows us how many people live in a certain area – whether an area is crowded, moderately or sparsely populated.

Global population is very unevenly spread. For example, nearly two-thirds of humanity live in Asia, yet this is only one-third of the land surface. Within each continent the uneven spread continues. Some areas are densely populated, whilst others are very sparse.

It is often easier to explain the virtually uninhabited parts of the world than many of the more densely populated parts. Mountainous, cold, or arid zones limit farming and mostly deter settlement although some people do inhabit hostile areas if there are, for example, valuable resources to exploit.

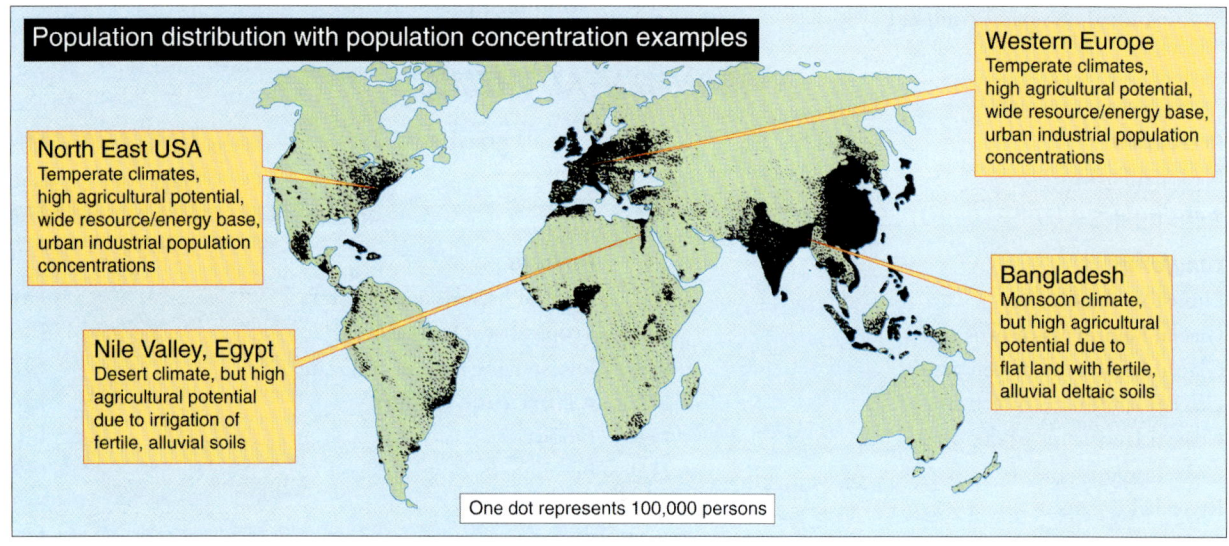

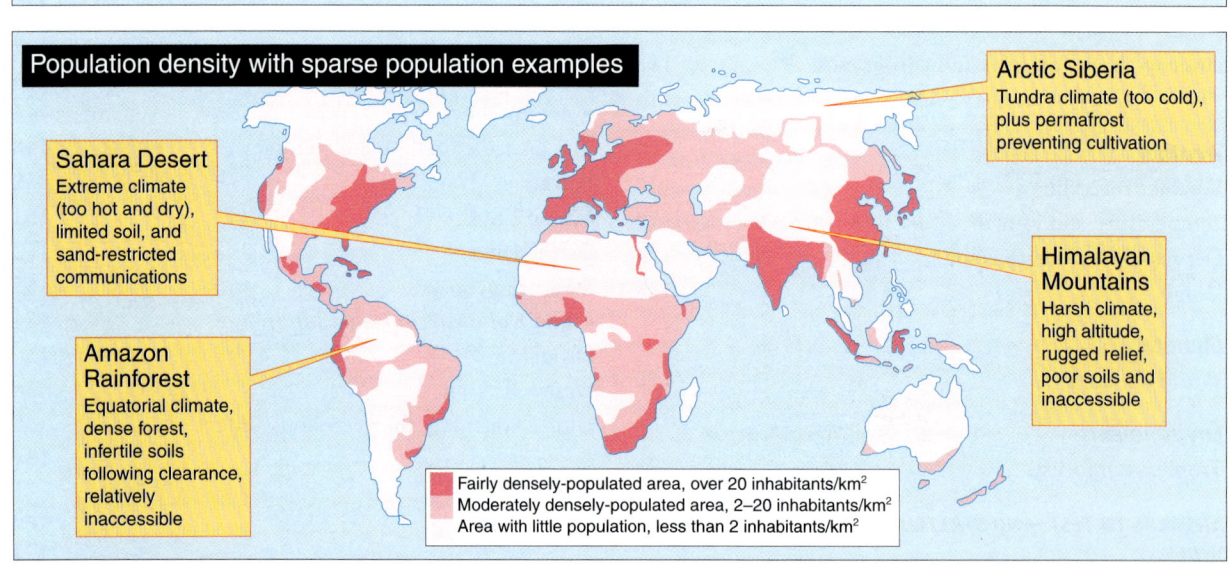

The table provides a list of the main factors encouraging and discouraging settlement:

Factors discouraging settlement		Factors encouraging settlement
Steep gradients and rugged terrain are difficult to cultivate and restrict movement.	**RELIEF**	Lowland plains and river valleys with gentle or flat relief encourage settlement.
There are few settlements above 5000m. The thinner atmosphere and low temperatures restrict comfortable habitation.	**ALTITUDE**	Of the world's people, 80% live below 500m, and over 50% below 200m.
Both extremes of temperature and aridity (dryness) deter settlers.	**CLIMATE**	Temperate climates (not too hot or cold, wet or dry) provide ideal conditions – yet vast numbers live in S and SE Asia, which has a monsoon climate (see page 126).
Thin and/or infertile soils limit farming.	**SOILS**	Rich, fertile, alluvial and deltaic soils encourage farming.
This can deter settlement if difficult to clear, or if cleared land is of low agricultural potential. (Tropical rainforest exploitation, for example, has been restricted until recent decades because of this.)	**NATURAL VEGETATION**	Areas easy to clear, such as European deciduous forests, often reveal fertile land to farm.
Areas with few or inaccessible mineral and energy resources limit development.	**NATURAL RESOURCES**	Readily available resources encourage exploitation followed by urban and industrial development.
Earthquake, flood, and tropical revolving storm zones prove less of a threat than logic might suggest. Pests, such as tsetse fly and mosquitoes prove a greater deterrent.	**NATURAL HAZARDS**	Tectonically stable areas offer no threat, just like moderate climates. Yet very dense populations are still found in the most hazardous locations, such as the flood plains of Bangladesh.

Test yourself

1. What is the difference between population distribution and population density maps?

2. Copy and complete the following sentences selecting from the alternatives given:

Population distribution/density is shown by choropleth mapping. This technique uses progressively darker/lighter shades to indicate increasing population distribution/density.

Stretch yourself

The world population distribution and density maps have been annotated with selected examples of both crowded and relatively empty areas.

Choose additional examples from areas studied, locate them on the maps, and plan appropriate captions.

World population growth

Key points

▶ *Human evolution is thought to extend over a million years.*

▶ *Numbers grew steadily, controlled by disease and conflict, until the 18th century.*

▶ *Today growth is moderate in rich economically more developed countries (EMDCs) – and rapid in poor economically less developed countries (ELDCs).*

The earth is 4600 million years old. However, human evolution can only be traced back, with any certainty, to just beyond 1 million years.

The oldest fossil remains of early human beings were found in sites in North and East Africa, most notably the Omo Valley in Ethiopia, and what was known as Mesopotamia in West Asia. People are unsure exactly how, and when, humans spread from these areas, westwards into Europe, and eastwards into Asia.

Clearly the racial characteristics associated with different parts of the globe indicate long periods of further evolution since these migrations.

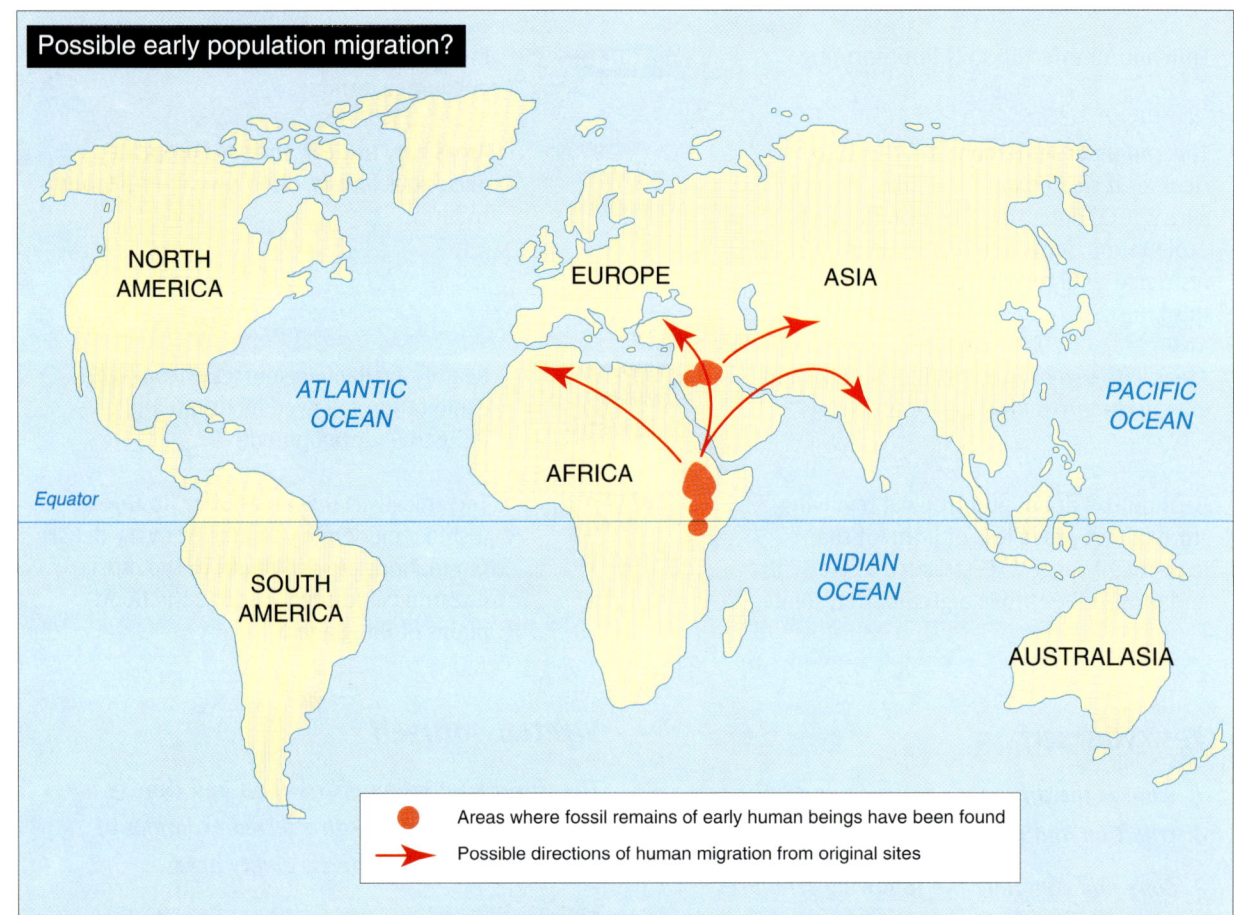

The growth shown is not uniform throughout the world. The rate of increase in rich, economically more developed countries (EMDCs) of the North is generally very slow, and in some cases virtually non-existent. The so-called population explosion is primarily a feature of economically less developed countries (ELDCs) of the South. But remember – it is not so much the numbers which are the problem, but how to feed, house, clothe, occupy and fulfil them.

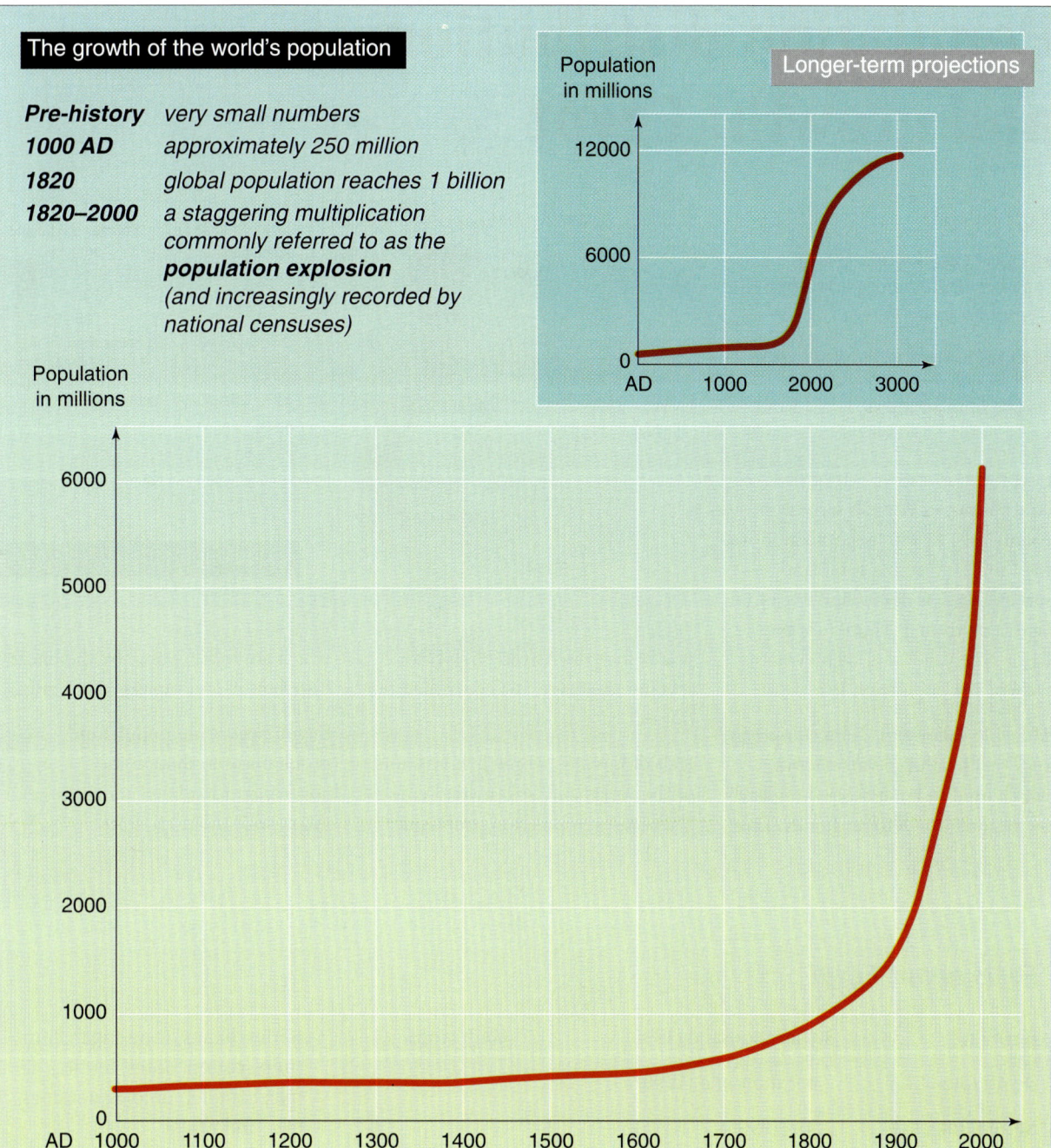

The growth of the world's population

Pre-history   very small numbers
1000 AD   approximately 250 million
1820   global population reaches 1 billion
1820–2000   a staggering multiplication commonly referred to as the **population explosion** (and increasingly recorded by national censuses)

Test yourself

1. What is the population explosion?

2. What relationship between births and deaths determines population growth rates? (Page 8 will help.)

Stretch yourself

The Longer term projections graph indicates gradual changes to the rate of world population growth. What assumptions have been made by these forecasters regarding economic development and population control programmes?

HUMAN THEMES • POPULATION

Population distribution and growth: Egypt

Key points

▶ Egypt's population is very concentrated along the River Nile and on its delta.

▶ Egypt's rapid population growth is now being addressed by sensitive planning.

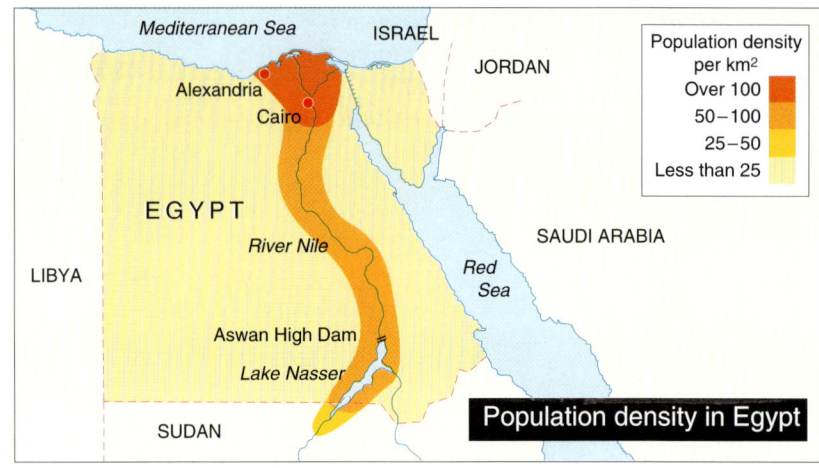

Population density in Egypt

Egypt, the so-called 'gift of the Nile', is one of Africa's largest countries. In 1996 its population was 63.7 million. Of the total land surface, 96% is desert and 4% of the land is cultivated. This 4% is the River Nile Valley and Delta where 99% of the population live.

The Nile Valley and Delta comprises very fertile alluvial volcanic silt, which used to be deposited regularly by the June to October floods. This was before the Aswan High Dam scheme (see page 56) controlled the flow.

Half of Egypt's people live in some of the world's most crowded cities. This causes population problems which are made worse by the linear distribution and rapid growth rate.

Egypt faces acute population problems even though the government has been addressing them since the mid-1950s.

Facts about Egypt

Birth rate	30 per thousand (1996)	Main crops	Barley, beans, cane sugar, citrus fruits, cotton, dates, lentils, maize, millet, onions, potatoes, rice, and wheat
Death rate	7 per thousand (1996)		
Natural increase	2.3% (1996)		
GNP per capita	$710 (1994)	Main products	Cement, cotton goods, fertilisers, iron and steel, processed food, and textiles
Official language	Arabic		
Religion	Islam (Sunni), also Christian minority	Major imports	Cereals and other foodstuffs, chemicals, hides, iron and steel, machinery, rubber, transport equipment, and wool
Ethnic groups	Egyptian Arabs. Also Nubian, Sudanese and Bedouin minorities		
Major minerals	Asbestos, iron, manganese, phosphates	Major exports	Citrus fruits, cotton, dates, onions, potatoes, petroleum products, and phosphates

A number of facts show the present situation:

- Egypt's population is growing more rapidly than domestic food production.
- Today over 50% of the country's food has to be imported.
- Egypt now has a greater total population than Britain, and four times its land area.
- The low rainfall virtually limits agriculture to the irrigated lands of the Nile Valley and Delta.
- As its population has grown, so has the cultivated area, principally through the construction of the Aswan High Dam during the 1960s.

One approach was via family planning.

Family planning clinics were slowly introduced but, even by the late 1970s, only one in five women benefited from their services. The initiative was only really successful in the largest urban areas, such as Cairo and Alexandria. In the rural areas of Upper Egypt people still saw it as important to produce sufficient children – to ensure parental security in old age and the maintenance of the succession.

The Egyptian approach was seen by some people to be too clinical, and too often male-dominated. It also came from an urban viewpoint, not universally acceptable in rural areas. Consequently, a more sensitive policy of village-based family planning was adopted. Known as the 'grass roots approach', the initiative centred on training respected female volunteers from the villages in many aspects of **primary health care** (see page 14). Education concentrated on the long-term benefits and means of birth control. One approach – house-to-house counselling, advice and distribution of contraceptives – has proved both successful and cost-effective.

Egypt's population growth rate has declined steadily since this new approach was adopted. Half the married women now use contraception and families are becoming smaller. The policy is also helping in the planning of similar programmes in other ELDCs.

Overpopulation

Egypt represents a situation of **overpopulation**. This is when an area has too many people for the available resources and technology. The population, on average, has an inadequate standard of living.
Overpopulation can occur in densely, moderately and even sparsely populated areas depending on their circumstances.

Most **population control programmes** aim to reduce growth rates in order to achieve an **optimum** (ideal) level whereby the population is at its most productive and enjoys a reasonable standard of living.
It is mostly the highly industrialised countries of Europe and North America that can support higher densities of population.

Too many people: too little space.

Test yourself

1. Study the map showing population density in Egypt. How does this show Egypt's population distribution to be linear?

2. What is primary health care? (Page 14 will help.)

3. Define overpopulation.

Stretch yourself

List the reasons why other ELDCs are adopting Egypt's revised approach to family planning programmes.

Reasons for population change

Key points

- ▶ Populations change due to births, deaths and movements (migrations).
- ▶ Death rates fall due to improvements in health, hygiene, diet and living conditions.
- ▶ Birth rates fall due to female emancipation, later marriages and schooling.
- ▶ The demographic transition model shows population change as a country develops.

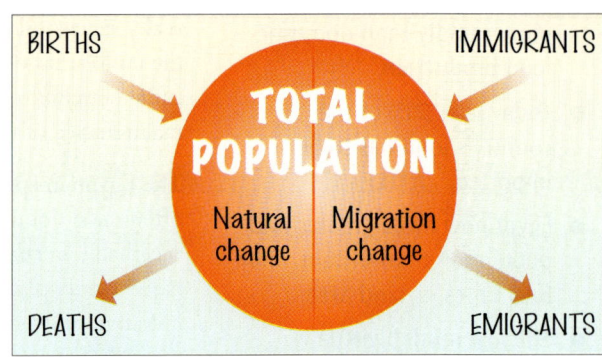

The **birth rate (BR)** is the number of live births for every 1000 members of an area's population in one year.

High birth rate: 50 per 1000 (Afghanistan, 1996)
Low birth rate: 9 per 1000 (Germany, 1996)

The **death rate (DR)** is the number of deaths per 1000 per year.

High death rate: 22 per 1000 (Afghanistan, 1996)
Low death rate: 7 per 1000 (Canada, 1996)

The natural increase (NI) is the difference between birth rate and death rate.

NI = BR − DR

The greater the difference between birth and death rate, the greater the natural increase – and so the faster the rate of population growth. A high rate would be more than 2.5% – a low rate less than 1%.

Changes in the death rate

Prior to the Industrial Revolution, high death rates due to plagues, diseases, famines, and other hazards controlled world population growth. Since then, hygiene and medical care have improved; more people survive long enough to have their own children, and they live longer. However, the improvements are not universally spread. In many countries, large numbers of people suffer from **debilitating diseases** (which make them unfit to work efficiently) and illnesses which kill.

The pattern is uneven. For example, the so-called **diseases of affluence**, such as heart disease and cancer, kill many in EMDCs. Infectious diseases, such as dysentery and malaria, tend to affect more people in ELDCs.

Infectious diseases are spread by insects, and contaminated food and water. Public hygiene, therefore, is very influential in reducing death rates. Likewise, inoculations and vaccinations prevent diseases spreading, and improved medicines allow more illnesses to be cured. Diets have improved, and famines reduced. This is due to improvements in agriculture, and to the distribution and storage of food. Of most note, however, is that all these advances have taken far longer to significantly affect the populations of ELDCs. It is only recently that 'death control' has become markedly evident in the South.

Changes in the birth rate

In ELDCs it is common for children to work, to grow food and to earn money. If children are not allowed to work, as in EMDCs, they must be supported by their parents, who are likely to have fewer babies as a result. Schooling, particularly of girls, is of key significance, and not simply as the alternative to employment. Studies in Latin America have demonstrated that schooling delays the age of marriage, so reducing the potential years of fertility. Educated women in both EMDCs and ELDCs have more career opportunities, and enjoy higher standards of living, with fewer children.

Parents in ELDCs, who have had schooling, are more likely to understand both hygiene and birth control. This enables them to plan their families with the confidence that their own children will survive. Government planning and provision of health care, pensions and welfare benefits reduces the need for children to support parents when illness, or age, prevents them from working. The encouragement of family planning programmes, such as in Egypt (see page 7), is normally a central component of ELDC development plans.

The demographic transition model

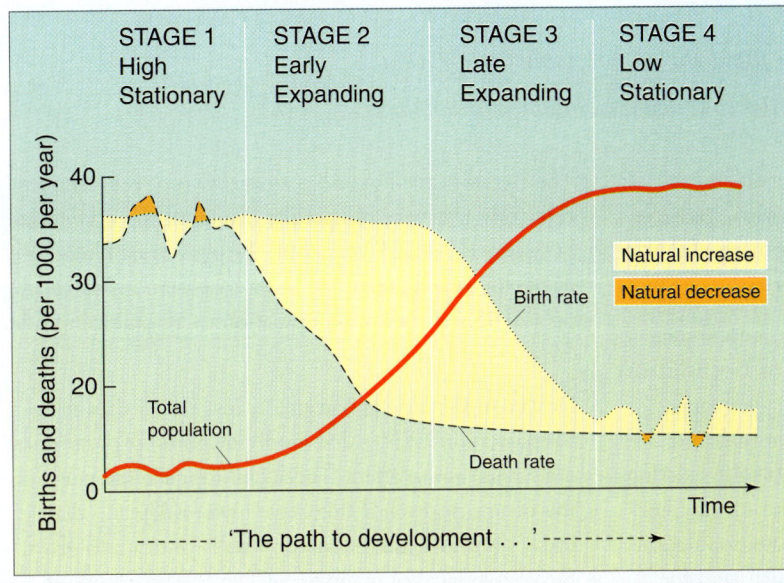

This model is based on Europe's experience of changing population. The four distinct stages could be viewed as 'a path to development' with many ELDCs currently in stage 2 or entering stage 3. Most advanced, industrialised EMDCs are now in stage 4 (there could even be need to recognise a stage 5 representing population decline). However, it cannot be assumed that all countries will pass through a similar demographic transition. Countries in Africa, Asia and Latin America have widely differing environments, racial, cultural and historical backgrounds. Foreign aid, and investment in agriculture, education and family planning programmes are certainly shortening the time scales within each stage.

Stage one (high fluctuating)
High birth rates are accompanied by high fluctuating death rates as population is checked by epidemics of disease, famine and war. Population growth is slow and intermittent. Europe was like this 200 years ago. Now, however, even the least economically developed countries of the South, such as Niger, are emerging from this stage.

Stage two (early expanding)
Birth rates stay high and may increase marginally, but death rates decline as diseases are controlled by better medical services, hygiene, sanitation and diets. Population growth is rapid and accelerating as the gap between birth rate and death rate widens. Britain went through this stage between 1780 and 1880, whereas now it is characteristic of many ELDCs.

Stage three (late expanding)
The birth rate starts to fall as economic development and education encourage smaller families, made possible by birth control. The lower death rate reflects the control of major diseases, and improved standards of health and sanitation. Population growth continues, but at a progressively slower rate. Britain went through this stage, slowly, between 1880 and 1940. Other EMDCs went through it very quickly, such as Japan from 1950 to 1960.

Stage four (low fluctuating)
Both birth rate and death rate fluctuate around a low level, resulting in occasional periods of population stagnation and /or decline. The stage is characteristic of highly developed societies where standards of living are high, such as Britain and Japan today.

Test yourself

1. Express as a percentage: (a) a high rate (b) a low rate of population growth.

2. What is meant by the terms: (a) debilitating diseases (b) diseases of affluence?

Stretch yourself

It has been said that 'development is the best contraceptive'. Why, in countries like Egypt, should this simple assumption be regarded critically?

Population structure

Key points

▶ Information about different age groups in an area is shown by population pyramids.

▶ Young populations, with potential for rapid growth, are common in ELDCs.

▶ Ageing populations in EMDCs represent a so-called population time bomb.

We tend to assume that the 'population problem' is simply one of 'too many people in the world'. Perhaps, however, the problem is one of age – too many children in ELDCs, and too many aged in EMDCs.

The ages of people in a country's population is shown diagrammatically using age-sex pyramids or **population pyramids**. These show us how different age groups within the population are divided between male and female. The shape of the 'pyramid' indicates the existing age-sex structure. From this we can work out the likely level of development, the proportion of the population dependent on others (the dependency ratio), and the probable immediate future growth trends.

The pyramid for Egypt has a narrow top, representing relatively few very old people. Much of the population is between 15 and 35 years old, the ages most likely to have children. Indeed, the wide base demonstrates a high proportion of the total population to be children under 15 years old.

However, the base is marginally less flared than it has been, demonstrating that family planning programmes are having some effect. These children are the parents of the future, so even if they have fewer offspring than today's parents, the population will continue to grow. Egypt is typical of many ELDCs in having a **young population**.

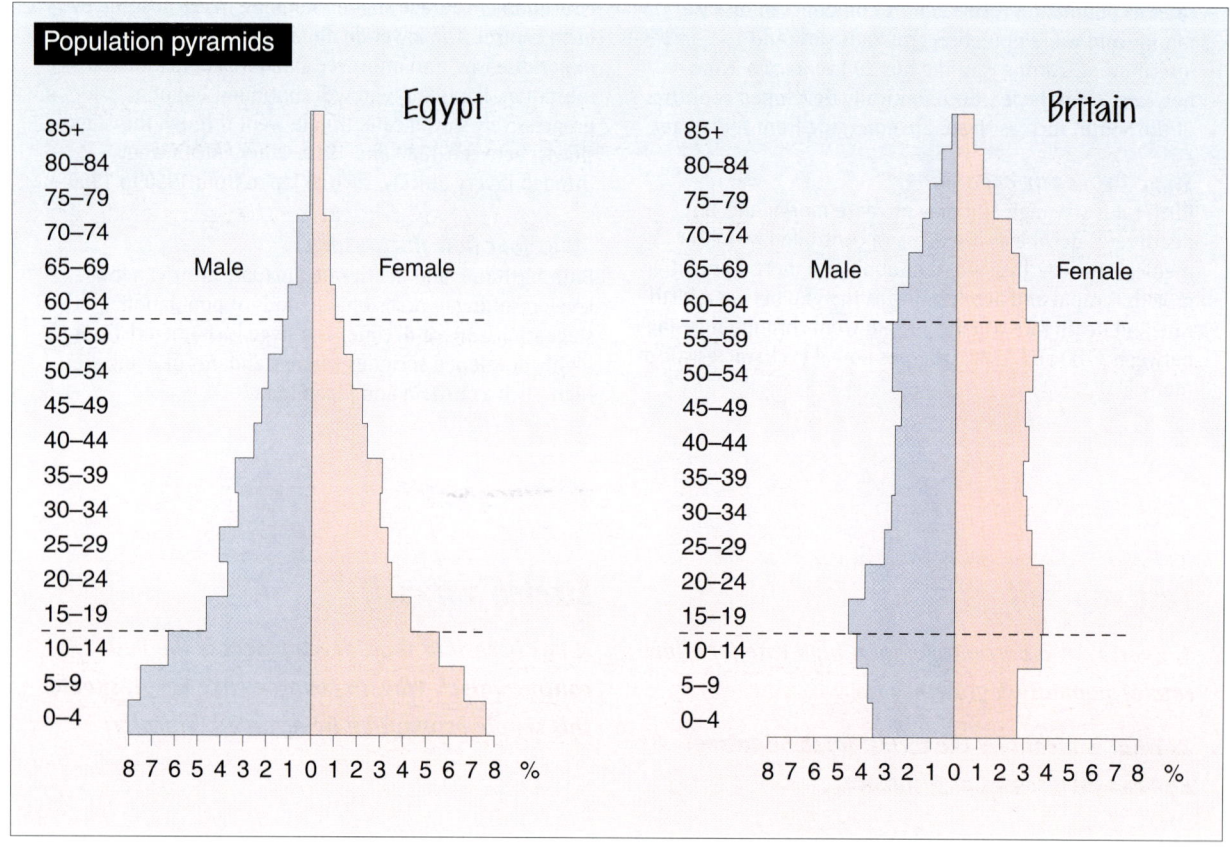

Population pyramids

HUMAN THEMES • POPULATION

In contrast, the pyramid for Britain is much more 'pillar like'. The wider top demonstrates the high proportion of elderly people, especially women, surviving beyond their seventies. Of particular note, however, is that there are relatively similar numbers of adults aged between 15-30 as children under 15. Should, as seems likely, these children grow up to have similar-sized families, then the numbers of babies born will stay roughly the same as now. Population growth will continue to be very slow, with occasional periods of stagnation and, even, decline. This British situation is typical of many EMDCs with an **ageing population**.

Dependency ratios show the number of children and elderly people that the working population has to support. The ratio compares the working population to the dependent population.

$$\text{Dependency ratio} = \frac{\text{dependent population}}{\text{working population}} \times 100$$

As a general rule, EMDCs have lower dependency ratios (50-70) than ELDCs (often over 100) – usually because of the high proportion of children in the latter. However, dependency ratios in EMDCs are getting higher as more and more people live longer, yet retire earlier.

Can we expect to live to 130?

Some biologists and demographers believe that with healthier environments and lifestyles, some children born today could live to be 130. Certainly, by the middle of the 21st century, such a life expectancy – double that of present – could be the norm. Key factors could include:

- *less polluting environments*
- *safer working conditions*
- *better diets*
- *less smoking and alcohol consumption.*

The social and economic consequences of such life expectancy could be alarming. It is already certain that, by the turn of the century:

- *there will be twice as many people aged over 60 as there were in 1970*
- *the over-80s will also double in this time period*
- *a dwindling proportion of tax payers will have to cover the pensions*
- *governments may have to shift resources from child welfare to, for example, geriatric provision*
- *immigration policies may need revision, in order to swell the workforce.*

All of these issues graphically demonstrate why long-term demographic planning is essential – now.

Test yourself

1. What is a population pyramid?
2. What is a dependency ratio?
3. Copy and complete the following sentences selecting from the alternatives given: Population problems in ELDCs could be summarised as too many children/aged and slow/rapid growth. In EMDCs, however, the problem is usually a/an declining/ageing population.

Stretch yourself

Outline the contrasting population problems facing ELDCs and EMDCs in terms of numbers, structures, and future prospects.

Cycles of misery

Key points

▶ Low productivity, poverty and ill health in ELDCs are interrelated in 'cycles'.

▶ Problems facing farming in ELDCs make these cycles difficult to reverse.

▶ Diseases in ELDCs are related to both poor diets and infections.

ELDCs probably have the potential to produce enough food for their ever-increasing populations. To realise that potential ELDCs need support (through finance, technology and advice) to break out of the poverty trap.

However, at present, low productivity is the norm, as many are trapped in vicious cycles of misery relating to ill health and poverty.

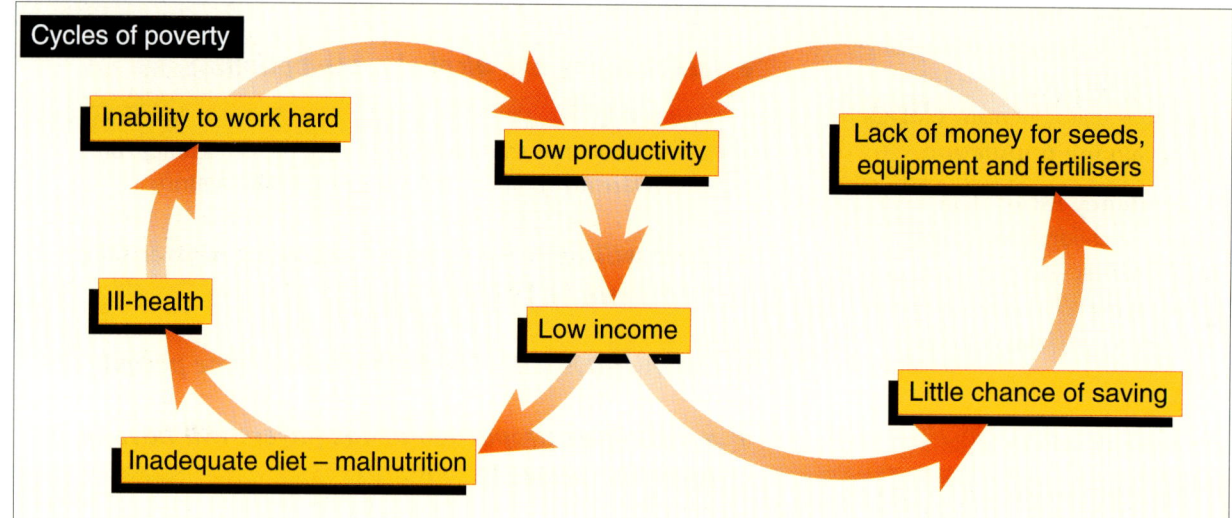

Problems facing farming in ELDCs

Climate
Many ELDCs have difficult climates. South Asian countries, such as India and Bangladesh for example, depend on the monsoon rains arriving on time. Semi-desert areas, such as Ethiopia, lack sufficient rain. Rainforest areas when cleared, such as the Amazon Basin, are exposed to soil erosion.

Pests
Eg. locusts, tsetse fly, cotton leaf worm. There may be little money for pesticides.

Diseases
Eg. malaria, bilharzia, river blindness. These affect crops, animals, and people. They also effectively restrict the areas where people can farm.

Lack of market
Some farmers probably could increase production if there was an incentive to do so – such as a market and the means to get to it.

Inaccessibility
Some areas are so remote that markets (even when they do exist) are inaccessible due to insufficient and poor roads.

Very small farms
Ever increasing population means less and less land to go round. Small inherited plots make it uneconomic to use machinery – even if it could be afforded.

Fragmented (scattered) plots
These are a particular problem where peasants are forced to rent additional land in order to supplement their own. As a result, land reform is a high priority for many governments.

Diets and diseases

Higher death rates are associated with a lower resistance to disease caused by malnutrition, and environmental conditions which foster germs or encourage pests.

Diet
Half the world is poorly fed – whether **undernourished**, with insufficient food, or **malnourished**, with an inadequately balanced diet.

A balanced diet should comprise:

- *60% carbohydrate*
- *20% protein*
- *20% fat*
- *roughage*
- *vitamins*
- *minerals.*

But an understanding of dietic composition requires education and the means to implement the knowledge.

Carbohydrates are common in abundant staple foodstuffs such as rice and maize. These foods are starchy, and in circumstances of rapid population growth may have to be relied upon for their bulk, rather than quality. Proteins, by contrast, are comparatively scarce. Frequently, only relatively wealthy countries can produce meat for human consumption. Also, some religions and cultures have moral objections to the eating of meat. **Deficiency diseases** caused by inadequate diet affect vulnerable, growing children with tragic results.

Diseases
Lethargy and **ill-health** related to water-borne diseases such as malaria and bilharzia (which affects 90% of Egypt's population) are proving difficult to cope with. Fly-borne diseases, such as sleeping sickness carried by the tsetse fly, likewise often quickly regenerate once the carrying pest develops a resistance to the latest pesticide.

The heat and high humidity of many tropical countries also encourages the breeding of insects and vermin. Malaria and river blindness are spread by water-borne flies. Polluted water spreads hepatitis and dysentery. Hookworm and yellow fever are also common. Natural hazards, such as floods, allow diseases such as typhoid and cholera to spread, especially when water supplies are disrupted, or relief camps overcrowded.

Increasingly, illnesses, once invariably fatal, are being brought under control. Smallpox, for example, has been virtually eradicated globally for well over a decade, due to a widespread UN inoculation programme. Also, the assumption of inevitably higher death rates in ELDCs is increasingly challenged as more and more people in EMDCs succumb to the 'diseases of affluence' associated with over-indulgence and the pressured pace of life.

Test yourself
1. What is meant by the terms: (a) low productivity (b) lethargy (c) deficiency disease (d) undernourished (e) malnourished?

Stretch yourself
Many argue that reversing vicious cycles of poverty and ill-health can be achieved, in localised situations, by appropriate investment of foreign aid or charitable donations. Assume an ELDC village situation, and substitute 'grant or loan' in the 'low income' box. Redraw the resulting cycles of virtue.

Primary health care

Home for too many people, a shanty town in Lima, Peru.

It is thought that 80% of all disease is caused by some form of polluted water, or inadequate sanitation. In consequence, the United Nations Organisation (UN) designated the 1980s as the Clean Water and Sanitation Decade.

This demonstrated an appreciation of a 'prevention rather than cure' philosophy. This belief now underlies much improvement and development planning in ELDCs. The approach will be visible in the adoption of appropriate technology to provide, say, village-based irrigation projects, or soil conservation measures. Health care, however, remains an emotive issue, not least because of the vulnerability of so many children to suffering and early death.

For example, 40,000 children die needlessly every day through measles and diarrhoea. The former could be prevented by immunisation, the latter through oral rehydration with a sugar and salt solution. Both measures are simple and cheap, certainly a realistic objective for many ELDCs, and lend moral weight to pressure for worldwide investment in primary health care schemes.

Primary Health Care (PHC) was devised by the World Health Organisation (WHO) in order to improve the health of poor people – especially children. Eight admirable and cost-effective elements have been identified:

- *Water and sanitation* – to provide everyone with clean water and basic sewerage.

- *Health education* – to inform people of the causes of ill health, the importance of hygiene, and good diet.

- *Food and nutrition* – to combat malnutrition by ensuring sufficient balanced foodstuffs are available and affordable.

- *Maternal and child health* – to promote family planning, pre- and post-natal care.

- *Disease control* – to organise inoculation programmes against common childhood diseases, such as measles.

- *Curative care* – to train village-based health workers in first-aid and diagnosis.

- *Traditional medicine* – to adopt and adapt, rather than scorn, traditional cures.

- *Essential drugs* – to identify, and manufacture locally, 200 affordable key medicines.

The cost of implementing the above is minimal when compared with global military expenditure. However, despite highly successful adoption in places such as Egypt (see page 7), worldwide implementation still remains a dream.

Primary health care ...

... self-help sanitation project, Guatemala.

... nutritional advice for mothers, India.

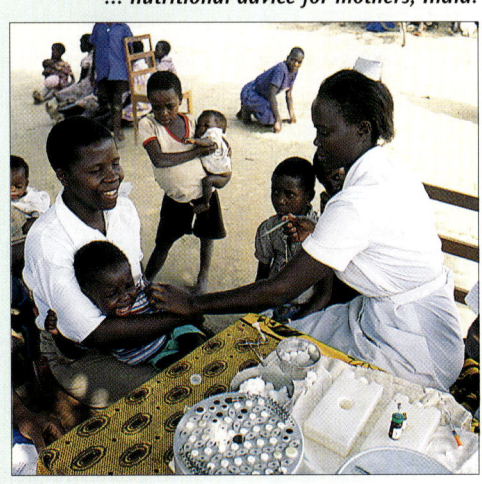

... inoculation in Uganda.

HUMAN THEMES • POPULATION   **15**

Types of migration

Key points

▶ *Migration can be temporary or permanent, voluntary or forced.*

▶ *Migration can be internal (within countries) or international (between countries).*

Migration is population movement, whether temporary or permanent, voluntary or forced. It can be at all scales, from local to international.

Temporary migrations include:

- diurnal (daily) movements to and from home, familiar to so many who commute from dormitory settlements to work or school.
- seasonal movements associated with agriculture eg. the annual cycle of transhumance still practiced in the Himalayas and Alps. (Transhumance involves animals being tended on upland pastures during the summer months, whilst fodder crops are grown in the valleys; the animals are then herded down for winter stall feeding.)
- international migrations eg. British and American oil employees working monthly, or longer, shifts in the Middle East.

Permanent migrations, by contrast, need much stronger motivations. This is because a permanent change of residence is involved.

Distance decay is noticeable with permanent migration. This means that, as distance increases, so the number of migrants decreases. For example, larger numbers move from rural to urban locations (urbanisation) within ELDCs than move abroad. Those moving abroad face the prospects of whole new cultures, climates and languages. There are also financial and legal disincentives. To make a permanent move the motivations must be very strong.

Motivation is the key difference between voluntary and forced migrations.

Voluntary migrations involve weighing up the advantages and disadvantages prior to a decision being made – normally based upon the perception that a better standard of living is achievable elsewhere. Immigration from the Caribbean to Britain in the decades immediately following World War II illustrates these dilemmas well.

Forced migrations follow natural disasters, persecution and wars. Again, the scale of such movements ranges from local to international. The numbers involved can be staggering. There were an estimated 60 million 'compulsory' migrations in the years before, during and after World War II! Such people are called refugees. Today these movements often outnumber the economic migrants discussed earlier.

The largest recorded movement in recent history followed tribal-based genocide in Rwanda, Africa. In 1994 over 1 million refugees escaped to neighbouring countries. Their plight characterised refugees of innumerable wars and famines in recent decades. Relief agencies, such as charities and the UN, are acutely aware of the extreme misery, poverty, hunger, uncertainty and fear that characterise refugees. It is their selfless workers who seek to address the suffering of these refugees – subsisting without citizenship, in sprawling camps lacking adequate shelter, water, provisions, health care, clothing and education.

Temporary dwelling in the Western Punjab.

West Indian immigration into Britain

1950s — Post-war labour shortages in Britain stimulated the government to attract many West Indians to fill specific jobs, such as with London Transport. Overpopulation and poverty in some Caribbean islands made the idea welcome.

1960s — Immigration laws were changing. Restrictions ensured that only dependant relatives or migrants with specific skills, such as doctors, could come to Britain.

1970s — Numbers were further restricted. Growth in the 'immigrant' population mostly limited to British born subsequent generations.

1970s on — Clustering in certain urban centres and districts persists with mixed consequences. The positive benefits of maintained cultural traditions are appreciated by most; the environmental and social problems associated with ethnic minority concentrations, reflect the fears and prejudices of others.

Multi-cultured Britain: opportunities for all?

In Britain, as across the world, discrimination against any ethnic, cultural or religious group different to the domestic majority is evident. British African-Caribbeans are not alone in suffering the self-perpetuating cycles of educational disadvantage, high unemployment, poverty, higher crime rates and strained police relations.

Britain is a multi-cultural (plural) society, but not, alas, fully appreciative of the national opportunities possible when all races, cultures and religions live and work together for the common good.

Test yourself

1. Give one example of each of the following types of migration: (a) temporary (b) permanent (c) voluntary (d) forced.

2. What is meant by the terms: (a) commute (b) dormitory settlement (c) economic migrant (d) refugee (e) push factor (f) pull factor?

Stretch yourself

Migration decisions are often summarised into combinations of push and pull factors.

For an internal and/or international example studied, list the relevant motivating push and pull factors.

Migration in the European Union

Migration into the countries of the European Union (EU), between them, and within them demonstrates distinctive patterns.

Immigration into EU countries

In the early years of the EU (see page 50) most countries in western Europe had more job vacancies than workers to fill them. This was because they needed to rebuild their economies and infrastructure following World War II. The 1950s, and to a lesser extent, 1960s, saw Britain and France encouraging immigration from their former colonies in, for example, the West Indies (see page 17) and North Africa.

West Germany attracted hundreds of thousands of Turkish and Yugoslav 'Gastarbeiter' (guest workers) into farming, manufacturing industry and construction. Many of these jobs were regarded, by increasingly affluent Germans, as unattractive and poorly paid. But income and living standards, internationally, are relative. The immigrants, therefore, were attracted by what they saw as higher paid work with better housing, health care and educational opportunities.

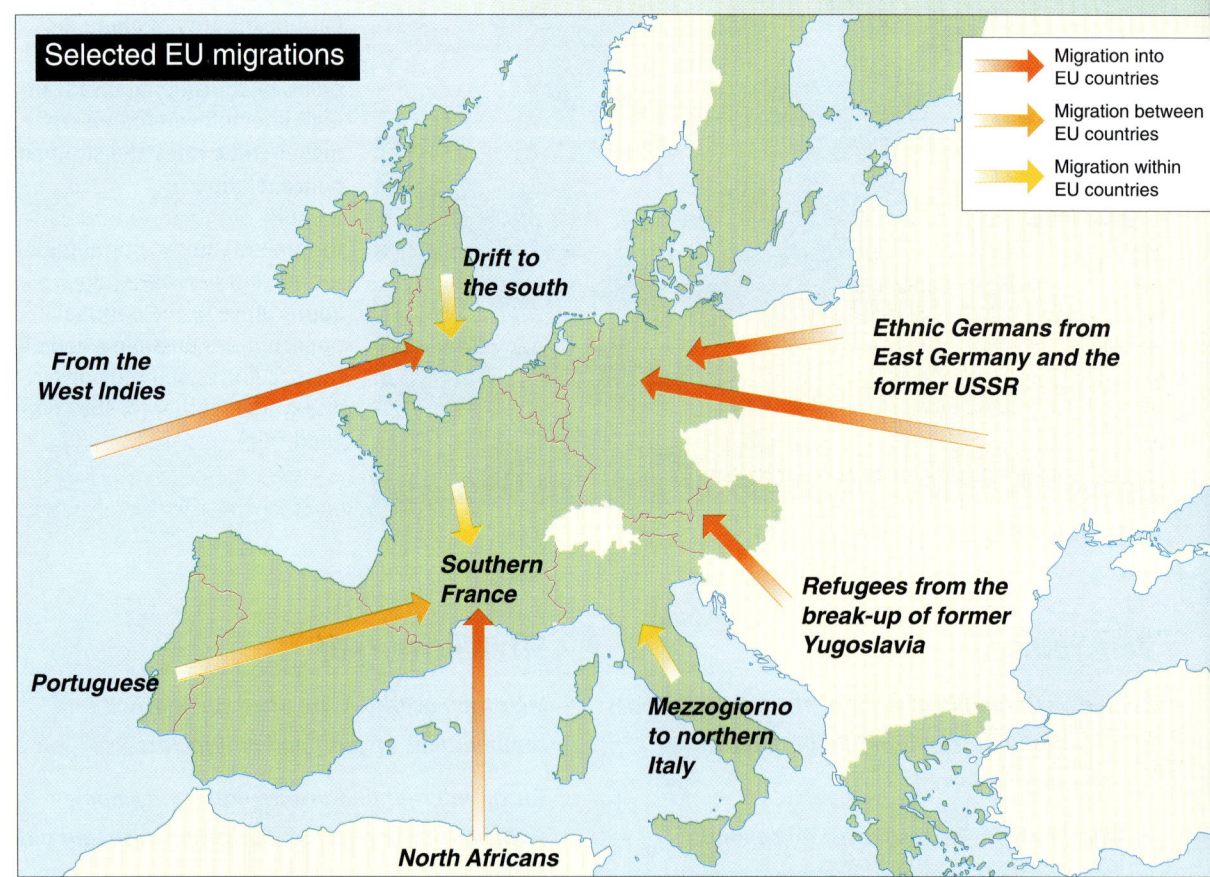

Selected EU migrations

- Migration into EU countries
- Migration between EU countries
- Migration within EU countries

Drift to the south
From the West Indies
Ethnic Germans from East Germany and the former USSR
Southern France
Portuguese
Refugees from the break-up of former Yugoslavia
Mezzogiorno to northern Italy
North Africans

By the mid 1970s, however, there was much stricter control. Britain, France, and West Germany introduced new laws preventing immigration for work, although families could still come to be reunited. Political asylum would be granted only to those who could prove that they were escaping persecution.

Also the economic recession of the early 1980s affected manufacturing industry; unskilled jobs were the first to go and immigrants suffered particularly bad unemployment.

The late 1980s and early 1990s saw a political transformation in Europe with the communist countries of the east turning to democracy. This stimulated vast movements, not least of ethnic Germans into the reunified Germany. These voluntary movements have since been considerably increased by forced migrations – for example, refugees from the break up of Yugoslavia.

Mass exodus, Serbs flee their homeland, August 1995.

Migration between EU countries

Migration between EU countries has been encouraged since the original Treaty of Rome. As the EU has grown, so have migration opportunities. Portugal, which joined in 1986, is one of the least urbanised European countries and particularly poor compared with other members. Relatively large families in rural areas, and increasing mechanisation in farming, has encouraged many younger Portuguese to seek temporary work elsewhere. Many went to France for better-paid farm work and jobs in construction and services. Just like 'guest workers' in Germany, many found themselves exploited by having to work long, unsociable hours, and endure crowded accommodation.

Today rising unemployment is encouraging resentment towards migrant workers. This bad feeling may be expressed as increasing racial tension.

Migration within EU countries

Far more migration takes place within countries than between them. Again, patterns can be seen, often because of problems in some areas and opportunities in others. The so-called 'drift to the south' in Britain (see page 79) and movements from the Mezzogiorno to northern Italy (see page 52) illustrate regional migration well. Currently the highest rate of rural depopulation in the EU is represented by migration from the mountainous Cevennes region to its coastal lowland neighbour Languedoc-Roussillon, in southern France.

Finally, at a local scale, migrations relating to both suburbanisation (see page 32) and counter-urbanisation (see page 24) are well established trends in many EU countries.

What is a settlement?

Key points

▶ Settlements are dwelling places – whether small or large, temporary or permanent.

▶ Most settlements have long histories, which help explain their situation and site.

A **settlement** is simply a place where people live. It may be permanent, such as a city, or temporary, such as a nomadic encampment. Size also varies, from single houses to sprawling urban areas formed by the merging of towns as cities. (These are called **conurbations** in Britain.) However, whatever its size, any settlement's location, function, growth and form will reflect its history.

Most of England's settlements, for example, are recorded in the Domesday Survey of 1086. Clearly, therefore, only by examining the past can most settlements be understood.

What factors are important?

In many cases, the **situation** (position) would have been determined by purpose – food provision, defence or trade. Physical factors would dominate this decision-making process. These might include:

- a fresh and reliable **water supply**, for people and livestock
- dry, sheltered, **fertile land**, such as on river terraces above a valley floor flood plain, for successful farming
- forest **wood supply** for construction and fuel
- a **defendable point**, even exposed on a hill top, for security.

Clearly, no one **site** could offer everything, so most locations involve compromise. The selection of a specific site, the actual land it is built on, would have followed after a comparison of alternatives.

Today, assuming piped water, brick, concrete and, not least, civil order, many of these early considerations are irrelevant. Settlements across the globe, whether temporary or permanent, will reflect a mix of physical and cultural characteristics, and past and present circumstances.

A defensive site, Cordes, a hill top village in France.

Settlement origin, growth, development and change: Kingston upon Hull

As described earlier, most settlements can be traced back for centuries.

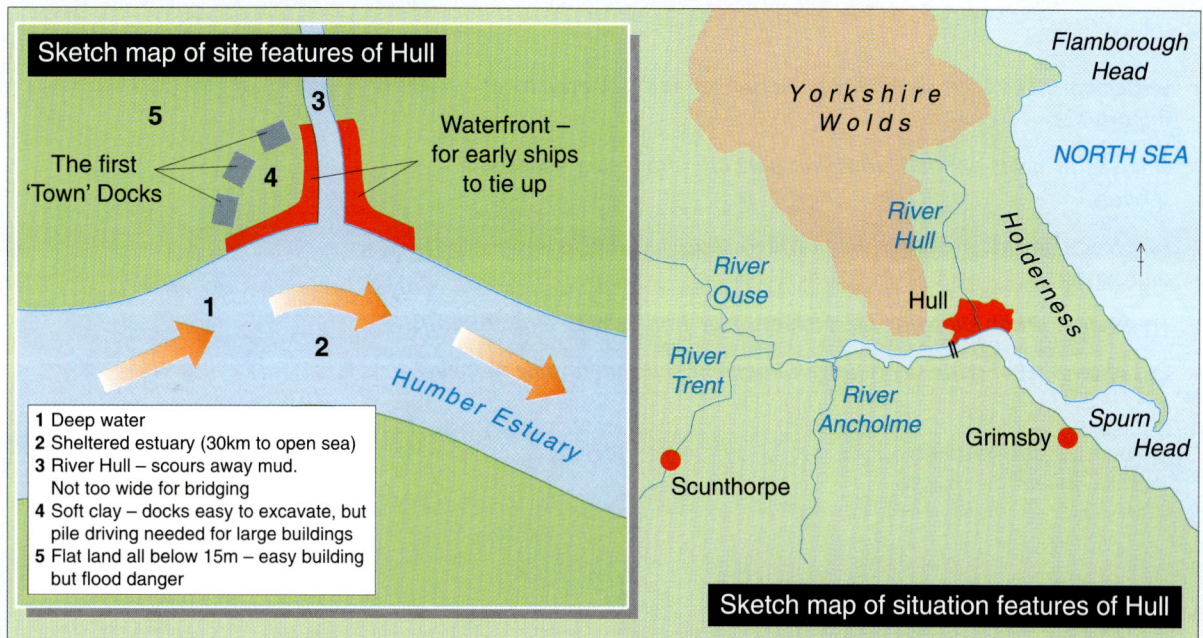

The port city of Kingston upon Hull, on the east coast of England, can be traced back to a 6th century Danish settlement called Wyke, near the mouth of the River Hull. It was in the 12th century, however, that Hull started to grow as a regional collection and distribution centre for wool from the Yorkshire Wolds. During the 13th century it was renamed Kingstown by Edward I and given a market charter. This allowed a weekly market which increased further its population and importance.

By the 14th century it had grown to be an important market town. However, it was only during the Industrial Revolution that it became a major port. Huge docks were excavated from 1773 onwards and manufacturing industry, including engineering and pharmaceuticals, developed. It also boasted a world renowned fishing fleet. But as with all settlements, evolution occurs. Today Hull's fishing industry is virtually gone, and whilst a wide variety of manufacturing and service industries thrive, the city is known best for the Humber Bridge (its spectacular link to the south) and its ferry service, the 'Gateway to Europe'.

Test yourself

1. What is a conurbation?

2. What is the difference between settlement site and situation?

3. (a) List the site factors most important to early settlers. (b) Which of these are usually irrelevant today and why?

Stretch yourself

For your home town, or any other named settlement you have studied, outline briefly the original location factors which explain its site and situation.

Settlement hierarchy, spacing, and service provision

Key points

▶ *Settlements, and their services, can be ordered into a hierarchy of importance.*

▶ *Small settlements are numerous, but only offer low order goods and services.*

▶ *Larger settlements are fewer, more widely spaced, but offer more goods and services.*

▶ *Traditional urban shopping hierarchies range from corner shops to CBDs.*

▶ *Out-of-town retail centres encourage convenient and comfortable shopping.*

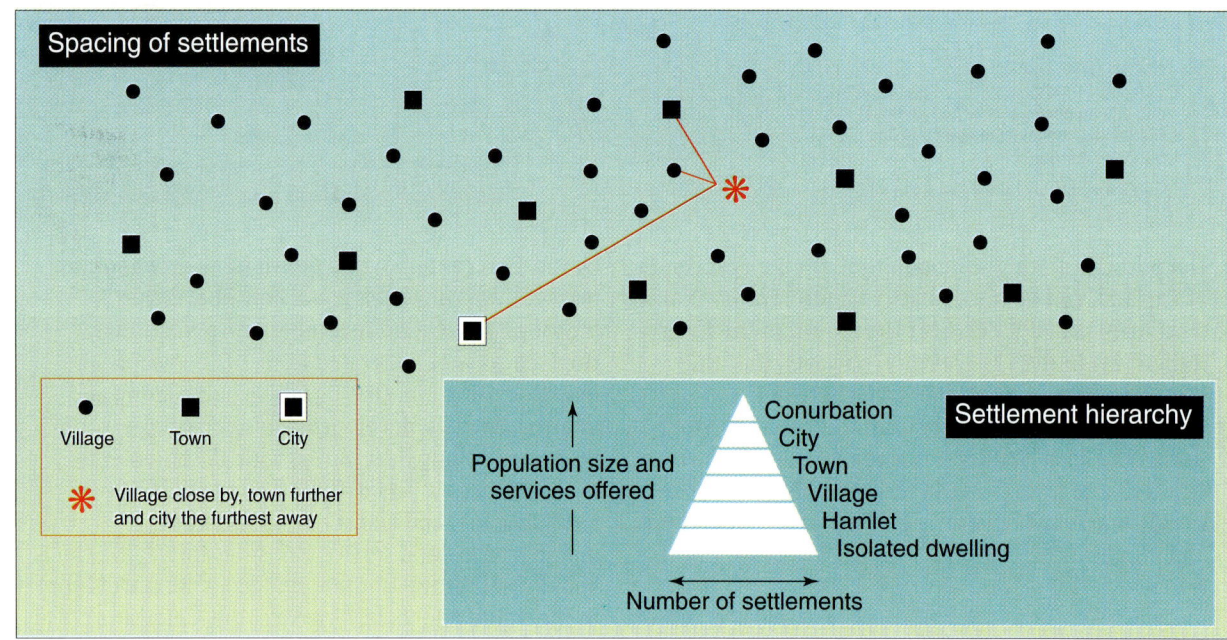

Settlements tend to form a hierarchy of importance. As a general rule, the bigger the settlement, the more important it will be – but the fewer there are.

Villages

Villages are spread across the landscape, often relatively close together. They may offer a few services, such as a public house, church and shop/post office. The latter is likely to offer only **low order (convenience) goods** such as daily necessities. Customers will only travel short distances for such low order goods. This distance is known as the **range**. However, by their regular purchases, only a relatively small number of customers may be required to keep the business going. This minimum number, required to cover the overheads (costs) of the business before profits are ensured, is known as the **threshold**.

Towns and cities

Towns and cities, by contrast, are bigger and so more widely spaced. They will offer a far greater variety of goods and functions including **high order (comparison) goods** such as clothes, furniture, and services such as lawyers and dentists. People buy and use these more expensive services less often, and so will be prepared to travel further for them. Due to less frequent use far more customers (measured in thousands) are needed to support the businesses. Both threshold and range, therefore, are higher.

Distinct **shopping hierarchies** within urban areas can also be determined. In Britain, for example, these include:

- numerous corner shops, catering for regular convenience shopping
- less common shopping parades, such as on estates
- the main shopping centre in the **central business district (CBD)** that caters for less regular shopping for higher order goods.

Recent decades have seen interference to this hierarchy caused first by supermarkets, then suburban hypermarkets. It is, however, the increasing number and popularity of **out-of-town retail (shopping) centres** that has had the most impact on our purchasing habits. Busy modern lifestyles emphasise the convenience and attraction of over 250 'retail parks', plus major regional shopping centres – such as those at Brent, Dudley, Newcastle, Sheffield, and Thurrock.

Such sites as these offer a range of attractions:

- abundant parking
- competitive prices
- vast choice
- familiar chain stores
- climate controlled malls
- catering and leisure facilities for all age groups.

Convenient shopping: The Merry Hill Centre, West Midlands.

Indeed, some regional shopping centres have so affected town and city centres, and caused such congestion on feeder motorways, that it is now government policy to use planning controls to discourage any more major developments. Planning emphasis is to be directed at encouraging the revitalisation of city centres, with sufficient parking, pedestrianisation etc. (see page 39). The aims are to ensure survival for CBD businesses and avoid the environmental and social problems associated with blight and decay.

Test yourself

1. Explain briefly the terms: (a) hierarchy (b) range (c) threshold (d) low order goods (e) high order goods and services (f) hypermarket (g) retail park.

Stretch yourself

Outline the changes over recent decades to most people's shopping habits, and preferences – as a result of greater affluence, choice, and mobility. Consider the reasons for each change.

HUMAN THEMES • SETTLEMENT

Urbanisation and urban growth

Key points

▶ Urban, built-up areas can be distinguished from rural surrounding countryside.

▶ Urbanisation is a proportional increase in the numbers of people living in towns and cities.

▶ EMDC urbanisation has slowed markedly of late and is reversing in some cases.

▶ ELDC urbanisation is so rapid, that by 2025 two-thirds of all humanity will be urban.

A large part of the world's population growth is occurring in urban areas (towns and cities). This is particularly true of ELDCs. An increase in the proportion of urban dwellers is the process called **urbanisation**.

Today, urbanisation in EMDCs, associated with economic development and industrialisation since the Industrial Revolution, is now virtually at an end. In EMDCs the percentage of urban dwellers is either remaining constant at around 80% of the total population, or slowly beginning to fall. This fall is known as **counter-urbanisation** and reflects greater affluence and mobility. People can commute daily from more environmentally attractive 'dormitory' settlements beyond the main urban centres.

As urban growth appears to be coming to an end in EMDCs, the predicted massive increases in the world's urban population (see graph) will take place almost entirely in the cities of the South. Already more than half of the world's urban population lives in a town or city in an ELDC, and by the end of the 20th century two in every three urban dwellers will live in the South.

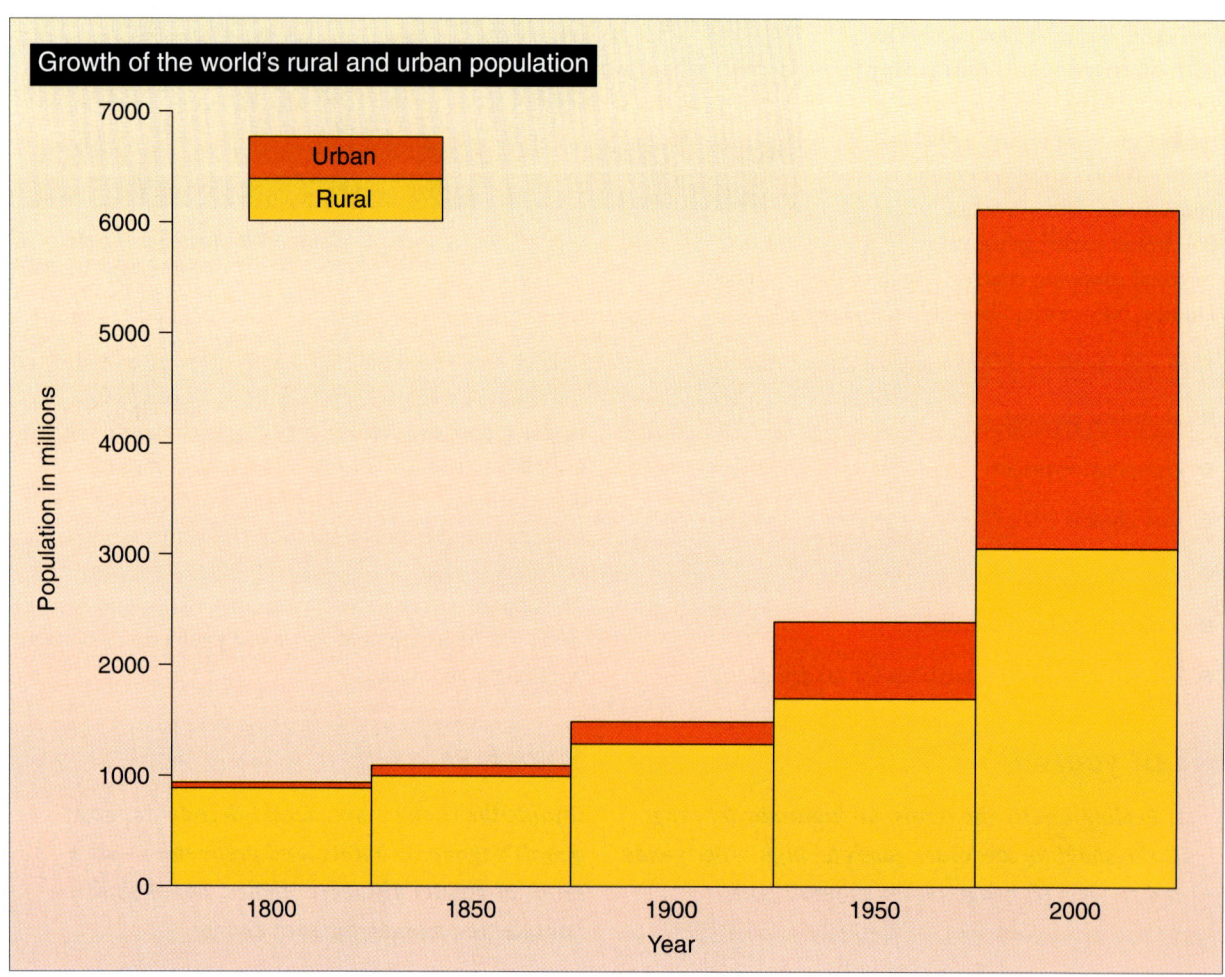

24 HUMAN THEMES • SETTLEMENT

Millionaire and super cities

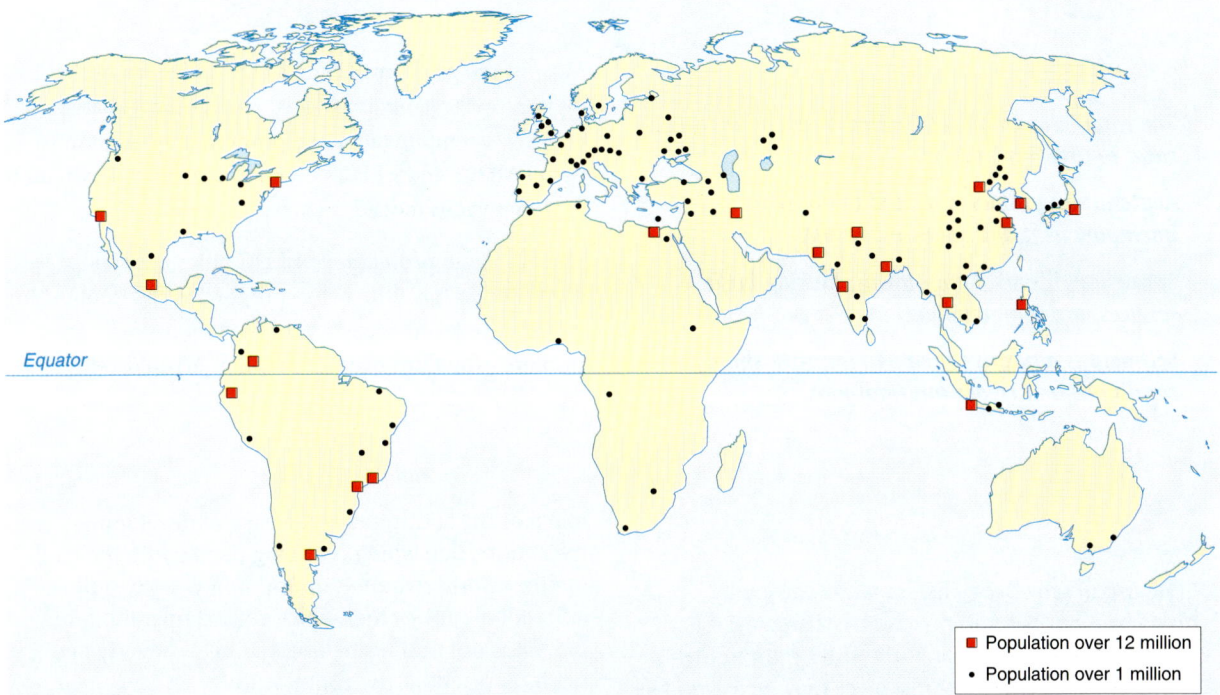

One indication of the speed of urban growth, particularly in the last 30 years, is the large increase which has taken place in the number of cities with population in excess of one million. It seems certain that the number of 'millionaire' cities will continue to grow in the near future, to exceed 300 early next century. Most of these new millionaire cities will be in the South.

The most rapidly growing cities of all will be the so-called 'super' cities whose populations exceed 12 million. Tokyo, New York, Shanghai, Calcutta, Mexico City (the world's biggest), and São Paulo (the world's fastest growing), are notable examples. Beyond the year 2000 there will probably be more than 20 super cities, most of them in the South. Many of those projected are not only capitals, but port cities too, with trading links all over the world.

Test yourself

1. What is meant by the terms: (a) urban (b) rural (c) urbanisation (d) counter-urbanisation?

2. Use an atlas to check the locations of the specific cities named above.

3. Does the world's most populated continent have the greatest number of millionaire cities in it?

4. Study the graph showing the growth of the world's rural and urban population.
(a) What was the world's rural population in 1900?
(b) What was the world's urban population in 1950?

Stretch yourself

Describe and compare the overall trend of world rural and world population growth.

HUMAN THEMES • SETTLEMENT

Urban problems – and solutions – in ELDCs

Key points

▶ *The rapid growth of ELDC cities is caused mainly by rural to urban migration.*

▶ *Acute urban problems related to poverty, unemployment and squatting result.*

▶ *Sprawling, illegal shanty towns, lacking basic services, are commonplace.*

▶ *Self-help is a positive theme to improve shanty conditions and create informal jobs.*

Most of the problems facing ELDC cities are caused by rapid growth. Many problems, such as inadequate housing, unemployment and poverty, are common to both EMDCs and ELDCs – and in the latter they tend to be very serious indeed.

The desperate problems of ELDC cities are vividly illustrated in India. Its urban proportion has doubled in recent decades to over 25% of the population – an absolute growth to over 200 million urban dwellers.

Rural to urban migration

ELDC urban growth has been mainly caused by migration, but natural increase has also played its part. Health care is better in the cities than in the countryside, and in some instances may be as good as in EMDCs. This produces low death rates – and with youthful populations and high birth rates, natural increase is rapid.

In Britain's period of rapid urbanisation in the 19th century, rural to urban migration was caused mainly by the attraction of industrial jobs. In India (as in much of the South today) it is lack of development in the countryside which is driving people into the cities. In other words, whereas in Britain it was the pull (attraction) of the cities which caused migration, in India it is the push (repelling action) of poverty and unemployment in the countryside.

Of course, some migrants do return to their villages – disillusioned with the city – but the overwhelming majority stay. Most would have little to return to. Although many have simply exchanged rural poverty for urban poverty, life seems to offer more hope in the city.

Pull factors
(attracting migrants to the cities)

- *better job opportunities and career prospects*
- *better medical and family planning facilities*
- *better educational opportunities*
- *better housing – with electricity, water supply and sewerage*
- *better social life and entertainment*
- *better shops, transport and communications*
- *higher wages and standards of living*
- *lower interest to pay on loans*
- *less threat from natural hazards*
- *relations may have already migrated.*

Push factors
(repelling migrants from the countryside)

- *unemployment and underemployment*
- *poor medical and family planning services*
- *few schools and colleges*
- *poor housing – lacking basic amenities*
- *limited socialising opportunities*
- *poor services and communications*
- *widespread poverty*
- *high interest loans and debt*
- *natural hazards such as drought, floods, and pests*
- *population pressure leading to insufficient land – often fragmented following inheritance.*

The most obvious problem within ELDC cities is poverty. There are few jobs within the sprawling, often illegal, **shanty towns** which house vast numbers of rural migrants. Shanties are spontaneous (unplanned) settlements of shacks, built at very high densities, by the incoming migrants. Constructed from materials scavenged from rubbish dumps and building sites, they are characterised by a lack of basic services, such as sewage disposal and drinking water.

In India, as in most ELDCs, the government does not like shanty towns, but has little option but to tolerate them. Positive measures to improve the conditions of the squatter population are employed. Shanty towns can be provided with piped water, drainage and electricity, and facilities made available for improving buildings, such as brick making units. This so-called **upgrading** employs local labour and is a cheap alternative to **rehousing** squatters in conventional, low cost housing schemes. (These have rarely proved successful because they are too often poorly built and ill-affordable – despite modest rents.)

Upgrading relies on **self-help**, low-interest loans and realistic planning. So called **site and service schemes** are the ultimate self-help projects. Often funded by UN agencies, building plots are provided and laid out with water, drains, roads, street lighting and, occasionally, clinics and schools. Squatters are given modest loans for building materials and are expected to build their own homes on prepared sites. Emphasis is placed upon harnessing the initiative and ingenuity of the migrants, in order to improve their living conditions.

The problem of **unemployment** exists simply because there are not enough urban jobs in manufacturing industry to satisfy demand. Once again, people have to rely on self-help. Many find work in the **informal**

Going nowhere! Living under the highway in São Paulo, Brazil.

service sector – collecting recyclable rubbish, shoe-shining, running errands, street trading, cleaning cars etc. However, such self-employment avoids the taxation system, so denying governments much-needed revenues for developing public services.

Many ELDCs, including India, show urban dwellers proving successfully that they can not only house themselves, but also create their own employment. Increasingly, governments are facing reality and encouraging this spirit of self-help. Governments provide squatter settlements with basic services, support site and service schemes, and remove legal obstacles to the squatters' ownership of land. Such a positive approach offers real hope for improving the quality of urban life for the people of the South.

Test yourself

1. (a) What are shanty towns? (b) Why are they called informal settlements?

2. What are site and service schemes?

3. What is the informal service sector of an ELDC economy?

Stretch yourself

Poverty is a relative and much misunderstood term. It can be better appreciated once you consider the expectations of the poor in Britain, with those of the poor in India. Compare and contrast indicators of poverty in both Britain and India. Consider basic requirements for housing; water supply; education; health care; food; entertainment.

Calcutta: a super city under pressure

Calcutta is India's largest city, with a population of 14 million (1997). It was originally founded in 1690 by the British East India Company, as its centre for trading activities in the area. The site was flat and marshy land located beside the Hooghly River, which forms part of the Ganges Delta.

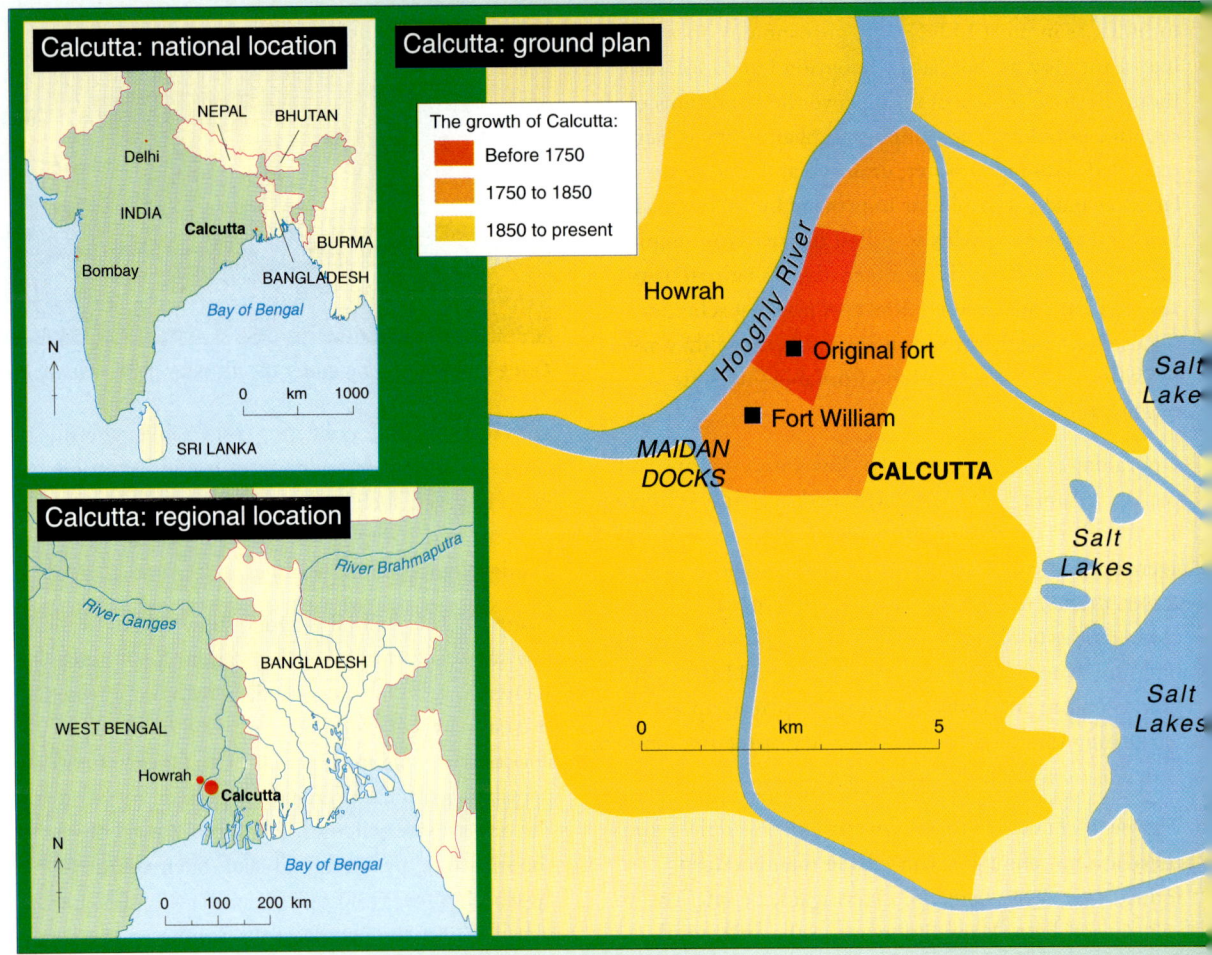

British colonial influence was evident in the city's early development. Until 1912 it was India's capital. It was important as an administrative centre, with grand government buildings, a military base and high class residential districts for Europeans. Calcutta also developed as a major port, with widespread industrial areas along and near the river, such as in Howrah on the west bank.

Throughout the 19th and early 20th centuries Calcutta grew steadily. The colonial authorities developed basic services for water supply and sewage disposal. However, unplanned tenement housing rapidly engulfed the early city. Today, in these blocks and compounds, hundreds of thousands live in cheap, single-room accommodation –

some even rent rooms in 'hot bed hotels 'where three or more residents rent a bed in eight-hour shifts.

Such has been the rate of urbanisation over recent decades that Calcutta's growth rate has exceeded that of India as a whole. A young, male-weighted population structure has resulted, with formal accommodation and services overwhelmed. Over 200,000 are thought to live on the pavements, with additional millions squatting (often illegally) in sprawling shanty towns known locally as bustees.

These settlements:

- *are found on waste land within the city, but especially at the margins*
- *consist of shacks built of scavenged scrap materials, such as sacking, corrugated iron and polythene sheeting*
- *provide barely adequate protection, especially from the monsoon rains*
- *possess few services such as electricity, schools and clinics*
- *have virtually no sanitation with contaminated stand-pipe water supplies and pit latrines the norm*
- *have rubbish dumped between the shacks which further encourages diseases, such as dysentery and typhoid.*

The Calcutta Metropolitan Development Authority has provided much needed employment for local labour in order to upgrade many of the bustees (see earlier) and to provide site and service plots. Despite these efforts the rate of urbanisation still outstrips services. Remember, shanty towns remain a familiar feature of urban areas throughout the South – but not all shanties are the same. Each should be viewed as having a unique set of characteristics.

In Calcutta, for example, many bustees are legal. Many now are rented to migrants by landlords, who evict those unable to maintain their payments. Migrants typically group in well-defined areas amongst those of similar origin and caste.

Whilst migrants may have exchanged rural for urban poverty, opportunities are certainly greater. Industrialisation, however, has not kept up with urbanisation. Unemployment is inevitably high. Many migrants have returned to home villages and it is clear that Calcutta is no longer attracting the numbers of previous decades.

Certainly, site constrictions and severe traffic congestion have slowed the rate of growth. Indeed, it is the youthful population, ensuring a high birth rate, that now accounts for much of the continued population growth.

Living on the streets in Calcutta.

Urban land-use zones and models

Key points

▶ *Although every town and city is unique, distinctive land-use zones can be found.*

▶ *Models of urban land-use help to explain how these zones develop.*

Clearly, some areas of a town or city are very different to others. The various functions of a town are never scattered randomly – but grouped in distinctive **zones**. Various processes operate to cause this zonation.

Retail, commercial, financial, legal and social services have traditionally benefited from being in the centre of a town. The centre is the place which can, theoretically, be reached most easily by the surrounding population.

Retailers particularly sought this location – to ensure maximum customer accessibility. As a result, high order retail outlets, such as department stores, clothes and shoe shops outbid other potential users. This increases the land value of the central business district (CBD). High building, traffic and pedestrian densities are the result.

Some services, such as legal, financial and administrative, benefit by close association, and so cluster together – hence the commercial zoning within many CBDs. Elsewhere, few want to live near the noise, dirt and smell of commercial and especially industrial areas, so these tend to be separated from residential areas and schools.

In this way, distinctive zones are normal. Only in recent decades have clear divisions between zones been noticeably complicated. Today, out-of-town shopping centres, industrial/trading estates and a car-mobile population allow greater variety in urban areas although functional zones still do exist.

High-density land-use, La Defense, Paris.

30 HUMAN THEMES • SETTLEMENT

Models in geography

A model is a simplification of reality designed to help us explain aspects of the real world. A number of models, including the three shown, have been developed to help demonstrate the urban processes described earlier, and so allow easier analysis of very complicated urban forms.

- The **concentric model** shows how cities have grown historically. By growing outwards from the centre, new building on cheaper suburban land allows better-off people to move to bigger houses. The less well-off do not have such choice, so live in higher density inner city locations.

- The **sector model** shows how cities grow for economic reasons. Until the 20th century, the size of cities was restricted by the need for workers to live within walking distance of their jobs. However, since then, improvements in public transport, and especially widespread car ownership, have allowed workers to live further away. Urban areas, therefore, can expand unevenly along main transport routes.

- The **multiple-nuclei model** shows how conurbations grow. As cities expand, so smaller towns and villages are engulfed. A well connected patchwork of zones, with many centres, results.

Both the concentric and sector models have been widely criticised as just too simplistic to cope with the complex nature of modern cities. The multiple nuclei model is generally accepted as more flexible, and so the most realistic of the three.

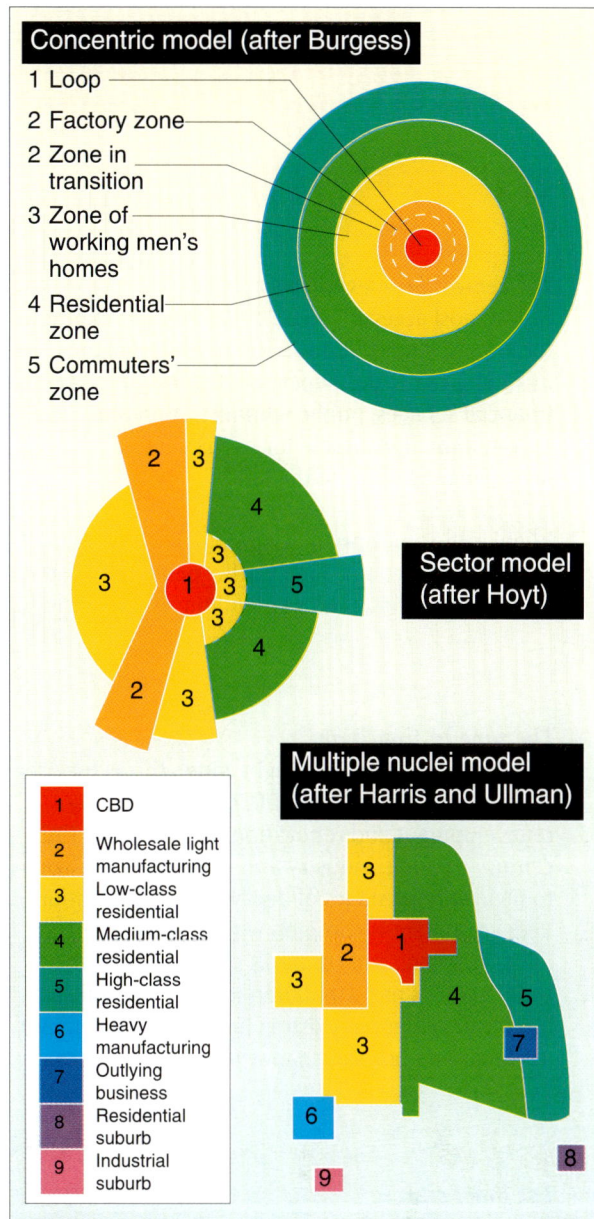

Test yourself

1. What land-use zone is likely to be found in the centre of an urban area and why?

2. (a) What is a model in Geography? (b) Why are they useful?

Stretch yourself

Whilst it is clear that towns and cities rarely grow haphazardly, most are so complex that it may require more than one model alone to represent any one settlement's development and current form. What, therefore, makes urban land-use models unrealistic? You might want to consider, for example, relief and landforms; changes through time; accidents of history; the role of planners.

Distinctive urban land-use zones in Britain

The central business district (CBD)
As the most accessible part of the city, competition for limited land is intense. High order functions, including chain and department stores, legal and financial services, public administration and entertainment, compete for prime sites, so increasing the value of the land.

'High' is the appropriate theme: high land values, high order functions, high traffic, pedestrian and building densities, and high buildings.

The zone of transition
Sometimes called the 'twilight zone', this is the area immediately beyond the CBD, characterised by redevelopment and renovation. High density 19th century housing, industry and workshops are likely to be in various stages of decay and/or renovation. Redevelopment is common with new commercial (CBD) functions and car parks spreading into the zone. There is net population loss (to the suburbs) but improvement of existing housing stock is now proving more popular than wholesale clearance.

The inner city
High density housing is common, built amongst the factories during the Industrial Revolution. Grid-iron patterns of, originally, cobbled roads ensured no waste of space, and ready access to work. The inner city today sees net out-migration to less congested, cleaner, more attractive suburban environments. This is known as suburbanisation.

Inner suburbia
Larger 'town houses', also in long terraces, or around 'squares' were built for 19th century factory owners and managers. These were the suburbs of their day, complete with servants' quarters in attics or basements. Conversion of these houses into health care surgeries, nursing homes, commercial offices, guest houses, student flats, and bedsitters, for example, is now the norm.

Suburbia or the 'urban fringe'
'Ribbon developments' of terraced, or more usually semi-detached, houses spread, during the inter-war years, along main roads. Characterised by front and back gardens, and distinctive bay windows, they represented the start of suburbanisation and 'urban sprawl'. More recent estates tend to reflect the fashions of the day, but low building density and variety are common themes, with cul-de-sacs to 'calm' the traffic.

Outer city council estates
Inner city slum clearance during the 1950s and '60s usually resulted in the construction of large council estates on the fringes of cities. High-rise tower blocks, maisonettes, terraces along crescents, and some semi-detached properties ensured variety whilst supporting a relatively high population density. Services vary. At worst the only facilities are convenience shopping 'parades', and public houses.

Commuter suburban villages
Within the urban–rural fringe, but not too distant to prohibit commuting, these 'dormitory' villages rarely maintain any rural character. The original cottages are usually expensively modernised, and surrounded by estates of high quality semi-detached and detached houses, of varying design and layout. These villages can be swamped by unchecked urban sprawl, unless protected from city expansion by strictly observed green belt legislation.

Organised urban change

Key points

▶ *Planners direct and monitor present day urban growth and development.*

▶ *Planning is a 'young' profession, with a much improved reputation of late.*

▶ *Planning now favours renovation rather than renewal.*

▶ *Planners now consider the social impact of their policies.*

▶ *Copenhagen's Finger Plan illustrates radical, influential yet flexible urban planning.*

Urban areas are dynamic – always changing. As older areas decay, new areas are developed. It is the job of **planners** to direct and monitor this change – to renew urban areas to the benefit of residents and businesses alike. Planners also have to cope with the problems that arise from their decisions, such as traffic congestion, or a threat to environmental quality.

Planners throughout Europe have enjoyed mixed reputations. In Britain, for example, they gained a bad reputation throughout the 1960s and 1970s because of policies favouring wholesale redevelopment of inner city areas. The construction of high-rise tower blocks, inner ring roads and new suburban estates and shopping centres, transformed familiar urban landscapes and lifestyles.

With hindsight, much of the redevelopment was logical in theory, but socially flawed. By the 1980s planning emphasis had, thankfully, changed for the better. By consulting the people who were affected, emphasis on renovation, rather than renewal, became the theme. Intimidating tower blocks were not the only answer to high density housing need. Communities were, and increasingly are, kept together, housed in developments with great attention paid to environmental quality and neighbourhood security.

Copenhagen: a planning example for all?

Copenhagen is the historic capital of Denmark. It is also a **primate city**, many times bigger than any other in the country. (The Greater Copenhagen region accounts for over one-third of Denmark's population.) Its situation is strategically important, controlling trade routes between Germany and Sweden, and separating the Baltic from the North Sea.

Copenhagen industrialised throughout the 19th and early 20th centuries, and grew rapidly outwards from the harbour core. By the mid-20th century, rural migrants and natural growth had swelled the population to a peak of 750,000.

Housing in the inner city was high density and poorly built. It was mixed with industry and polluted by congested traffic. Wealthier families were starting to move out, to be replaced with poorer, often single people. Suburban sprawl, inner city traffic congestion and urban decay had become problems. The city was in urgent need of attention from the planners.

Three separate plans, encouraging controlled decentralisation of population, were devised to address the problems. These have proved controversial yet very influential to planners throughout the world.

- The **1947 Finger (Linear) Plan** was accepted at a time of rapid population growth. Development was confined to five linear sectors, served by road and railway, radiating from the city centre – rather like fingers from the palm of a hand. Wedges of open space between the fingers were theoretically protected from development to give recreational countryside for the population. However, population growth exceeded expectations. Suburban sprawl and 'finger link' roads encroached on the 'green wedges'.

- In **1960, a revised and stricter plan** was adopted, deliberately enlarging the two fingers pointing west and south-west, in order to protect the particularly attractive, and vulnerable, northern areas. By 1970, the population of Greater Copenhagen was static, but the demand for further high quality, low density suburban housing continued. Given rising living standards, this was not unexpected; it was also due, in part, to the trend towards more single person households and childless families.

- Copenhagen then saw the **1973 third evolution of the original plan**. Population decentralisation was still the key, but each finger was now to contain a major industrial and service centre too. (The creation of so many jobs beyond the city boundaries would reduce commuter congestion within Copenhagen itself.) Each centre would be situated where 'finger link' roads cross the main radial routeways (at the knuckles and nails). Overall, much emphasis has been placed upon extending the existing transport system especially with new motorway links and suburban railways.

In conclusion, it must be noted that, throughout the period, professional planners and politicians continued to debate the merits of decentralising population and employment rather than replanning and redeveloping within the city itself.

In Copenhagen, as elsewhere (see page 23), planners are now concerned about the detrimental effects of decentralisation and are addressing the needs of the inner city.

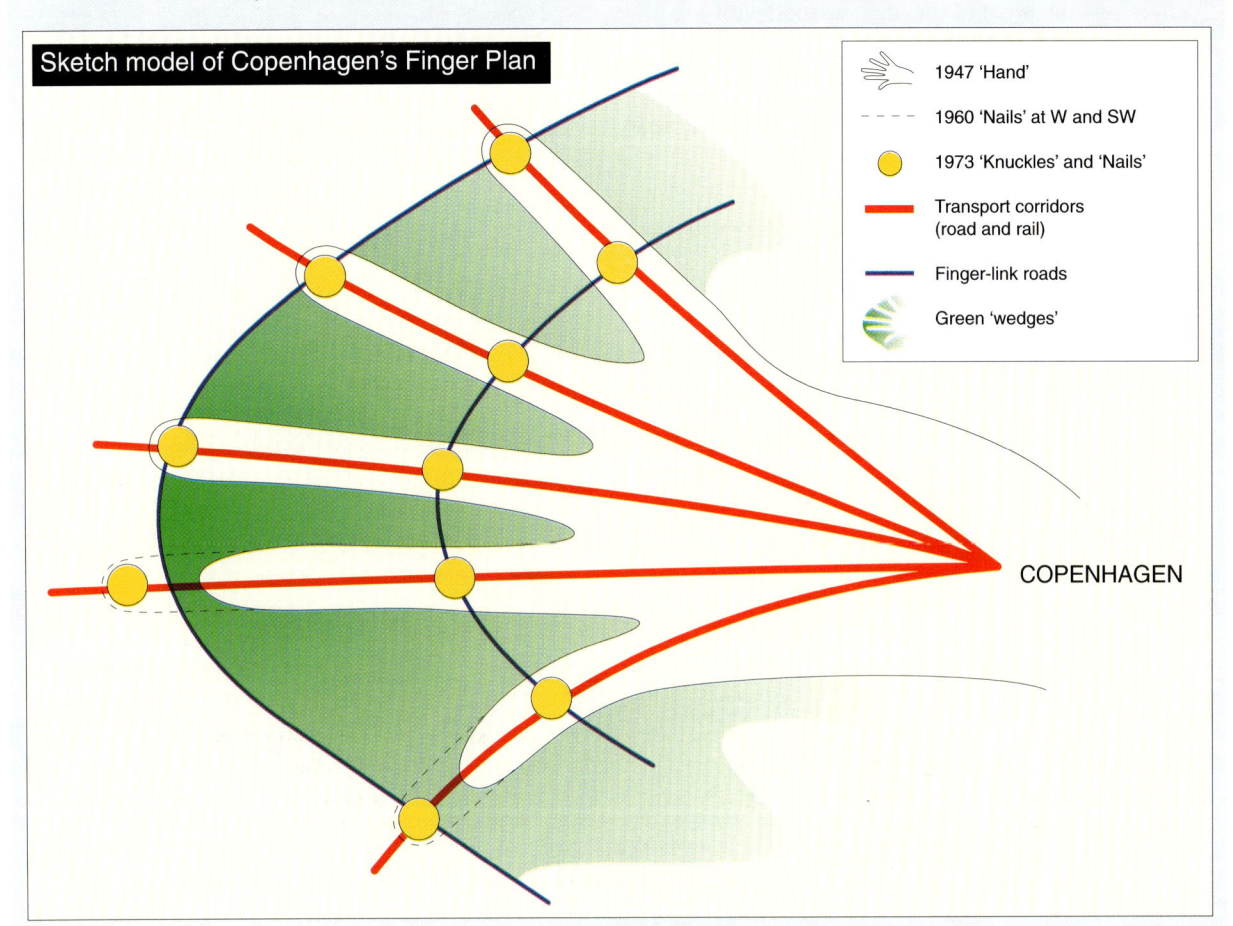

Sketch model of Copenhagen's Finger Plan

Legend:
- 1947 'Hand'
- 1960 'Nails' at W and SW
- 1973 'Knuckles' and 'Nails'
- Transport corridors (road and rail)
- Finger-link roads
- Green 'wedges'

COPENHAGEN

Test yourself

1. Describe briefly the job/role of a planner.

2. What do planners mean by: (a) suburban sprawl (b) green belts (c) green wedges?

Stretch yourself

Successful urban planning involves the people to be affected, keeps communities together, and creates desirable living and working environments. Often an overall theme holds the total planning objective together. What was the general theme in Copenhagen's case?

HUMAN THEMES • PLANNING

London Docklands redevelopment

During the Industrial Revolution the Port of London grew to be the busiest in the world. By the 1960s, however, it had started to decline, and was losing business to the more efficient containerised Tilbury Docks, further down the Thames. From the late '60s to the early '80s over 50,000 port jobs had gone, plus 200,000 in dependent trades. The Isle of Dogs, effectively the heart of the area, was left with:

- **more than half of its land derelict**
- **its 19th century housing in urgent need of repair**
- **few basic services or leisure facilities**
- **a poor transport system likely to hinder any revival.**

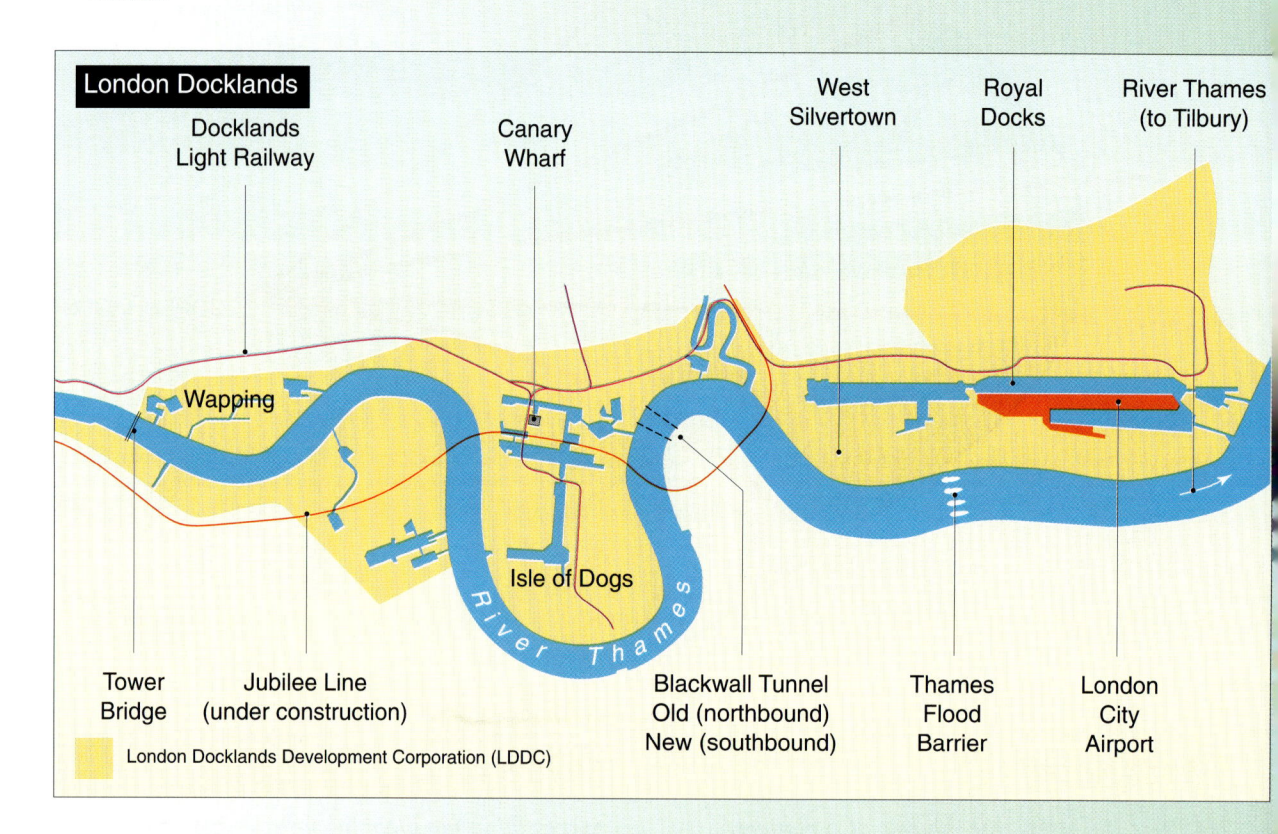

Consequently, in 1981 the area was granted Enterprise Zone status and funding, and the London Docklands Development Corporation (LDDC) was set up to buy land, plan its future and oversee its regeneration and redevelopment. In other words, their enormous task was to transform the area's economic, social and environmental conditions.

London Docklands

Docklands Light Railway · Canary Wharf · West Silvertown · Royal Docks · River Thames (to Tilbury)

Wapping · Isle of Dogs · River Thames

Tower Bridge · Jubilee Line (under construction) · Blackwall Tunnel Old (northbound) New (southbound) · Thames Flood Barrier · London City Airport

London Docklands Development Corporation (LDDC)

Economic regeneration has been tackled by using government Enterprise Zone grants, and the promise of low business rates, to attract new firms. But regeneration required improved public utilities and transport. Some road improvements, for example, have taken advantage of derelict land, but it is in public transport that the most exciting developments have occurred.

The Docklands Light Railway, built above ground to provide a 'ten-minute link' to central London, has since been extended beyond the original Docklands area. This has opened up the Royal Docks further east, where the London City Airport has been successfully developed. The Jubilee underground line extension, opening in 1998, will further improve access. Financial institutions, high tech firms and newspaper publishers have moved to Docklands, creating thousands of jobs.

The new jobs, however, have been mostly in skilled occupations unlikely to employ former port workers. It can be argued that social conditions have changed rather than improved. Most of the new private housing, including warehouse conversions, has been expensive. Only affluent new residents, rather than established locals, could afford them. New shopping and leisure developments, such as restaurants and a marina, have tended to cater for these new residents, rather than the original 'Eastenders'.

It is only very recently that more emphasis has been on the provision of low-cost housing, and there is still insufficient social services provision, such as health care and support for the elderly.

One other sign of positive change for all are a number of environmental improvement initiatives, backed by conservation groups. These have included:

- *transforming derelict wastelands into attractive public open spaces*
- *opening up ecological parks, conservation areas, waterside walkways, cycle paths – even a city farm*
- *planting and transplanting over 100,000 saplings and mature trees in Europe's largest urban tree planting programme.*

As a planning exercise, the redevelopment of London's Docklands is of major significance. However, any such programme, involving so many interested parties, is unlikely to progress without problems. Economic recession throughout the early 1990s increased unemployment, reduced investment, and delayed full occupation of the 'flagship' Canary Wharf project.

Fortunately fears that the scheme could fail altogether have proved unfounded. There is great optimism for the future, based on ambitious plans to continue redevelopment further east around the Royal Docks and the Thames Flood Barrier. There are plans, for example, to build 'urban village' communities such as West Silvertown and a new university.

The 'new' Eastenders: the Canary Wharf Development.

Transport and urban traffic management

Key points

▶ *Transport involves the moving of people and goods between places.*

▶ *Transport is central to the running of a successful economy, but associated with problems too.*

▶ *Modes of transport cater for different needs – whether by road, rail, air, or water.*

▶ *Urban traffic management has become a global planning necessity.*

What determines mode of transport? Both the frequency of journey, and the volume/number of goods or people to be moved, for example, are relevant considerations. But it is distance, cost and time which influence transport decisions most, with each method having relevant advantages and disadvantages.

	Advantages	*Disadvantages*
Road	Numerous routes Door-to-door convenience No timetables Cheap over short distances	Heavy congestion Vulnerable to bad weather Limited loads Noise and air pollution
Rail	Fast over long distances Only affected by extreme weather More people/goods carried safely Cost-effective for large, bulky loads	Only main urban centres connected Restricted to timetable Vulnerable to delays Loads need transferring at stations
Air	Very fast over long distances Relatively cheap for long journeys Very safe Minimal congestion in the air	Not ideal for bulky goods Relatively few airports Vulnerable to extreme weather Bad pollution – especially noise
Water	Cheap for freight Can be luxurious Limited/rare pollution Great weight/bulk carried	Restricted to waterways and seas Uncomfortable in stormy weather Oil tanker pollution notable Relatively slow

The history of transport is one of changing fortunes. In Britain, for example, three phases have been noted:

- during the early stages of the Industrial Revolution, **river** and **canal barges** were essential to the movement of raw materials and manufactured goods
- the 19th century development of the steam engine stimulated the expansion of a **railway network**
- since the 1940s **road transport** has steadily increased in importance, and now, with the widespread interconnected **motorway** network, dominates the movements of both goods and people.

The dominance of road transport is causing concern – particularly in urban areas. The car may have increased the mobility of shoppers, and increased the trade of city centre shops, but it has also led to increased problems such as congestion, accidents, insufficient parking, noise and air pollution.

The conflict between too many vehicles and too many people wanting to use the same streets at the same time is one of the foremost planning issues of our time. Typical attempts at solutions include multi-storey car parks, one-way streets, traffic free pedestrian precincts and ring roads.

Traffic management in Kingston upon Hull

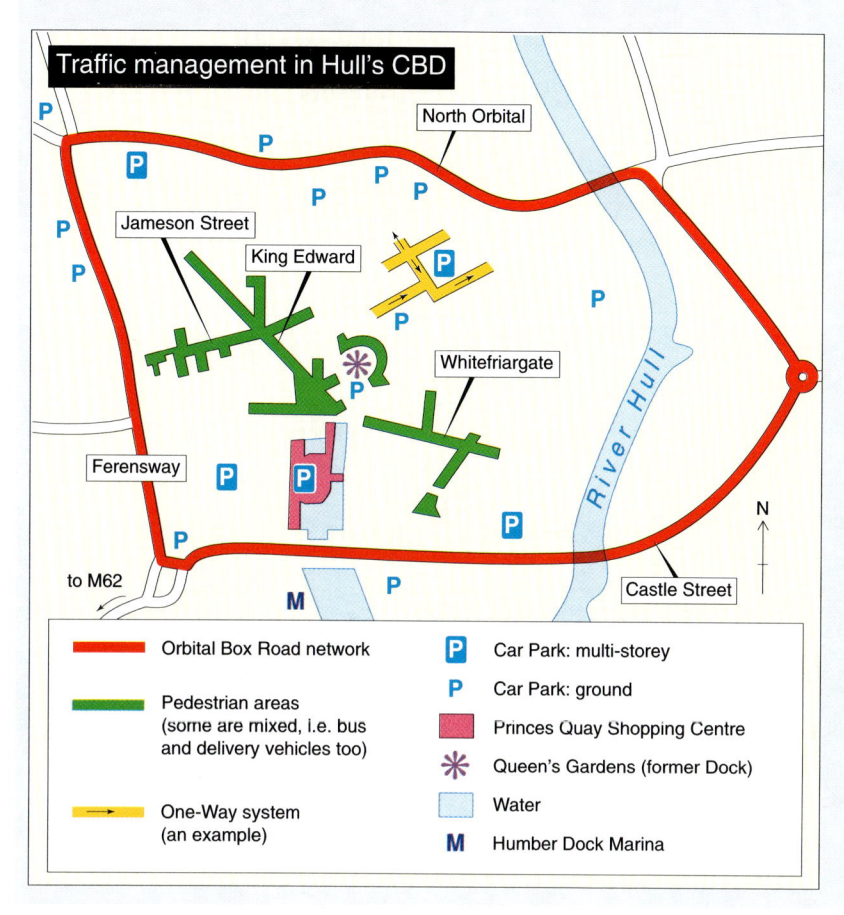

Traffic management in Hull's CBD

Map features: North Orbital, Jameson Street, King Edward, Ferensway, Whitefriargate, River Hull, Castle Street, to M62

Legend:
- Orbital Box Road network
- Pedestrian areas (some are mixed, i.e. bus and delivery vehicles too)
- One-Way system (an example)
- P Car Park: multi-storey
- P Car Park: ground
- Princes Quay Shopping Centre
- Queen's Gardens (former Dock)
- Water
- M Humber Dock Marina

Kingston upon Hull faced its pedestrian/vehicle conflict in the late 1980s. Key roads at the margins of the CBD were designated for redevelopment as a high capacity inner ring road system. Over a five year period, existing streets were improved, and additional links and car parks constructed. An 'Orbital Box' network was created to divert all through traffic from the city centre. Key shopping streets within the CBD were pedestrianised, with paved areas enhanced by landscaping with shrubs and trees, and the provision of street furniture.

Kingston upon Hull's approach is typical. Similar schemes can be found throughout Europe. Planners have become very skilled in reconciling the needs of shoppers, retailers, delivery drivers, office workers and so on. In recent years we have learned through experience.

Shrubbery, for example, has proved too often to be more attractive on the drawing board than in (litter attracting) reality. Materials for street furniture have to be vandal resistant, with the use of highly polished marble and granite facings an attractive, albeit expensive, alternative to concrete. Public transport initiatives can play a part in addressing the pedestrian/vehicle conflict too. For example, underground rail systems in Glasgow and Newcastle, and now 'supertrams' in Sheffield and Birmingham, all contribute towards cleaner, safer city centres.

Test yourself

1. What is meant by: (a) transport mode (b) transport network (c) the pedestrian/vehicle conflict?

Stretch yourself

For your home town, or any major settlement you have studied, briefly outline its traffic management problems, needs, and responses.

Farming as a system

Key points

▶ Farming is a global industry – producing our food and many raw materials.

▶ Farming systems operate with inputs, processes, outputs and feedbacks.

▶ Farming can be arable, pastoral, or mixed – commercial, or near-subsistence.

▶ Intensive farming systems (the opposite of extensive) invest much into small areas.

▶ Sedentary farming is tied to a location; shifting cultivation regularly moves.

Farming, like any other industry, involves:

inputs

processes and

outputs.

A **systems diagram approach** can be applied to any farm, anywhere in the world.

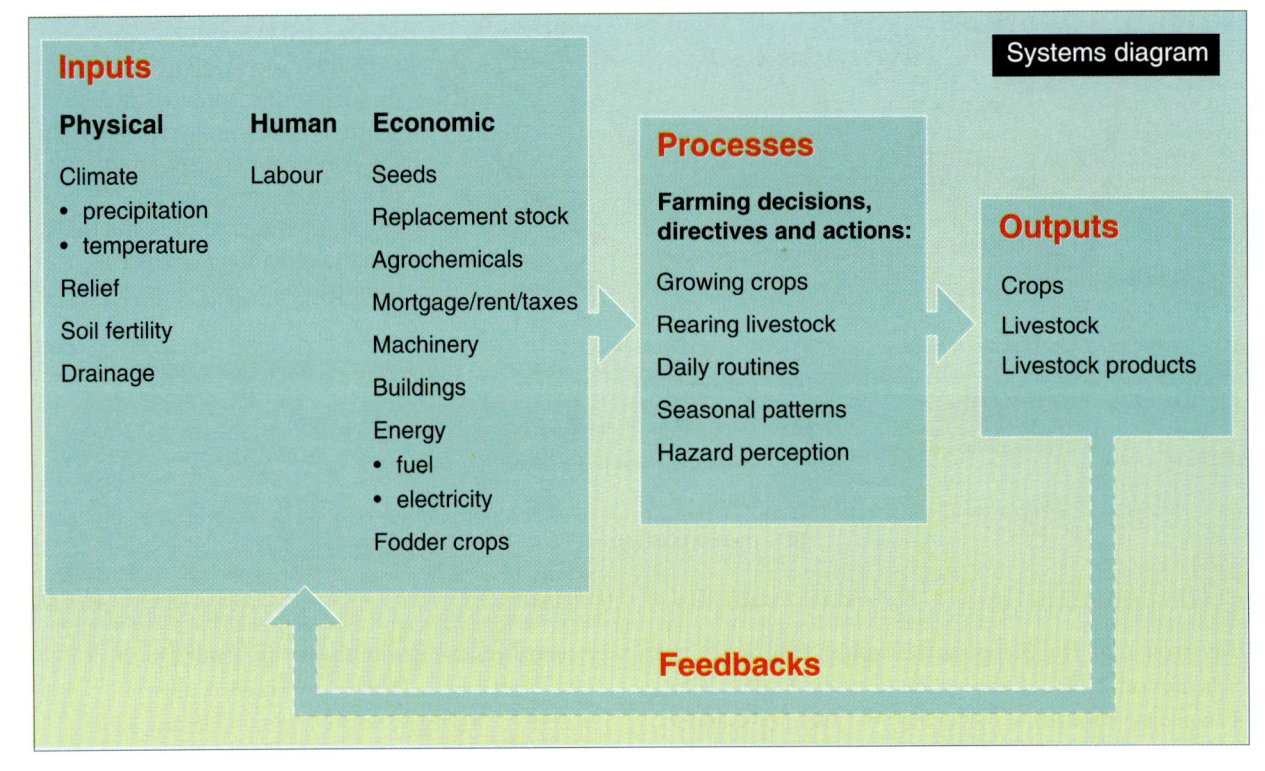

Systems diagram

Inputs

Physical	Human	Economic
Climate	Labour	Seeds
• precipitation		Replacement stock
• temperature		Agrochemicals
Relief		Mortgage/rent/taxes
Soil fertility		Machinery
Drainage		Buildings
		Energy
		• fuel
		• electricity
		Fodder crops

Processes

Farming decisions, directives and actions:

Growing crops
Rearing livestock
Daily routines
Seasonal patterns
Hazard perception

Outputs

Crops
Livestock
Livestock products

Feedbacks

- **The inputs** – physical, human, and economic factors – determine the type of farming found in any particular location.

- **The processes** (farming methods) will vary according to these inputs, but also due to the levels of technology available.

- **The outputs** are the crops cultivated and animals reared.

- There are also **feedbacks**, for example, the use of manure as fertiliser and the use of fodder crops produced for feeding livestock.

With environmental and cultural diversity across the world, different areas have different farming systems. The number and variety of these systems could be limitless, hence the need to classify farming into broad types:

- **Type of output** – Farming can be **arable** (growing crops), **pastoral** (rearing animals) or **mixed** (doing both).

- **Destination of output** – Farms are either **near-subsistence** (output mostly retained to feed the farmer's family) or **commercial** (output sold at market).

- **Scale of input and output** – Farms can be **intensive** (high yields per hectare, due to large inputs of labour, or capital invested in machinery, agrochemicals, and so on); intensive farms are, usually, relatively small. Or farms can be **extensive** (low yields per hectare, due to small inputs of labour or capital, or due to poor physical inputs such as a difficult climate, poor soils, and so on); extensive farm sizes can be very big.

Other categories have been suggested, such as whether the cultivation is **sedentary** (fixed in one location), or **shifting** (moving regularly from area to area), and whether the farm is owned or rented.

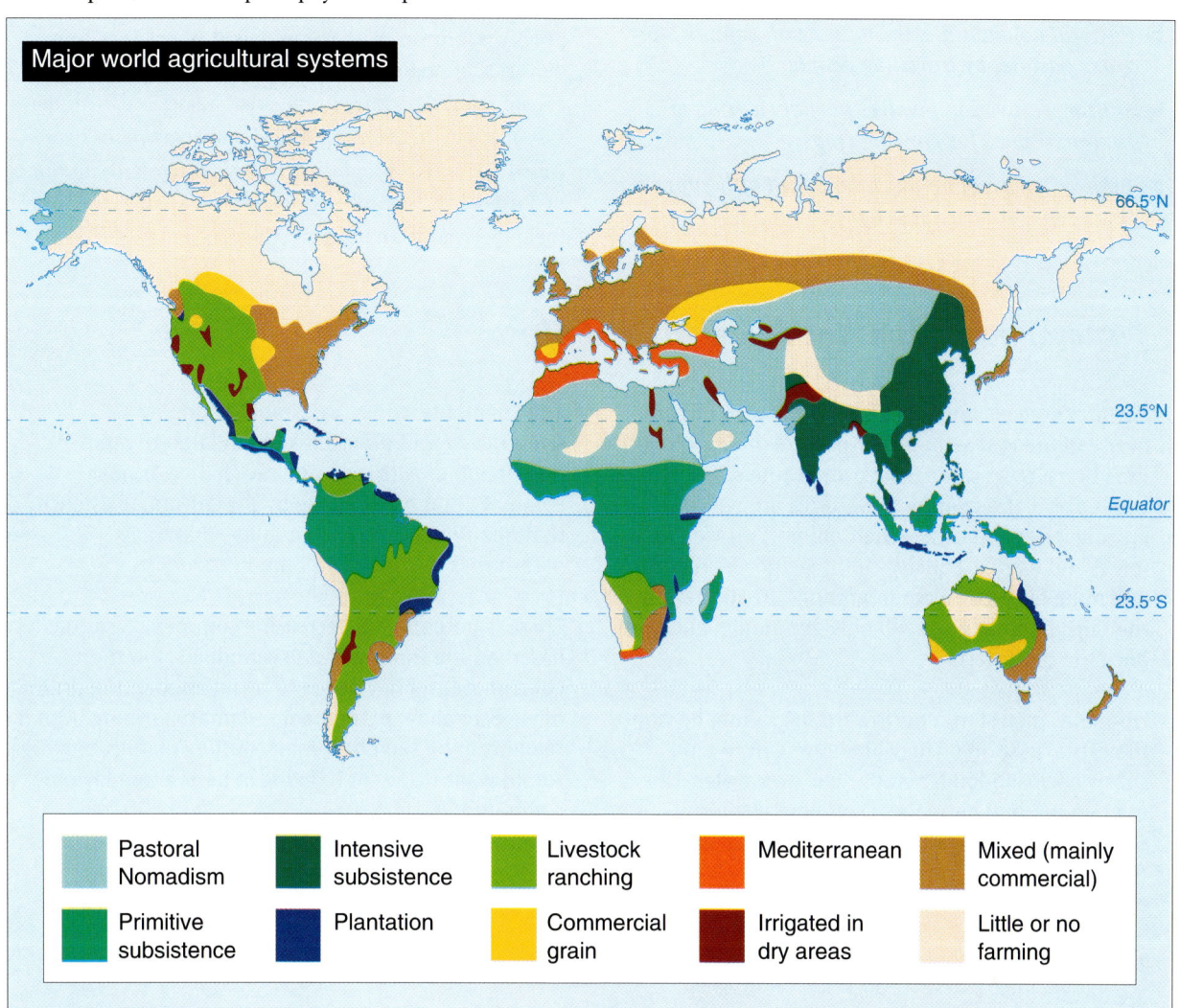

Major world agricultural systems

Legend:
- Pastoral Nomadism
- Intensive subsistence
- Livestock ranching
- Mediterranean
- Mixed (mainly commercial)
- Primitive subsistence
- Plantation
- Commercial grain
- Irrigated in dry areas
- Little or no farming

Test yourself

1. Which of the following is a farm output?
A Fertiliser. B Land. C Barley. D Tractor. E Workers.

2. Outline the differences between the following forms of farming:

(a) arable and pastoral

(b) near-subsistence and commercial

(c) intensive and extensive.

Stretch yourself

For any farm, or type of farming studied, summarise its key characteristics under the three main headings of inputs, processes and outputs.

ECONOMIC THEMES • FARMING   41

ELDC extensive farming systems

Key points

▶ Simple, extensive farming systems are ecologically sound, but under threat.

▶ Pastoral nomadism is the herding of animals, to graze pasture, by travelling people.

▶ Shifting cultivation involves partial clearing of rainforest plots for growing crops.

▶ Both systems require much land, but only support a few people at near-subsistence.

Simple **extensive farming systems**, for example, **pastoral nomadism, shifting cultivation and bush fallowing** represent some of the longest established and most ecologically balanced, agricultural practices. However, they can only support very low densities of population. Rapid population growth puts considerable pressure on the areas associated with these systems. Furthermore, political embarrassment over so-called 'primitive wandering tribes', often with no sense of nationality, is another pressure threatening the future for these simple farming practices.

Pastoral nomadism: the Fulani of West Africa

Pastoral nomads are travelling people who migrate over vast areas of semi-desert pasture in order to graze livestock such as cattle, goats, and camels. The Fulani tribes of Sahel regions in West Africa are typical – grazing long-horn cattle. Their animals provide food (meat and dairy products), clothing and shelter (skins), and dung for fuel. Fulani migrations are dictated by the rains because grass will only germinate, and grow, once the rains start.

Normally, men start a northward migration, herding the cattle, in spring. The women remain to tend subsistence and fodder crops near river water. The men set up semi-permanent settlements on sub-Saharan pastures before returning south at the end of the rainy season.

These seasonal migrations are dictated by environmental factors. Tsetse fly infestations (which are fatal to cattle and cause sleeping sickness in humans) are another limiting factor, preventing movements towards the more humid conditions further south.

The Fulani lifestyle is, inevitably, changing. Overgrazing and desertification, related to rapid population growth and climatic change, is now common, and made worse by the cultural insistence that quantity, rather than quality, of animals determines the owner's status.

There is potential for increasing commercialisation, based on the trading of dairy products. But more government money needs to be invested in the drilling of wells to allow permanent sedentary farming. Also it remains to be seen how many of the Fulani could, or would want to, adapt to living in permanent farming communities.

A Fulani tribesman.

42   ECONOMIC THEMES • FARMING

Shifting cultivation: the Amerindians of Amazonia, Brazil

Shifting 'slash and burn' cultivation is a traditional form of agriculture associated with tropical rainforests. Rapid commercial development of rainforests is, however, hastening the decline of this farming system; it is now only found in particularly inaccessible regions.

The rapidly declining Amerindian tribes of western Amazonia in Brazil, for example, illustrate what is probably the simplest of all farming systems.

An Amerindian-made clearing in the Amazonian rainforest.

- *Several football pitch sized patches of forest are cleared near to the village in August (the least rainy time of year).*
- *Stone axes and machetes are used to cut the trees to shoulder height.*
- *The branches, once dried, are burnt, and the fertile ashes spread between the stumps.*
- *Wooden digging sticks are then used to plant the main crop of manioc (for cassava bread), plus yams, pumpkins, peppers, beans and occasionally maize too.*
- *Hand weeding is necessary because both crops and weeds grow rapidly in these hot, wet conditions.*
- *Cultivation and cropping are continuous for around 3 to 5 years until the clearings lose fertility.*
- *They are then abandoned, along with the village, and the tribe 'shifts' to another area – ideally not to return for 20 to 30 years, so allowing the rainforest vegetation to regenerate naturally.*

Contemporary population pressure is reducing this fallow period, with reduced soil fertility in consequence. Also government pressure to develop the rainforest (see page 129), and encourage Amerindians to live on reservations, is threatening the system further.

Test yourself

1. Give two examples of ELDC extensive farming systems.

2. Why are such systems under threat today?

Stretch yourself

Both the farming systems described may be 'wasteful' of land, but can support people in harmony with what are fragile environments. This can be illustrated further by considering how shifting cultivation protects the soil. Outline the specific soil conservation advantages of: (a) small separated clearings (b) trees cut to shoulder height (c) clearings abandoned after 3 to 5 years.

ELDC intensive farming systems

Key points

▶ *Intensive farming ensures high productivity through labour, or capital investment.*

▶ *Rice is the world's most important food – highly nutritious and easy to store.*

▶ *Plantations are labour and capital intensive, and often owned by multinational companies.*

The main advantage of **intensive systems** of agriculture is that they are very **productive**. Intensive effectively means high yields per hectare – more people supported. In **near-subsistence** farming systems, with limited or no surplus food for sale, the high yields are obtained by high input of labour. Intensive subsistence rice cultivation in the Ganges Valley, India, illustrates this well.

Intensive **commercial** agriculture, in ELDCs, is well established too. It can be seen in the plantation systems specialising in producing cash crops for export.

Crops grown on plantations include:

- tea
- coffee
- cocoa
- palm oil
- bananas
- cane sugar
- tobacco
- rubber.

Plantations are found throughout the tropical world, frequently close to rail links to a port. This is because most were founded by European and North American merchants, in the 18th and 19th centuries, for export.

Monoculture is usual – allowing efficient organisation of the large labour force required, with cost-effective use of the necessary resources eg. machinery, agrochemicals.

Monoculture also makes plantations vulnerable to disease, soil deterioration, and especially fluctuations in demand caused by changing tastes.

Plantation agriculture: rubber in Malaysia

Tapping for latex, Malaysia.

Malaysia produces more than half the world's natural rubber, which comes from latex. Although originally an Amazon plant it thrives in Malaysia's hot, wet, equatorial climate. A typical plantation can extend over thousands of hectares.

'Cheap' local labour is needed to work in the nurseries, clear the forest, plant new trees, and 'tap' the mature ones. Rubber trees, planted in orderly rows, will yield latex once they are five years old – but they need replacing after twenty-five. The liquid white latex is allowed to weep from bark, peeled daily in strips, into a suspended cup. Experienced tappers can cover 500 to 600 trees a day!

The latex is then processed on site, into rubber sheets, prior to transport by rail or road to the nearest port. It is of note that since the 1940s, synthetic rubber, suitable for tyres, has badly affected demand although increasing worldwide demand for condoms has recently reversed the trend.

Intensive subsistence rice cultivation: Ganges Valley, India and Bangladesh

The tropical monsoon climate, and flat, fertile, alluvial flood plains of the Ganges Valley, provide ideal growing conditions for so-called 'wet' rice varieties. ('Dry' rice varieties are associated with irrigated hillside terraces.) Rice is rich in carbohydrate, fibre, and vegetable protein. It also stores well. It is the mainstay of the diet in this region – and represents the staple food for well over half of humanity! Everything associated with rice farming is highly labour intensive.

Ploughing the padi, Bangladesh.

Before the monsoon (April/May)
The process begins with preparation and manuring of the nursery seed beds.

The monsoon begins (May/June)
As soon as the rains start, the rice seeds can be planted. They need to grow for up to 6 weeks before they will be tall enough not to drown once transplanted. This allows time for digging irrigation channels where necessary, levelling and manuring the padi fields, plus checking and building their retaining banks (bunds) prior to flooding. (In some cases the padi fields will even be stocked with fish – a protein rich supplement to the diet, plus further fertiliser for the soil.)

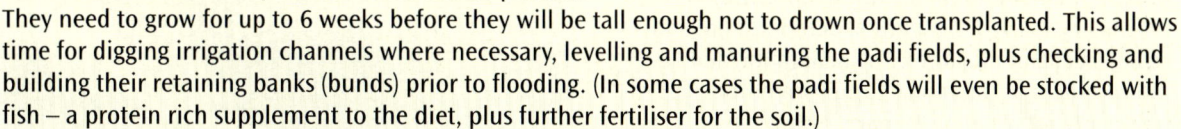

Working the padis (July/August)
Women and children transplant individual seedlings, from the nursery seed beds, by hand. Once in the padi fields, the rice grows very quickly, but it needs constant weeding right through to harvesting in drier conditions towards the end of the year. Again, all of this is very labour intensive.

Harvesting (October/November)
The cut rice is then threshed, and winnowed, to separate the rice to be stored from straw and other chaff which can be used for anything from fodder for animals, to weaving hats, mats, and baskets.

Re-using the padis (January)
Providing sufficient irrigation water is available, other crops, such as beans, lentils, and wheat can be cultivated, or even a second rice crop planted for harvesting in April.

Test yourself

1. Give two examples of ELDC intensive farming systems.

2. What is the main advantage of these systems?

3. What qualities make rice the most important food in the world?

Stretch yourself

It can be argued that the large labour requirements for the two farming systems described are highly appropriate given ELDC population growth, under- and un-employment. However, you should be aware that plantation agriculture offers both advantages and disadvantages for 'native' workers. Advantages include the provision of social facilities within plantations, such as housing, schools, clinics, and general stores. What are the disadvantages?

The Green Revolution

Rapid population increase in ELDCs has placed many traditional farming systems under considerable strain. The so-called Green Revolution refers to the many important agricultural developments which have allowed food production, at a global scale, to generally keep pace.

Changing farming techniques?
One key feature of the Green Revolution is the application of modern farming techniques, common in EMDCs, to ELDCs. In particular, agricultural productivity has been increased by making more intensive and efficient use of the land. That said, one painful lesson learned has been that the adoption of large-scale 'western' style projects can prove wholly inappropriate in, say, tropical climates. The ploughing of large areas, for example, using sophisticated machinery, has led to rapid soil deterioration, and costly mechanical failures. The adaptation and improvement of traditional farming methods frequently proves to be of more lasting value.

Changing crops?
Another key element has been the development of new varieties of crops, achieved through hybridisation (cross-breeding). Indeed the origins of the Green Revolution are often quoted as hybridisation experiments in countries such as the UK, Italy, the Philippines and Mexico.

Transplanting rice seedlings in the Philippines.

In Mexico, for example, hybrid maize and wheat strains were developed to withstand heavy rain, strong wind and diseases. Maize yields consequently doubled, whilst wheat tripled! Animals have also been cross-bred in order to improve their tolerance to difficult environmental conditions, such as aridity. But it is the development of improved 'miracle/super/wonder' rice varieties in the Philippines, such as IR8 (improved rice version 8), which have gained most attention.

Sixfold increases in yield were reported from the first harvest of IR8, and before long 10% of India's padi fields were planted with it. But such high-yielding varieties (HYVs) have proved to be vulnerable to pests and new diseases. Consequently, they require continuing development. We had IR36 by the 1970s, and IR58 in the '80s!

Inspecting the 'super' rice crop, Manila.

Improvements have certainly been remarkable – with a 'super rice' in 1994 quoted as 25% higher yielding than IR8!

Changing the environment?

Another important aspect of the Green Revolution has been the extension of water control and irrigation schemes. These range from the installation of relatively inexpensive wells and pumps, to the development of large-scale multi-purpose river projects, such as Egypt's Aswan High Dam (see page 56).

The increased use of agrochemicals such as fertilisers, pesticides, fungicides and weedkillers is also very important. Chemical fertilisers alone have doubled crop yields in tropical areas, and locust plagues, for example, are now rare due to control by the pesticide, aldrin.

Synthetic hormones have also been developed – to control plant sizes and growth rates, so allowing growing seasons to be adjusted. Other innovations include the improvement of crop storage, handling, and processing, in order to reduce wastage. Appropriate mechanisation has also been possible, often accompanied by land reform, such as the reorganisation of small, irregular-shaped fragmented plots into more regular fields. Soil conservation measures, such as contour ploughing and intercropping, have been introduced too.

Assessing the results

The Green Revolution has not been all about success. The Green Revolution has successfully lessened the threat of food shortages in many ELDCs, but on an individual level it has proved socially divisive – rich farmers have got richer, whilst the poor, poorer. Just consider the following issues:

- ***The financial and social costs associated with many of the initiatives can prove very high.***
- ***Only the richer farmers can normally afford to buy and run tractors, for example, and unemployment increases as a result.***
- ***Demand for agrochemicals may have created industrial jobs, but their production and use can prove dangerous.***
- ***Education is needed to ensure productive cultivation of HYVs, given their frequent special irrigation and agrochemical requirements.***

Irrigation boosts the cane sugar crop in Zambia.

Farming in Britain

Key points

▶ British farming is big 'agribusiness' – influenced by both physical and human factors.

▶ Different regions in Britain are associated with different forms of farming.

▶ The EU's Common Agricultural Policy both supports and constrains farmers.

Farming is a very important and highly efficient industry in Britain. It is affected by:

- **physical factors** (climate, landscape and soils) which mean certain areas are more suited to certain types of farming than others.
- **human factors** (type and quality of transport routes and nearness to markets) influence which form of farming is best suited to any particular location.

Remember, farmers should be thought of as **satisficers**, seeking to achieve satisfactory profits and living standards. They need to decide upon the most appropriate form of farming. Their decisions will be influenced by the directives of the European Union's **Common Agricultural Policy** (see page 51).

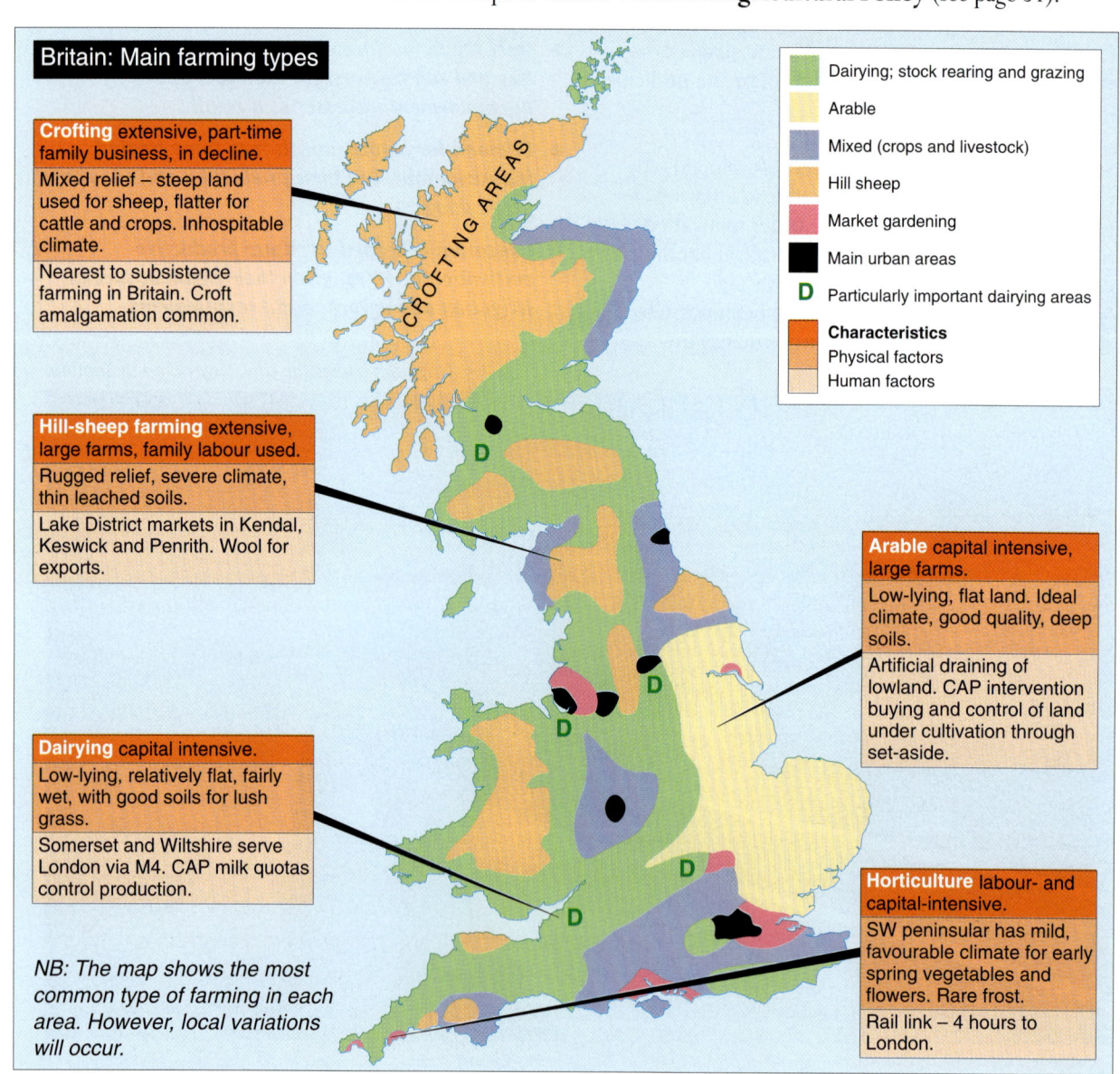

Britain: Main farming types

Crofting extensive, part-time family business, in decline.

Mixed relief – steep land used for sheep, flatter for cattle and crops. Inhospitable climate.

Nearest to subsistence farming in Britain. Croft amalgamation common.

Hill-sheep farming extensive, large farms, family labour used.

Rugged relief, severe climate, thin leached soils.

Lake District markets in Kendal, Keswick and Penrith. Wool for exports.

Dairying capital intensive.

Low-lying, relatively flat, fairly wet, with good soils for lush grass.

Somerset and Wiltshire serve London via M4. CAP milk quotas control production.

NB: The map shows the most common type of farming in each area. However, local variations will occur.

Legend:
- Dairying; stock rearing and grazing
- Arable
- Mixed (crops and livestock)
- Hill sheep
- Market gardening
- Main urban areas
- D Particularly important dairying areas

Characteristics
- Physical factors
- Human factors

Arable capital intensive, large farms.

Low-lying, flat land. Ideal climate, good quality, deep soils.

Artificial draining of lowland. CAP intervention buying and control of land under cultivation through set-aside.

Horticulture labour- and capital-intensive.

SW peninsular has mild, favourable climate for early spring vegetables and flowers. Rare frost.

Rail link – 4 hours to London.

48 ECONOMIC THEMES • FARMING

Britain: Annual rainfall

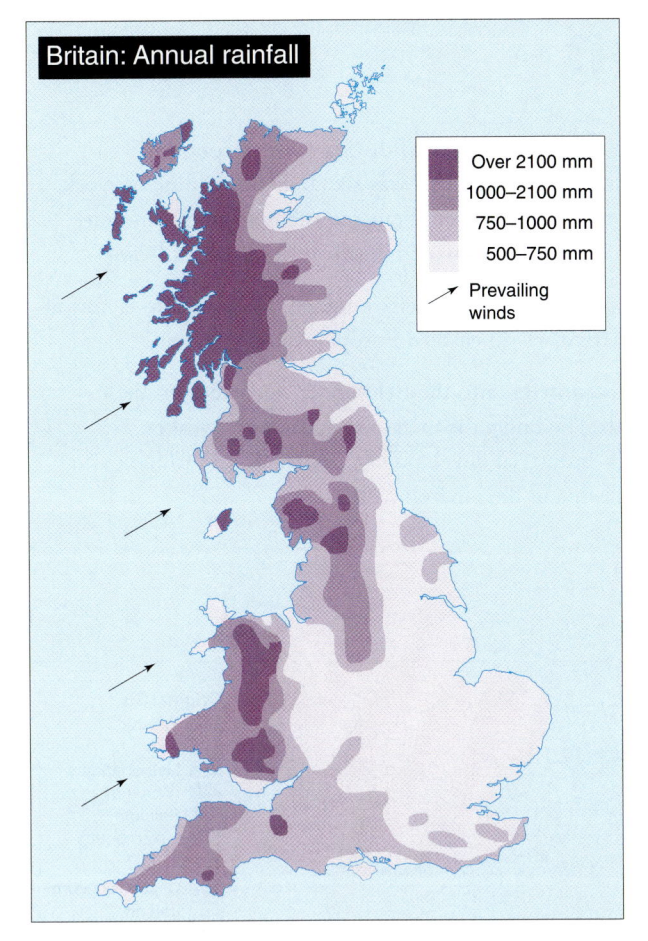

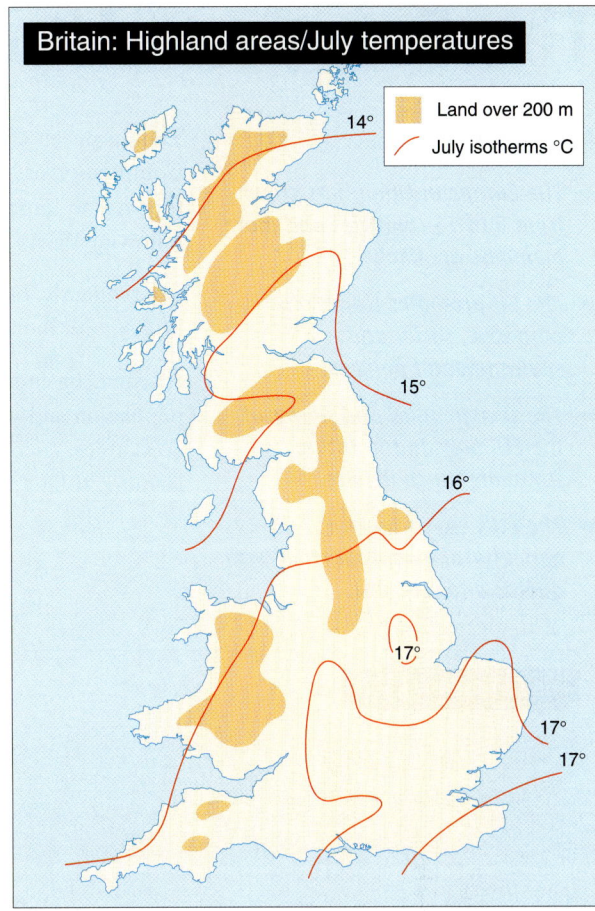

Over 2100 mm
1000–2100 mm
750–1000 mm
500–750 mm
↗ Prevailing winds

Britain: Highland areas/July temperatures

Land over 200 m
July isotherms °C

- **CAP opportunities** include guaranteed prices assured through intervention buying, in addition to, for example, tree planting grants.
- **CAP constraints** include, for example, milk quotas, and pressure to 'set-aside' fields in order to reduce overproduction.

Indeed, farmers must be both willing and able to respond to economic and technological change. The EU is under considerable pressure to reduce the amount it spends on agriculture. Consequently, CAP farm subsidies are increasingly less generous, forcing many farmers to change their land-use, such as by diversifying into leisure and recreation, in order to stay in business.

Test yourself

1. List the factors which determine what type of farming is practiced in different areas of Britain. Use two headings: (a) Physical factors (b) Human factors.

Stretch yourself

Although less than 3% of the British workforce are employed in farming, around 80% of the land is devoted to it. The Main farming types map shows the distribution of major forms of farming in a simplified, generalised manner. Assess the relationships between relief, precipitation, likely soils, and July temperatures. What influence are they likely to have in determining which type of farming predominates in any particular region?

ECONOMIC THEMES • FARMING

The European Union

Key points

▶ The European Union has grown from 6 to 15 countries and more members are likely.

▶ The EU promotes trade, plus economic, social and environmental policies.

▶ The specific roles and power of the EU, now and in future, stimulate much debate.

▶ The EU's CAP is tackling agricultural overproduction with quotas and set-aside.

The European Union originally started as the European Economic Community, or 'Common Market'. This was six countries aiming to work together to improve relations between them and rebuild their economies following World War II. These aims would improve standards of living.

Consequently, other groups of countries have joined. Membership is now at fifteen with more, particularly in eastern Europe, wanting to join.

All member countries contribute to the EU budget, according to their population and wealth. The budget is then used to support weaker economies, encourage industrial development and trade, and to look after farming, fishing, tourism and the environment.

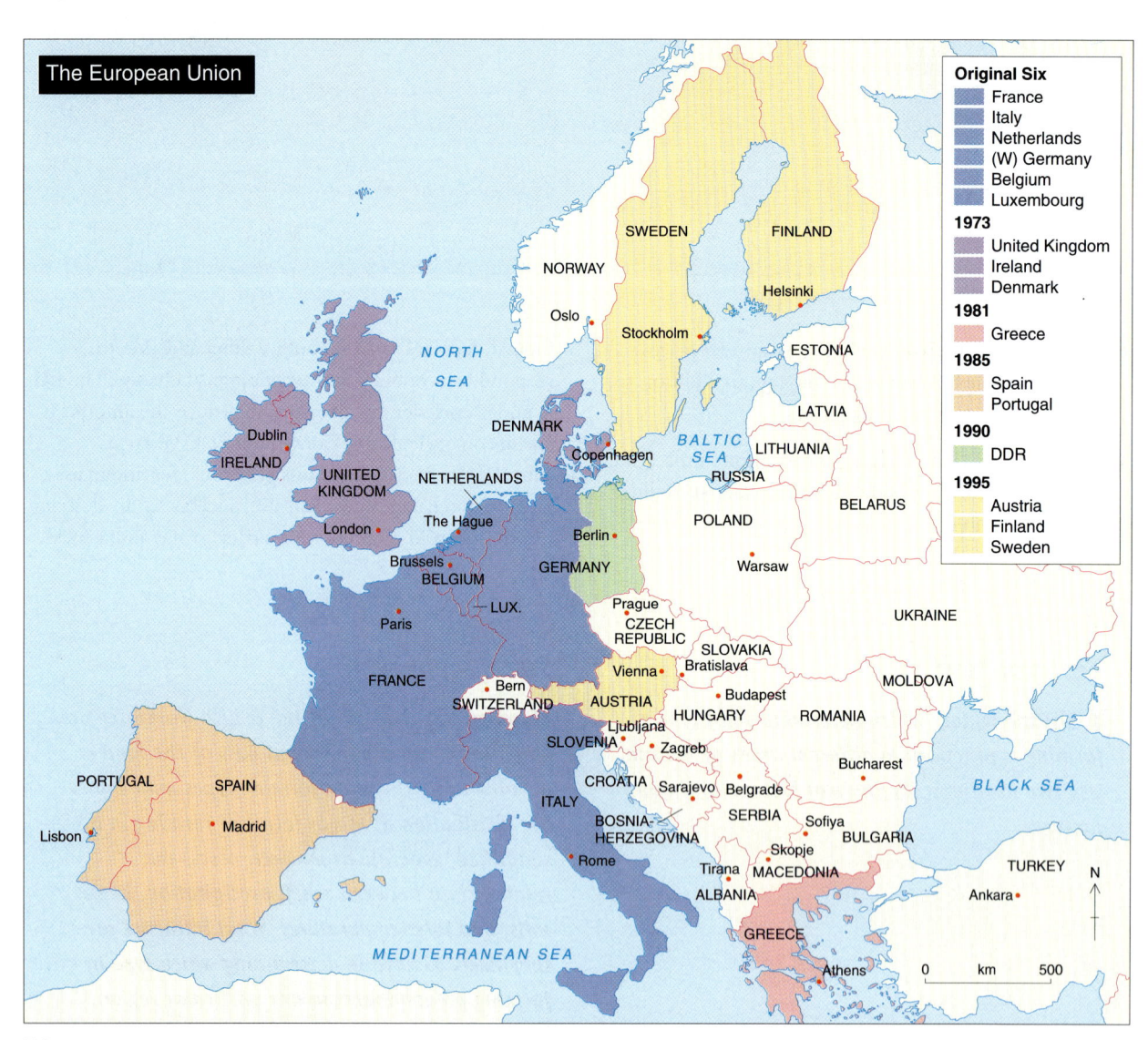

The European Union

Original Six
- France
- Italy
- Netherlands
- (W) Germany
- Belgium
- Luxembourg

1973
- United Kingdom
- Ireland
- Denmark

1981
- Greece

1985
- Spain
- Portugal

1990
- DDR

1995
- Austria
- Finland
- Sweden

The specific roles and powers of the EU cause much debate. This is often generalised into 'pro-' and 'anti-European' standpoints. CAP issues used to dominate discussions but today it is the extent that 'European' decisions affect national activities.

Also there is much debate about whether or not all members should move towards greater political unity – including a **common European currency** – which would bring the EU closer to the ideals of the original Treaty of Rome.

The Common Agricultural Policy (CAP)

European 'agribusiness' is dominated by the Common Agricultural Policy (CAP), run from Brussels. To summarise, the aims of the CAP are:

- *to assure the EU's essential food supplies*
- *to keep prices for the consumer stable*
- *to give farmers a secure income.*

The EU effectively represents a single market of over 370 million people. Within this market there is, normally, free movement of farm products, so countries do not have to pay duties on the goods they export. The CAP has protected EU farmers from cheap imports by imposing **trade tariffs**, and by giving them **subsidies** to produce certain crops.

Many essential products like grain, meat, and milk had a guaranteed minimum price. Whenever market prices fell to this level then the EU bought the produce from the farmers and either stored it until the market improved, or sold it off to non-EU countries. But the efficiency of most farmers, and the guaranteed prices ensured massive **overproduction** – stored as vast surpluses of such items as grain, frozen beef, powdered milk and olive oil. These stockpiles became known, infamously, as 'mountains' and 'lakes'.

Dumped cucumbers, Gran Canaria, Spain.

The 1980s saw much CAP attention addressed to reducing these stockpiles. Quotas have been introduced, for example, to reduce production of milk and beef, and the number of sheep reared. Subsidies on cereals and beef are being progressively reduced each year. Also, farmers are now paid to set-aside up to 15% of their land – either to leave it fallow, or to develop it for non-agricultural purposes, such as recreation (golf courses, caravan sites and so on) and woodland.

Test yourself

1. Study the EU map. List the current member countries.

2. Explain briefly the CAP terms: (a) intervention buying (b) quotas (c) subsidies (d) set-aside.

Stretch yourself

Not only the spreading European Union, but the changing political map of the rest of Europe, raises quite an interesting challenge.

Just how many countries and capital cities do you still struggle to identify? If only for peace of mind, and to avoid embarrassing gaffes, the names on this map are well worth learning.

An EU problem region: southern Italy

Key points

▶ Italy, south of Rome – the Mezzogiorno – contains the EU's poorest regions.

▶ In the 1950s many of the Mezzogiorno's problems could be likened to an ELDC.

▶ Since the 1950s various schemes have improved farming, industry and services.

The Mezzogiorno contains regions, such as the Neapolitan Riviera, much loved by tourists. Historic ruins, and villages 'clinging' to cliffs, overlooking warm, clear Mediterranean waters, have attracted visitors for decades. The importance of tourism, however, also emphasises just what little else southern Italy offered from an economic standpoint. The Mezzogiorno has long suffered from an **overdependence upon farming**, with limited industrial and commercial development and poor services. This has been related both to a lack of mineral and energy resources, and the area's inability to produce and retain sufficient skilled labour.

The way in which these problems have been tackled, since the 1950s, has attracted much attention. Some feel they have been successful – others disagree.

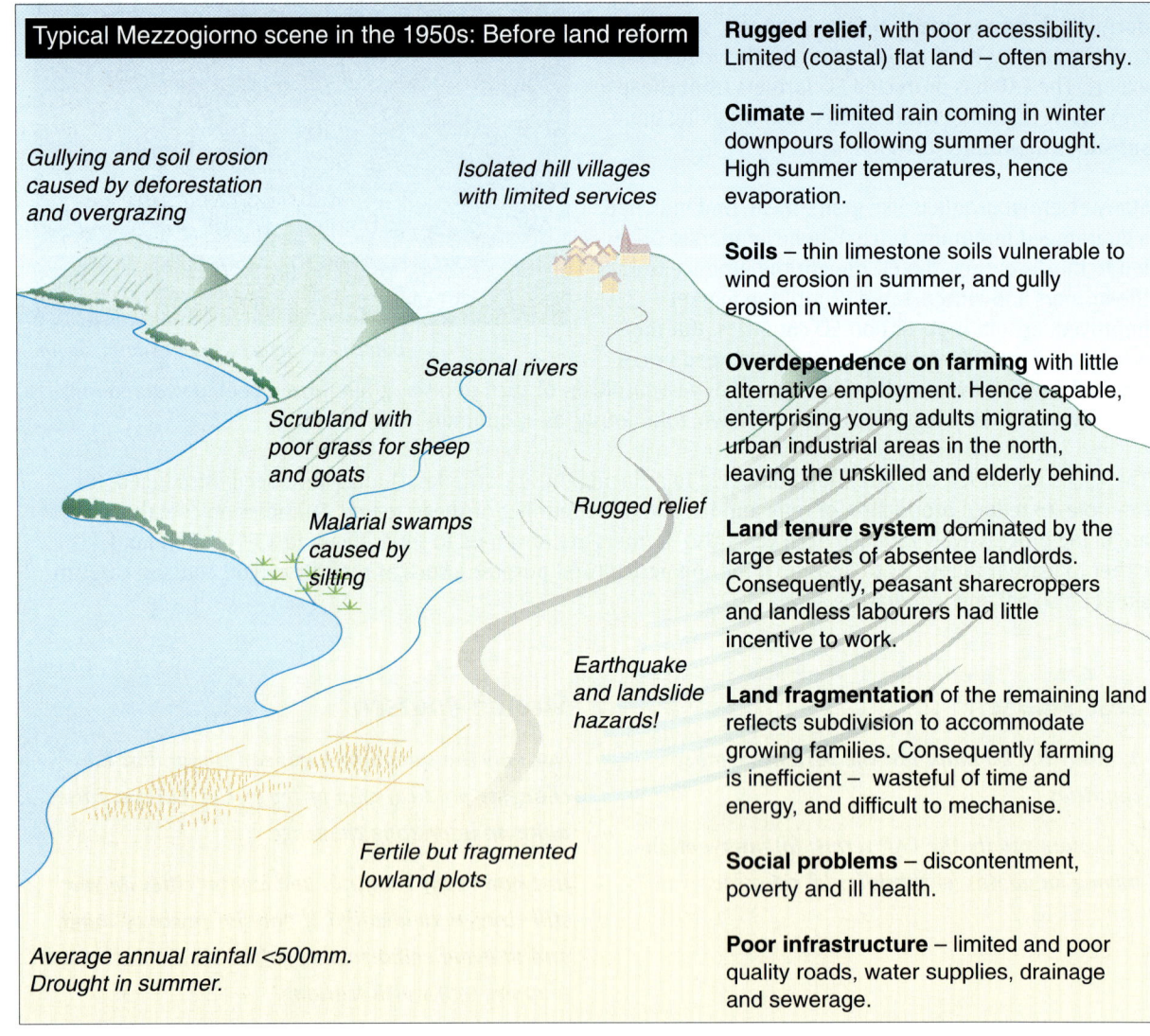

Typical Mezzogiorno scene in the 1950s: Before land reform

Gullying and soil erosion caused by deforestation and overgrazing

Isolated hill villages with limited services

Seasonal rivers

Scrubland with poor grass for sheep and goats

Malarial swamps caused by silting

Rugged relief

Earthquake and landslide hazards!

Fertile but fragmented lowland plots

Average annual rainfall <500mm. Drought in summer.

Rugged relief, with poor accessibility. Limited (coastal) flat land – often marshy.

Climate – limited rain coming in winter downpours following summer drought. High summer temperatures, hence evaporation.

Soils – thin limestone soils vulnerable to wind erosion in summer, and gully erosion in winter.

Overdependence on farming with little alternative employment. Hence capable, enterprising young adults migrating to urban industrial areas in the north, leaving the unskilled and elderly behind.

Land tenure system dominated by the large estates of absentee landlords. Consequently, peasant sharecroppers and landless labourers had little incentive to work.

Land fragmentation of the remaining land reflects subdivision to accommodate growing families. Consequently farming is inefficient – wasteful of time and energy, and difficult to mechanise.

Social problems – discontentment, poverty and ill health.

Poor infrastructure – limited and poor quality roads, water supplies, drainage and sewerage.

Massive **government investment** was a key part of the plans. A special 'Fund for the South', known as the 'Cassa per Il Mezzogiorno', with some money from the EU's CAP, has been used. This aimed to develop more industry, construct related infrastructure and provide other services. But it has been the reform of farming which has been the central theme.

Land reform agencies were set up to buy, and then break up, the existing large and inefficient estates. Once the owners were compensated, the estates could be sold off as sensibly sized farms.

Other initiatives included:

- soil conservation
- afforestation programmes
- marsh drainage
- hillside terracing
- reservoir and dam construction
- irrigation schemes.

Co-operatives were set up, for the marketing and bulk buying of machinery, seeds, and agrochemicals. Finally, processing factories, schools, hospitals, and agricultural training centres, with all their necessary infrastructure, completed the new landscape. However, although the Mezzogiorno is markedly improved, it remains a relatively impoverished EU region. It is still too dependent on farming, in what are still difficult physical conditions.

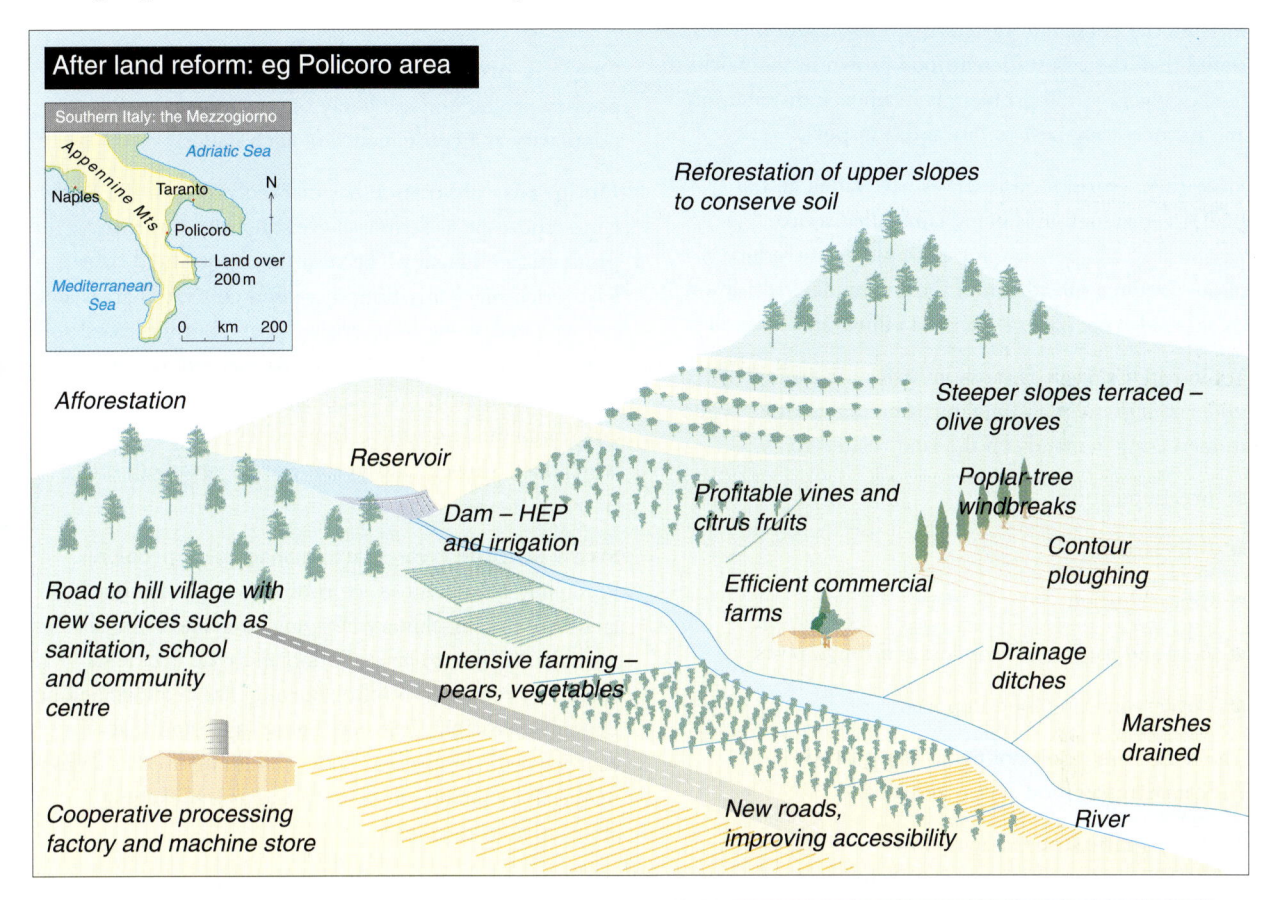

Test yourself

1. Express Italy's North-South divide in a sentence.

2. Which of the Mezzogiorno's problems could be described as: (a) physical (b) human?

Stretch yourself

Italy is a founder member of the EU, yet before this land reform programme its southern regions demonstrated many of the characteristics of ELDCs.
(a) Summarise the similarities between the Mezzogiorno before land reform and a typical ELDC.
(b) Why might the solutions adopted in this case study be less easy to implement in ELDCs today?

ECONOMIC THEMES • FARMING

Farming and public awareness

Key points

▶ The world can and does produce enough food, but consumption inequalities persist.

▶ 'Factory farming', stubble disposal, hedgerow clearance and chemicals provoke debate.

▶ Soil erosion, associated with bad farming practices, is a global problem.

In 1986 the Food and Agricultural Organisation (FAO) stated that 'there is sufficient food grown in the world to feed everyone – the problem is its uneven distribution and its increasing cost to buy and transport.'

Since then, world food reserves have fallen and, in EMDCs, production is being controlled more responsibly. EU policies, for example, to introduce quotas, reduce subsidies and the area under cultivation by set-aside (see pages 49 and 51) illustrate this well.

Yet in ELDCs, such as those in Africa for example, undernourishment and malnutrition persist; this is due to increasing demands on the land related to:

- overpopulation
- soil erosion
- desertification
- field and harvested crop losses through pests
- poverty limiting food imports.

The frustrating reality of persisting **global inequalities** in food supply remains.

Yet it is **agribusiness** issues closer to home which progressively dominate public consciousness.

The general public are increasingly more aware of what they consume, and how it is produced. There is widespread comment, informed and otherwise, on numerous issues including:

- **Factory farming** of beef, pork, poultry and eggs – intensive production has undoubtedly reduced prices to the consumer, but prompted concern over issues concerning animal rights and produce quality.

- Veal calf production and transportation, 'battery' hen conditions and egg quality, chicken and turkey breeding and husbandry techniques, and the abuse of growth hormones and antibiotics in beef production.

- The BSE ('mad cow disease') scare and the 'openness' of both food producers and governments concerning health-related issues.

- **Genetic engineering** of both crops and livestock raises questions as to what, exactly, we might be eating in future.

Organic production techniques, such as 'free range' poultry production are likely to gain increasing popularity as a consequence of such issues.

Hedgerow clearance has markedly altered the British rural landscape as farmers have sought to improve production efficiency. The resulting larger field sizes have aided mechanisation, increased cultivated areas and reduced hedgerow maintenance costs. But increased soil erosion, concern over lost wildlife habitats and the **overproduction** discussed earlier have led to more environmentally sensitive approaches being adopted which have slowed, and in some areas reversed, the trend.

Straw stubble creates farm management problems. Ploughing it back into the ground costs the farmer in labour hours, machinery clogging, weed and fungal growths. Yet due to air pollution and road accidents caused by reduced visibility, burning has been banned in Britain since 1993. It is now being suggested that reprocessed, compressed straw should be used as a raw material for building insulation and as a packaging alternative to cardboard.

Pesticide spraying undoubtedly improves crop quality, but also kills harmless insects such as bees. Whilst farmers can wear protective clothing and masks, environmentalists fear for the public exposed to chemicals carried 'on the wind'.

Agrochemical residues and **farm waste (slurry)** contain nitrates which leach through the soil into rivers and groundwater aquifers. Consequently, water supplies are polluted.

The real cost of cheap eggs.

Pollution from burning stubble.

Soil erosion and management: Loch Leven, Scotland

Loch Leven is an example of a place where soil erosion has been caused by changes in farm practices.

The highest slopes, cleared of woodland, have been overgrazed by sheep. Meanwhile, lower slopes have been intensively cultivated. The upland deforestation and overgrazing, and lower slope hedgerow clearance and plough furrow compaction have resulted in vast amounts of fine topsoil being washed into the loch.

Furthermore, agrochemical residues – particularly phosphates – carried in the topsoil have caused nutrient enrichment of the loch leading to algal growths. Rapidly growing algae poison the water with toxins and use up much of its oxygen. Consequently, fish stocks in Loch Leven have fallen.

Simple, but effective soil conservation measures have, however, now been introduced. Most notable have been the grass banks around field edges and along drainage ditches leading into the loch. These have checked the erosion, yet allow water to soak naturally through the soil. Leaching is reduced, algal growth is checked and fish stocks are less endangered.

Test yourself

1. If there is sufficient food grown in the world to feed everyone, why is malnutrition and undernourishment still common?

2. Find out the main differences between 'factory' and 'organic' farming methods.

Stretch yourself

Soil erosion is associated across the globe with bad farming practices. With reference to named examples from EMDCs and/or ELDCs you have studied state the conservation initiatives associated with: (a) deforestation (b) hedgerow clearance (c) overgrazing (d) upslope ploughing (e) overcultivation.

A multi-purpose river project: the Aswan High Dam, Egypt

Key points

▶ The Aswan High Dam provides Egypt with HEP, flood control and irrigation water.

▶ The project has, however, created economic, social and environmental problems too.

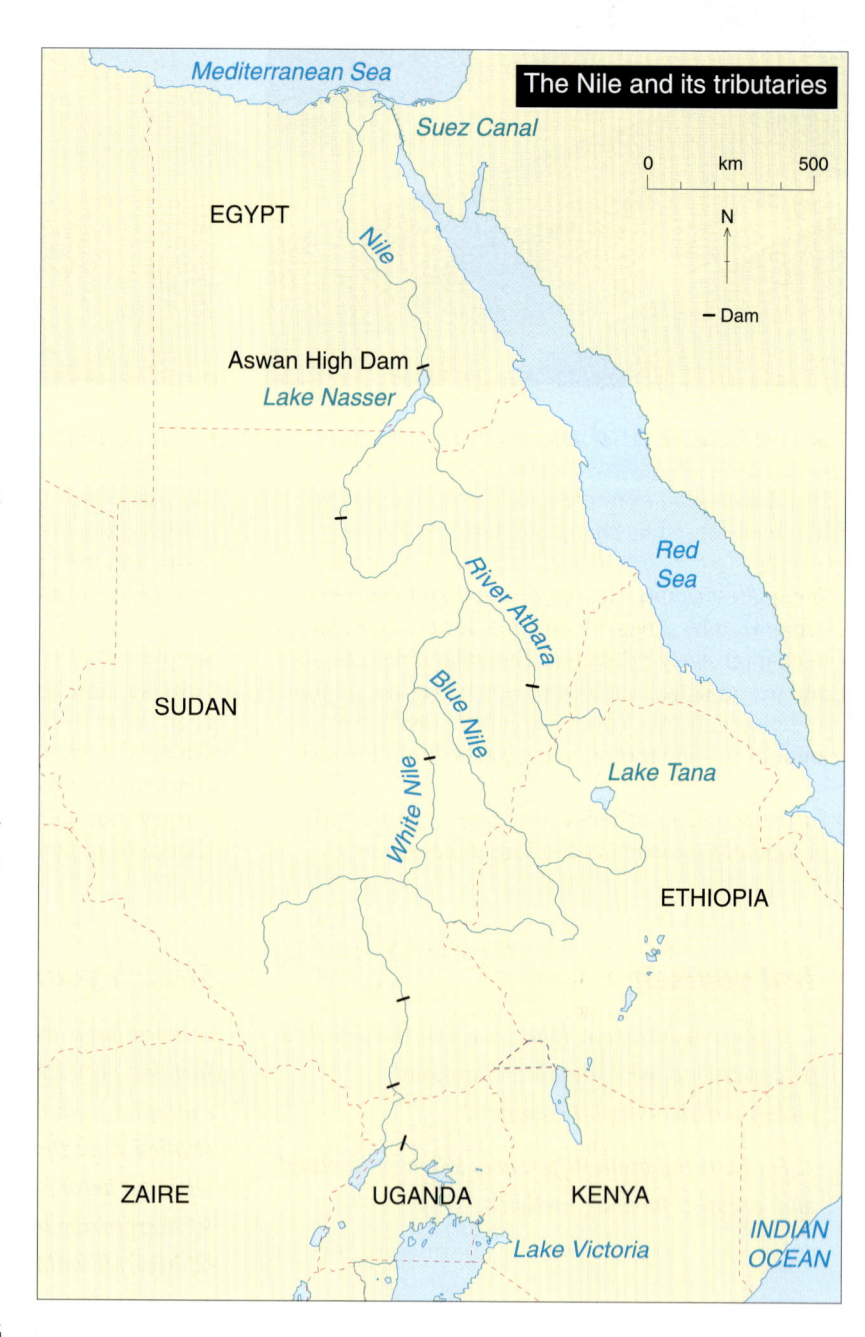

The Aswan High Dam was constructed during the 1960s, 8km south (upstream) of an earlier, less effective scheme. Behind the dam Lake Nasser was formed – a reservoir as long as England! The original scheme could neither prevent the Nile flooding, nor produce electricity all year round – the Aswan High Dam can.

HEP from the old dam had stimulated some industrialisation at Aswan. However, the now abundant power has allowed further industrial development, not least chemical fertiliser plants (needed to replace the alluvial silt no longer flooding the Nile Valley). The electricity is also used to pump irrigation water, and supply domestic demand from Aswan to Cairo.

An extra 800,000 hectares of land are now irrigated, leading to greater cash crop yields of cane sugar, citrus fruits, cotton, dates, onions, potatoes, and maize. Egypt enjoys a healthier balance of payments as a result. Lake Nasser also supports many fishermen.

The **benefits** of the project, therefore, include **river control**, and **HEP** generation. Furthermore, more water for **irrigation** can be supplied, and the previously unreliable level of the Nile is now constant, allowing **navigation** all

The Nile and its tributaries

The hydroelectric station at the Aswan High Dam.

year round. It has created a 5000km waterway to Sudan, thus improving **trade**. Finally, both the spectacular dam and Lake Nasser are proving great **tourist attractions**.

However, **economic**, **social**, and **environmental problems** have been caused by this major project:

- At the time of construction, for example, transporting raw materials and equipment proved very difficult and expensive. Although unskilled labour was in abundance, high level management and technical specialists had to come from abroad. Indeed, the £40 million it finally cost to build is still being paid back, mostly to the USA and the International Monetary Fund (IMF).

- The flooding of Lake Nasser lost 50,000 Nubians both their land and homes. Consequently, they had to be relocated.

- Many antiquities, associated with Egypt's ancient civilisation, were also threatened, and much had to be transported to museums abroad. The famous Abu Simbel temples would also have been lost had they not been dismantled meticulously and rebuilt again – elevated above the lake!

- Silt settling in Lake Nasser has allowed fish to thrive, but in the long term will need to be dredged if the whole reservoir is not to be silted up. Meantime, less silt and nutrients now reach the Nile delta, which is more vulnerable to erosion as a consequence.

- With no annual flooding to wash Mediterranean salts from the coastal fields, **salinisation** is increasing. Both fishing and farming in the delta is, therefore, under threat.

- **Evaporation** losses, both from Lake Nasser, and the increased number of irrigation channels, are worryingly high in this desert environment.

- The increased numbers of irrigation canals and drainage ditches have increased the **bilharzia** snail's breeding areas. Consequently this debilitating disease is spreading.

Test yourself

1. Writing no more than two short paragraphs summarise the benefits and problems of the Aswan High Dam project.

Stretch yourself

Study the location map showing the course of the Nile, and its main tributaries. What political problems might arise as a result of so many countries sharing these waters?

Sources of energy

Key points

► *Energy is essential for all economic and domestic activity.*
► *Energy sources are primary (direct use) or secondary (indirect).*
► *Energy resources are either non-renewable fossil fuels, or renewable.*
► *Electricity is the most flexible, convenient, secondary energy source.*

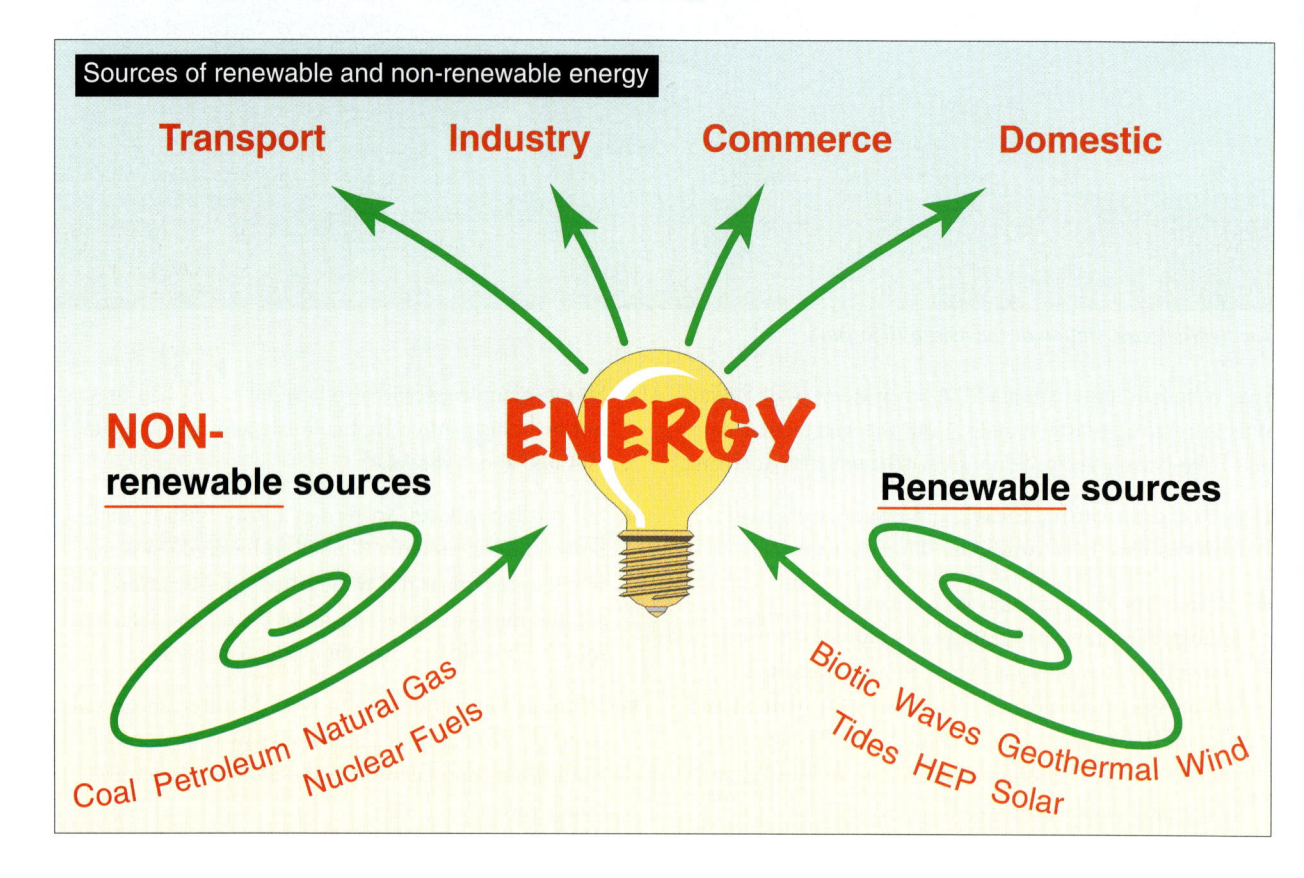

Sources of renewable and non-renewable energy

Transport   Industry   Commerce   Domestic

ENERGY

NON-renewable sources
Coal Petroleum Natural Gas Nuclear Fuels

Renewable sources
Biotic Waves Geothermal Wind
Tides HEP Solar

Transport, industry, commerce and homes all need energy of some kind. Today there are three main energy providers:

- coal
- petroleum refined into fuels such as petrol
- electricity generated by both renewable and non-renewable energy resources.

Energy sources are categorised as **primary** and **secondary**.

Primary sources such as coal and oil, are often converted into the latter, electricity. Electricity can be switched easily and quickly to the places where it is needed. The only constraint is a maximum **transmission** distance of 800 km. This ensures that energy sources for generation are appropriate to the region.

As a result, coal-fired power stations are located at coal fields, oil-powered power stations near oil terminals, and so on.

In Britain, for example, a **supergrid** of major electricity transmission cables on pylons carries the main supply from **thermal** power stations (coal, oil, gas or nuclear powered) and from hydro-electric power stations, to the major market areas. The most populated areas show a denser grid, from which smaller transmission lines distribute the electricity locally.

Power in Britain

Legend:
- Coal
- Oil
- Natural gas
- Oil pipeline
- Gas pipeline
- Oil imports
- Selected power stations:
  - ● coal, oil, gas
  - ■ nuclear
  - ⤳ hydro

Oil/gas fields labelled: Brent, Beryl, Forties, Auk, Morecombe Bay, West Sole, Viking

Electricity supergrid

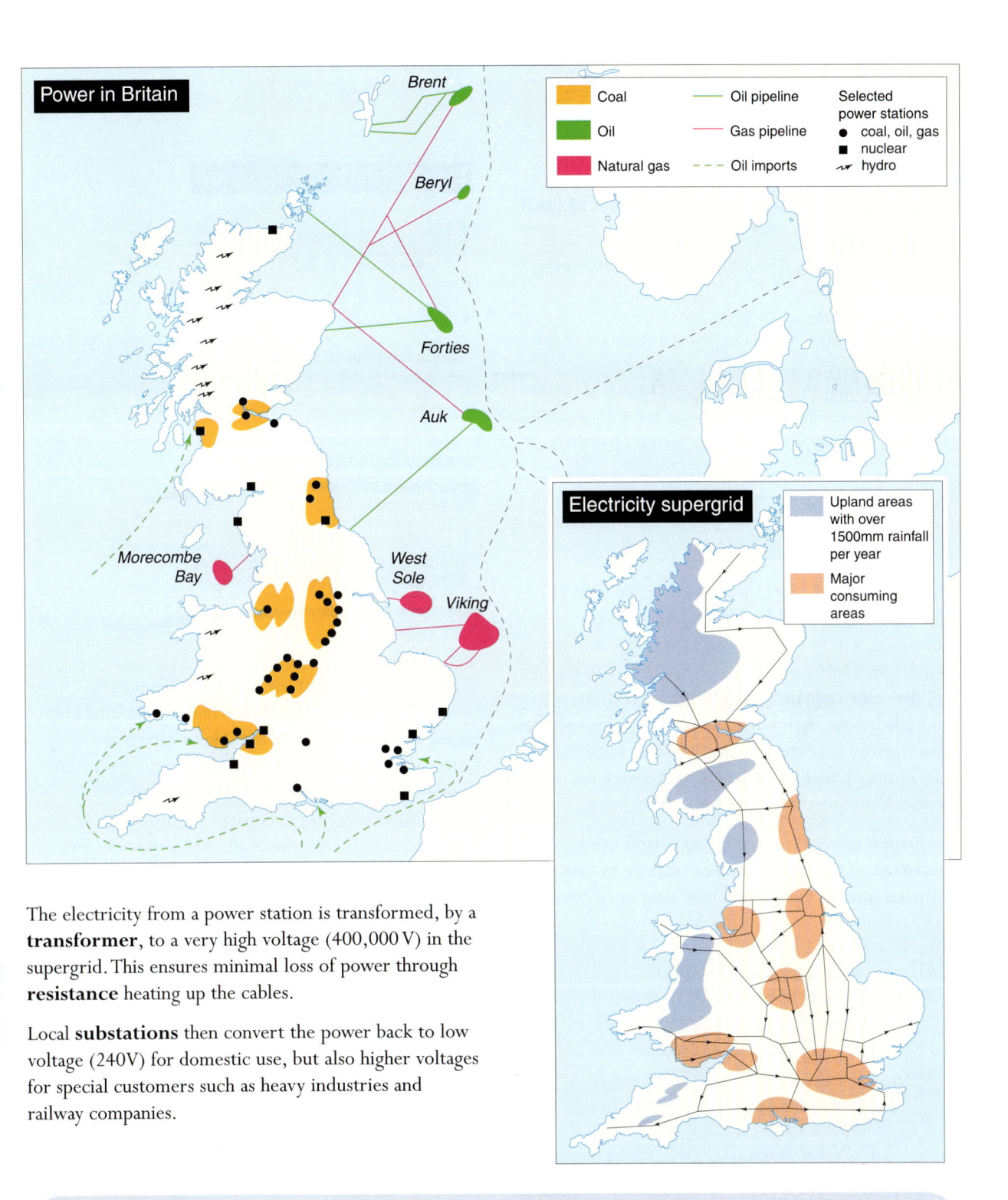

Legend:
- Upland areas with over 1500mm rainfall per year
- Major consuming areas

The electricity from a power station is transformed, by a **transformer**, to a very high voltage (400,000 V) in the supergrid. This ensures minimal loss of power through **resistance** heating up the cables.

Local **substations** then convert the power back to low voltage (240V) for domestic use, but also higher voltages for special customers such as heavy industries and railway companies.

Test yourself

1. With reference to examples, outline the difference between renewable and non-renewable energy sources.

Stretch yourself

Study the two maps. Describe and explain briefly the relationship between the electricity supergrid, types of power stations, their distribution, and the main market areas.

ECONOMIC THEMES • ENERGY

Coal in Britain

Key points

▶ Coal is a sedimentary rock formed millions of years ago, and found in layers.

▶ Modern mining is highly efficient, but controversial and in decline.

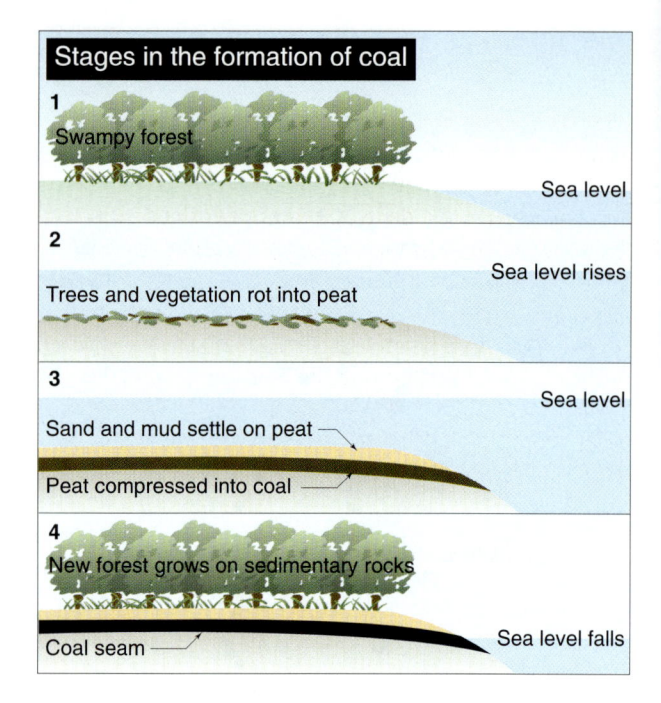

Around 300 million years ago, towards the end of the Carboniferous period, Britain was covered by vast swamps and mud-flats. Dense tropical forests also grew in the hot humid climate. Rises in sea level drowned the forest and enabled peat to form from the rotting trees and vegetation. This peat was then buried by sand and mud. Layers of **sedimentary rocks** were formed by compression from the weight above – sand to sandstone, mud to shale, peat to coal.

Repeated rises and falls in sea level over the next 20 million years produced layer upon layer of **coal measures**. Rarely, however, are such reserves found in their original horizontal layers. Some 280 million years ago, the rocks were deformed by distant tectonic activity and folded above sea level. Some of these folded **strata** form what we now know as the Pennines. Erosion has since removed the tops of the folds, exposing the coal measures, exploited since the 18th century.

The earliest mines exploited the **exposed coal measures** on the surface and near-surface by **adits** and **bellpits**. Most of these mines have long since closed, either because the coal has run out or because they were too small and inefficient. Newer mines were invariably bigger, more mechanised, and able to exploit the **concealed measures**. **Deep-shaft** mining remains possible through the use of high technology. **Trepanners** for cutting, efficient pit-propping, ventilation and flood control all reduce the risks for miners. In recent decades, coal's main use has been for electricity generation.

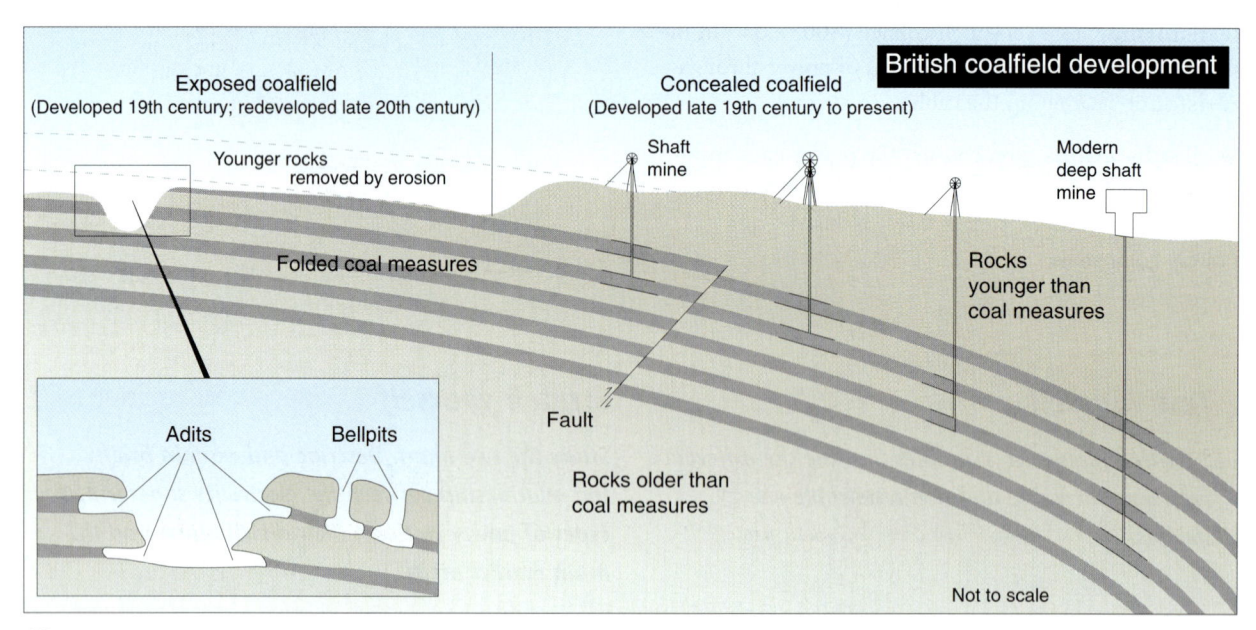

Selby: a future for deep coalmining?

In spite of vast remaining coal reserves, Britain's coalmining industry has contracted markedly in recent years. The reason may be political; central government has encouraged the development of a wider energy base for the electricity-generating companies in order to reduce the impact of coal industry strikes. Today the privatised electricity-generating companies, such as National Power, are no longer legally obliged to buy British coal; they often buy cheaper foreign coal.

Apart from buying abroad, electricity companies have also indulged in the so-called 'dash for gas'. Recently built natural gas-powered stations pose a real threat to the coal industry, and more and more mines have closed. Only the most efficient, productive coalfields, such as Selby in Yorkshire, are likely to compete effectively with foreign competition and new **open cast** quarries.

But even deep coalmining is controversial, as illustrated by the arguments stated for and against Selby during production planning in the 1970s:

Arguments for Selby

- **Rich reserves** from seams 4 m thick.

- Very pure **high-grade coal**, hence minimal waste, and no surface slag heaps because all the waste will be packed underground.

- Only **one exit shaft**, at Gascoigne Wood, serving five collieries, so minimising visual disturbance.

- **Pithead towers landscaped** and screened by trees.

- **High technology** allowing high productivity.

- A large **ready market** from local thermal electricity power stations such as Ferrybridge, Eggborough, and Drax, linked to Gascoigne Wood by special merry-go-round trains which load and unload automatically.

Arguments against Selby

- Low-lying land is prone to **flooding**.

- **Subsidence** could occur should abandoned flooded workings collapse.

- **Farmers** fear that the slightest subsidence will crack field tile drainage systems.

- **Production costs** are higher than anticipated because of flooding.

- **Wildlife and plant communities** of special importance, such as at Skipworth Common, face disturbance.

- **Visual pollution** of mine workings.

- The London to Edinburgh **railway line** has had to be diverted, to avoid mining disturbance, at a cost of £35 million.

Test yourself

1. Briefly explain the difference between open cast and deep shaft mining.

Stretch yourself

Outline the political, environmental, and social controversies raised by the coal industry.

Oil and natural gas

Key points

▶ *Oil and natural gas are highly efficient, popular, flexible, and therefore valuable fossil fuels.*

▶ *Oil and gas discoveries in the North Sea have created a major industry in Britain.*

▶ *Oil pollution is one of the environment's greatest threats, and not always accidental.*

Oil (more correctly known as **petroleum**) and **natural gas** are similar to coal. Both:

- are of organic origin
- were formed from seabed decay and burial of plants and animals
- were buried over hundreds of thousands of years under an enormous weight of sedimentary rocks
- changed chemically into oil and (lighter) natural gas.

They differ from coal in that, to relieve the pressure, they will move upwards, through **porous rocks**, until trapped by a **cap rock**.

There are four main stages from exploration to refining:

1. **Exploration** using seismic surveys, and test drilling, may represent a large proportion of total exploitation costs.

2. **Production** involves replacing the floating exploration rig with a fixed steel or concrete production platform. Several drill 'strings' may radiate from this rig to pump oil from throughout an oilfield.

3. Gas is **transported** by pipe to coastal terminals. Here, to assist detection of leaks, a smell similar to coal gas is added before distribution to consumers. Oil is either piped ashore, or taken by tanker to refineries.

4. **Refining** the oil is so efficient nowadays that very little is wasted. Not only are refinery products a major energy resource, but also the raw material for a vast petrochemical industry, from fertilisers to plastics.

Stages in the formation of oil

Dead sea plants and fish collect on the seabed

Sand settles on the seabed, burying the organic matter

24-hour activity: an oil-rig in the Cromarty Firth.

62 ECONOMIC THEMES • ENERGY

North Sea oil and gas

Both homes and industry made a major switch from coal to oil and gas following the discovery of plentiful oil supplies in the Middle East in the 1950s and 1960s. The process was accelerated when gas was discovered in the North Sea in 1965 and oil in 1970. But extracting these high-quality resources from the North Sea demanded massive investment and the development of new technologies. The problems included:

- great water depth
- sea-bed unevenness
- storm severity
- long distances from shore
- the concerns of conservationists (fearful of oil spillages).

Despite the difficulties, Britain was self-sufficient in oil (with surplus to export) within a decade of discovery. Thousands of jobs have been created constructing, operating and supplying rigs, pipelines and onshore facilities. Such has been the success of this industry, particularly in major centres such as Aberdeen, that fears about exhausting the oil reserves are inevitable. But successful exploration in the North Atlantic, and developing technology even further, is likely to ensure the oil industry's long-term future.

The Sea Empress lies wrecked off the Welsh coast ...

... but her cargo comes ashore.

The oil industry and the environment

Oil pollution can arise from blow-outs and explosions on oil rigs, fractures in underwater pipelines and even tankers running aground. For example, the so-called 'coffin ship' *Braer* spilled 85,000 tonnes of light, toxic crude oil on Shetland in 1993. Fortunately severe storms dispersed much of this, preventing major environmental damage. However, The *Sea Empress*, grounded off Milford Haven in 1996, proved far more destructive to the fishing industry, bird life and coastal wildlife habitats in one of Britain's most sensitive marine reserves.

Worldwide, serious pollution is caused by illegal, **deliberate discharges** of sea water tanker ballast. This is done offshore by ship owners avoiding expensive recovery charges prior to loading a fresh cargo.

Test yourself

1. Outline the advantages and disadvantages of the North Sea oil and gas industry to Britain.

Stretch yourself

What practical measures can reduce oil pollution?

Hydroelectric power

Key points

▶ Hydroelectric power (HEP) is renewable, but not always located conveniently.

▶ Pumped storage schemes are especially practical, flexible and cost-effective.

▶ HEP's 'environmental friendliness' should be questioned thoughtfully.

The power potential of running water has long been recognised. For example, hundreds of years ago waterwheels on fast rivers ground corn. Today **hydroelectric power (HEP)** stations use water power to drive turbines, attached to electricity generators. However, since fast-flowing rivers that never dry up are rare, the flow of water has to be ensured by damming water in reservoirs, and feeding it through pipes (**penstocks**) to the power stations.

HEP location requirements

- **Heavy reliable rainfall**, over 2000 mm per annum ideal.
- **Large drainage basin** (catchment area) to collect sufficient water.
- **Steep-sided valleys**, of impermeable rock, for dam and reservoir construction.
- **Steep gradients**, for penstocks, to provide a good 'head' (drop) of water.
- Relatively **near main markets**, to reduce transmission losses.

The hydroelectric power station at Trollhättan, Sweden.

In Britain, for example, the necessary conditions are frequently too remote from urban areas to allow economic HEP production. Indeed, all viable HEP sites in Britain have now been developed.

Pumped storage schemes, such as at Dinorwig in Snowdonia National Park, prove an excellent alternative. Pumped storage schemes are a renewable, clean and relatively cheap power source. They are popular because mains electricity cannot be stored, and demand fluctuates markedly according to the time of day, weather, and season. Flexible power sources, readily available to meet surges in demand, can therefore save the enormous cost of always producing sufficient electricity to meet any anticipated circumstance.

Such is the flexibility of pumped storage schemes that they can be ready in around ten seconds! They can meet massive surges in demand caused by, for example, commercial breaks in popular television programmes.

Pumped storage schemes use the fact that thermal power stations are uneconomic to switch off. They utilise cheap, **off-peak** electricity to pump water to upper reservoirs during the night. At peak demand times the water is released to generate power. The water is constantly recycled and provides a sufficiency of electricity generating capacity even during periods of prolonged drought.

The pump storage station at Dinorwig.

HEP tends to be regarded as environmentally friendly. Supporters point out that rainfall and gravity are free, and effectively non-polluting. Dam and reservoir construction, however, involves flooding large areas of land – often that which is the most habitable and cultivable. Also, penstocks, transmission pylons and cables are unsightly in a highland context (Dinorwig's underground concealment is unique in this respect). As with all energy issues, therefore, there are advantages and disadvantages to consider.

Test yourself

1. Outline the factors dictating daily and seasonal fluctuations in electricity demand.

2. Why do popular television programmes cause such predictable surges in demand?

3. Why have pumped storage schemes been described as 'power sponges'?

Stretch yourself

What are the environmental advantages, and disadvantages, of HEP schemes?

Nuclear power

Key points

▶ Nuclear power is more contentious than any other energy or environmental issue.

▶ Nuclear power issues affect the whole world.

▶ Transportation of nuclear fuel and waste causes widespread concern.

Nuclear power is an emotive issue. The 'what if' factor colours informed debate. Those opposed to nuclear power can quote the 1986 Chernobyl disaster in support of their cause. Thousands of square kilometres of previously rich Ukrainian farmland were left contaminated for years. Radioactive rain affected every European country. Fall-out was detected in Japan and the USA.

Advocates of this enormously effective power source argue that Chernobyl was a ghastly exception caused by a combination of human error and unforgivable cost-cutting. Given the fail-safe measures adopted as the norm in the nuclear industry, nuclear power is seen by many as the answer to a clean, efficient, energy future, in both EMDCs and ELDCs.

Nuclear power location factors

Two factors dominate the location of nuclear power stations:

- safety
- nearness to large amounts of water for cooling.

In Britain all nuclear reactors are on the coast – an inland (lakeside) one has closed. Remote locations, such as Wylfa on Anglesey, were often chosen as 'likely to be quickly evacuatable in case of emergency'. The most recently built stations have usually been on the same site as earlier ones, such as Hinkley Point.

This reflects public objections to new 'greenfield' developments. Indeed, the British nuclear power programme is now in abeyance with older reactors being decommissioned, and no new ones planned. For many, Chernobyl represented the 'final straw' for British public opinion on this issue.

Picturesque at night, an eyesore by day. The Three Mile Island Nuclear Power Station, Pennsylvania, USA.

So what are the arguments for and against this powerful energy resource?

The nuclear debate

First 'We must have nuclear power. The world's fossil fuels, especially oil and gas, could run out within decades, rather than generations.'

Reply *'We don't need it, because more efficient machinery, insulation, lighting and so on, in energy-saving homes and industries, will reduce electricity consumption in future.'*

Second 'Nuclear power is very cost-effective. One tonne of uranium ore produces as much electricity as 25,000 tonnes of coal.'

Reply *'Nuclear power stations not only cost a lot to build, but are also relatively expensive to run.'*

Third 'But so much research and development has gone into nuclear power that it is virtually foolproof. Indeed, safety precautions make the chance of an accident very, very unlikely.'

Reply *'A major nuclear accident would kill thousands, and undoubtedly ruin an area for future generations. And they do happen. Who could forget Chernobyl – and there was Three Mile Island in the USA as well.'*

Fourth 'OK, so what about coal? It is notoriously difficult to mine safely and, just like oil-burning power stations, pollutes the atmosphere with waste gases, worsening the greenhouse effect and producing acid rain. In fact, coal is especially dirty to use – unless expensive 'scrubbers' filter the smoke.'

Reply *'Nuclear radioactivity is always a fear. In Britain, leukaemia clusters near Sellafield and Dounreay surely can't be coincidence – and even at the end of its working life, a nuclear power station takes over a century to make safe.'*

Fifth 'Nuclear waste is limited and can be stored perfectly safely underground. You'll get more radiation from your wrist-watch!'

Reply *'I'm not convinced. There are just too many doubts for me. Future energy research should be concentrated on renewable sources, with minimal environmental impact.'*

Test yourself

1. What fuel is used in a nuclear power station?

2. State the two most important location factors for a nuclear power station.

Stretch yourself

Use the key arguments in the nuclear energy debate to discuss this suggestion: 'Only by understanding different points of view can we come to informed decisions'. (Remember, examiners are not allowed to mark your opinion, but they will assess the quality of the argument put forward in its support.)

ELDC energy: a case for alternatives?

Key points

▶ EMDCs use 80% of the world's energy, but ELDC demands are growing.

▶ Renewable and alternative energy sources offer great practical potential for ELDCs.

All societies depend on energy, whether it is electricity generated in a nuclear power station or simply an ox drawing a plough. Generally, the more advanced a society's technology, the greater the amount of energy consumed per person. The South has more than 80% of the world's population, yet uses only 20% of the world's energy.

However, population in ELDCs is rising, and the trend away from agriculture to urban industrialisation is established. As a result, the demand for energy is increasing rapidly.

Although a large proportion of the energy use in ELDCs is free – firewood, dung, and animal power – rural energy shortages are normal. Consequently, destruction of forests for firewood, and use of dung as fuel rather than as a fertiliser, leads to soil erosion and, in places, desertification. It is therefore essential that ELDCs expand both the 'non-commercial' and the 'commercial' energy sectors.

Examples of electricity generation using coal, oil, gas, even nuclear power (adopted in India and Pakistan, for instance) can be found throughout the South. But an emphasis on **appropriate technology** and renewable resources would seem to be most sensible in ELDCs.

Multi-purpose river projects such as the Aswan High Dam in Egypt (see page 56) have enormous potential, but this comes with environmental consequences. This 2100 megawatt scheme has made Aswan 'the Pittsburgh of Egypt', supporting chemical and fertiliser industries, steel mills and electronics factories. The energy produced also provides abundant electricity for agricultural irrigation schemes, and domestic use as far away as Cairo.

But such projects, despite their undoubted benefits, must always be considered in their totality. Some environmentalists, and particularly displaced locals, would argue that the disadvantages outweigh the advantages.

Today much research into **renewable sources of energy** is taking place in many ELDCs and NICs (newly industrialised countries), often to supplement the use of expensive oil.

The spread of civilisation? Solar-powered TV in Niger.

Renewable sources of energy

In Brazil, for example, **biomass** is proving a cheap alternative to petrol in suitably modified vehicles. It is produced from fermenting:

- plantation crops, such as cane sugar
- root crops, such as cassava
- cereals, such as maize and sorghum.

Biogas, such as methane, can also be produced from farm waste.

Solar energy offers considerable potential, whether involving the collection of heat or converting sunlight directly into electricity. With significant year-long daily hours of sunshine, ELDCs in tropical latitudes could benefit markedly. 'Solar villages', in locations distant from conventional power sources, are increasingly common in India.

Isolated locations throughout the world are particularly suited to **wind-powered electricity** generators, as long as battery or diesel back-up is integrated into the system.

Geothermal energy, generating electricity from steam, produced by water pumped down into volcanically heated sub-surface rocks, was associated with rich EMDCs in tectonically active regions, such as Iceland, New Zealand and California. Today Central American NICs and ELDCs, such as Mexico and Nicaragua, have successfully adopted this technology.

Tidal and **wave power** offer further scope for development and, most importantly, hope for future alternatives to traditional fossil fuel power sources which are polluting, diminishing and increasingly expensive.

A wind-powered water pump, Brazil.

Geothermal power, Mexico.

Test yourself

1. Make a list of renewable energy resources.

2. What is the most important reason for ELDCs adopting renewable energy sources?

Stretch yourself

Outline the renewable energy resource developments and potential in a named EMDC, such as Britain, and a named ELDC, such as Egypt.

Energy and the environment

Key points

▶ Energy exploitation can harm the environment, through various forms of pollution.

▶ Fossil fuels pollute the most, but alternative energy sources are not entirely 'green'.

Any energy exploitation has an environmental impact. For example the burning of fossil fuels and the transport of energy can have major polluting consequences (pages 63 and 80). Even apparently clean HEP schemes provoke angry protests in support of the people, wildlife and flora likely to be displaced.

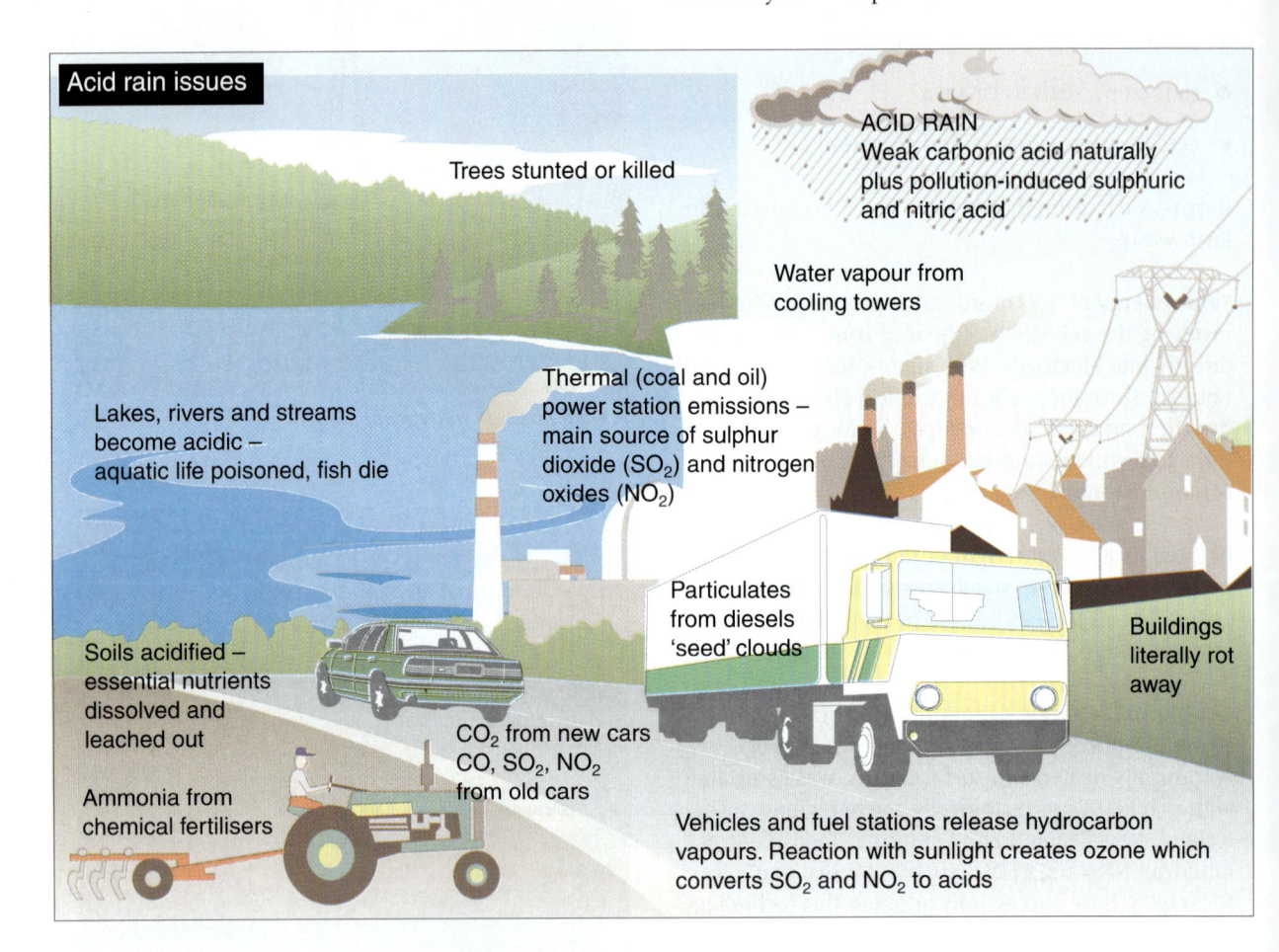

Acid rain issues

Trees stunted or killed

ACID RAIN Weak carbonic acid naturally plus pollution-induced sulphuric and nitric acid

Water vapour from cooling towers

Thermal (coal and oil) power station emissions – main source of sulphur dioxide (SO_2) and nitrogen oxides (NO_2)

Lakes, rivers and streams become acidic – aquatic life poisoned, fish die

Particulates from diesels 'seed' clouds

Buildings literally rot away

Soils acidified – essential nutrients dissolved and leached out

CO_2 from new cars
CO, SO_2, NO_2 from old cars

Ammonia from chemical fertilisers

Vehicles and fuel stations release hydrocarbon vapours. Reaction with sunlight creates ozone which converts SO_2 and NO_2 to acids

Acid rain is one polluting effect of energy exploitation that clearly demonstrates some of the problems.

Like nuclear energy, acid rain is an international issue because aerial pollutants do not respect international frontiers. For example, the sulphur dioxide scrubbers, costing millions of pounds, to be installed at Drax and other Yorkshire coal-fired power stations are much more likely to benefit Scandinavia than Britain. This is because the very tall chimneys ensure that smoke is carried well out to sea by prevailing south-westerly winds.

Geographers cannot ignore the problems of urban industrial pollution in all its forms including:

- forests dying directly from leaf loss or (indirectly) from nutrient deficiency in soils leached of their goodness

- lakes and rivers poisoning aquatic life

- historic buildings literally crumbling away.

Nor can governments postpone, indefinitely, support for **conservation programmes** that might reduce energy consumption or **active corrective enterprises** such as the liming of rivers and lakes to neutralise acidity.

Energy production: the effects on the environment

source of energy	land pollution	air pollution	water and coastal pollution	visual pollution
gas	short-term during pipe-laying but surface 'greens over' quickly	minimal	none	none
oil	more/less toxic depending on grade	global warming acid rain	oil slicks and detergents poison fish and bird life	unsightly installations, refineries, etc
coal	long-term during mining – dirt, dust, waste tips, open cast quarry scars	greenhouse gases global warming acid rain	minimal	dirt and smoke blacken buildings
HEP	land lost to flooding	none	none	unsightly dams and penstocks
nuclear	high-level radioactive waste disposal must be secure for generations	none unless an accident spreads radioactive fall-out	low-level waste disposal at sea	huge installations unsightly
alternative	minimal	none	tidal power disrupts marine ecosystems	wind farms unsightly and noisy

Test yourself

1. Review your understanding of (a) fossil fuels (b) acid rain (c) pollution (d) conservation.

Stretch yourself

Consider critically the concept of 'green energy'. Why must any energy exploitation, whether non-renewable or renewable, have environmental consequences?

Employment structure

Key points

▶ Industry can be defined as any form of economic activity.

▶ Industry is classified into primary, secondary, tertiary and quaternary categories.

▶ The proportion of workers in each category suggests a country's level of development.

Economic activity – better known as **industry** – has traditionally been classified into three groups or sectors – **primary**, **secondary** and **tertiary**. However, as economic organisation has become increasingly complicated, a fourth group – **quaternary** – is often referred to. The quaternary group includes those services involving expertise, specialisation and information.

You should note that, unless otherwise stated, the quaternary sector is included within the tertiary (service) grouping.

Salt extraction, Namibia.

Chemical plant, Netherlands.

Banking services, Birmingham.

The sectors of industry

- **Primary** industry refers to direct, extractive use of the earth's resources. Agriculture, fishing, forestry, mining and quarrying provide much of the fuel and raw materials for other industries. **Renewable resources** such as crops, trees and fish are reproducible, whereas **non-renewable** or **'wasting' resources**, such as fossil fuels and iron ore can never be replaced.

- **Secondary** industry, or **manufacturing**, changes raw materials into products of more value to people – eg. iron ore into steel, steel into motor vehicles. The secondary sector includes mechanised factories as well as craft (cottage) industries using hand skills, such as weaving. Mechanised production is divided into **heavy manufacturing**, like using bulky raw materials such as coal, limestone and iron ore in the production of steel, and **light manufacturing** where high value luxury goods, such as electrical items and processed foods, are produced.

- **Tertiary** industries provide **services** to assist other industries and to make life easier for us all. For example, people and goods are transported, products are marketed, machines and buildings maintained. There are also financial, social and cultural services covering everything from education to administration, health care to tourism, banking to insurance.

The development level of a country is reflected in its employment structure.

- The poorest ELDCs are in a similar position to Britain 150 years ago. They are in the early stages of economic development with most of their population still working directly on the land in primary occupations, such as near-subsistence farming.

- NICs such as Brazil have more developed economies, with up to 40% of their population employed in secondary (manufacturing) industries.

- EMDCs have mature economies, with up to 70% of their workforce in tertiary and quaternary service occupations.

Industrial structure triangular graph

As a country's economy matures, the proportion of people employed in each sector of industry changes. This may be plotted on a triangular graph.

	Primary %		Secondary %		Tertiary %	
	1960s	1980s	1960s	1980s	1960s	1980s
Brazil	49	30	17	24	34	46
Burundi	89	84	4	5	7	11
Ethiopia	86	80	6	7	8	13
South Korea	58	34	13	29	29	37
United Kingdom	3	2	46	37	51	61
United States of America	5	2	36	32	59	66

Triangular graph axes hints
- Always read the obtuse angle
- Plot with two values – check with the third

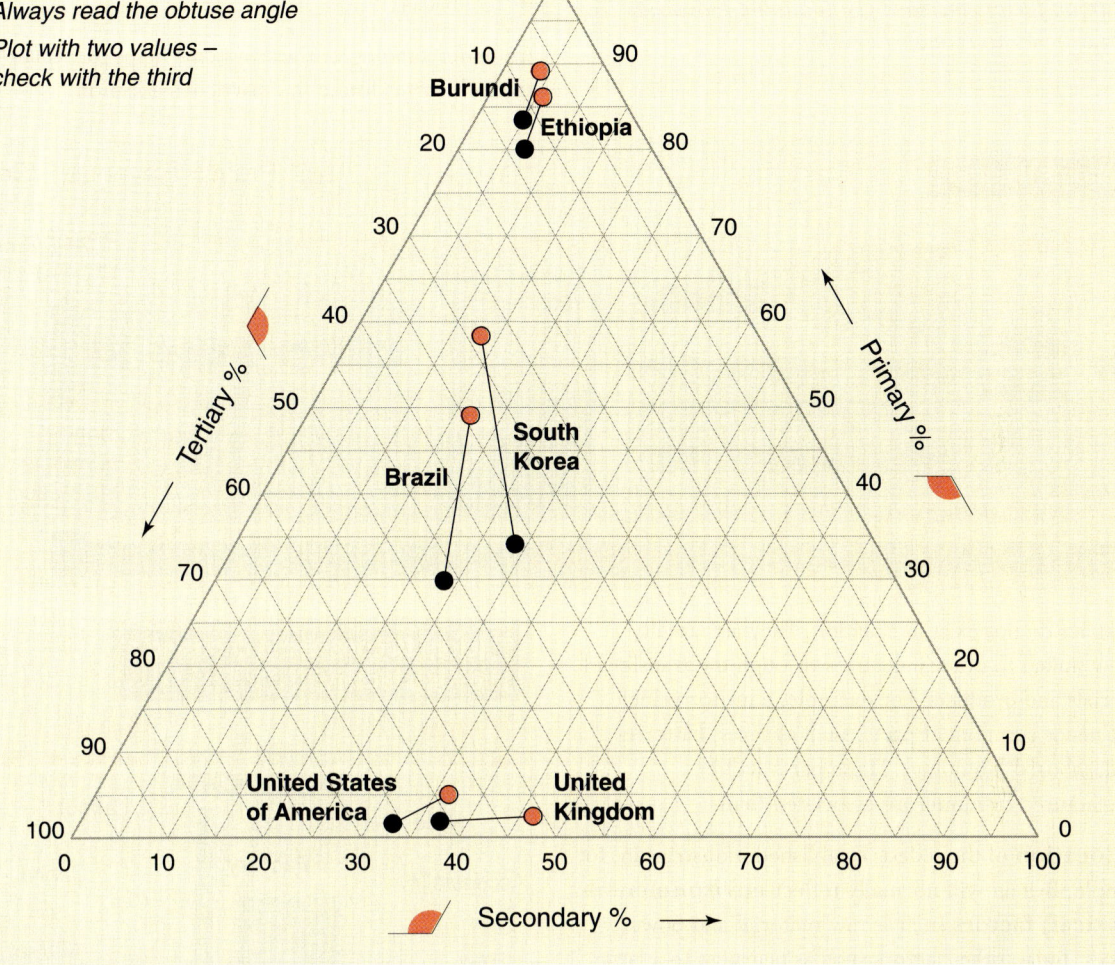

Test yourself

1. Study the triangular graph. (a) Group the countries plotted into ELDCs, NICs, and EMDCs. (b) Describe and explain briefly each group's position on the graph. (c) As a country develops over time, what happens to its position on the graph?

Stretch yourself

How does the graph on this page indicate the rate of economic development?

ECONOMIC THEMES • INDUSTRY

Industrial systems and location factors

Key points

▶ *Industries function as systems of inputs, processes, outputs and feedbacks.*

▶ *Industrial locations are influenced by both environmental and human factors.*

▶ *Human factors increasingly dominate industrial location as an economy develops.*

Industry functions as a **system** of:

- inputs
- processes
- outputs
- feedbacks.

An understanding of these systems helps to explain why any industry is found in a particular location.

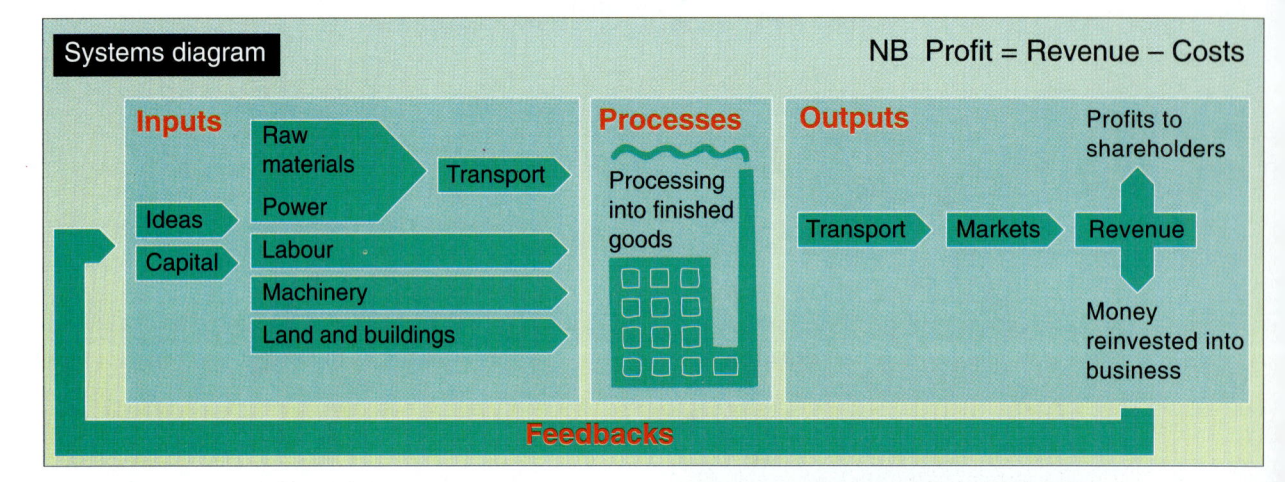

Systems diagram

NB Profit = Revenue − Costs

Inputs: Ideas, Capital, Raw materials, Power, Labour, Machinery, Land and buildings → Transport

Processes: Processing into finished goods

Outputs: Transport → Markets → Revenue → Profits to shareholders / Money reinvested into business

Feedbacks

Industries do not exist in isolation. They are usually closely linked to other industries through the transfer of materials and products. For example, a motor vehicle plant needs component parts, such as tyres, batteries, and dashboard mouldings. These parts will be manufactured by numerous associated firms.

The **location** of the oldest, established industries in, for example, Britain will normally reflect **environmental (physical) factors** such as raw material and power sources. Today, other factors such as nearness to a large market, the availability of skilled labour, and government planning policies tend to be more important.

These **human and economic variables** take precedence over environmental conditions. Where many sites are available, the firm or company will choose the most profitable location – a site where the costs of raw materials, energy, land, transport and labour are minimised, and where there is an accessible large market for the product.

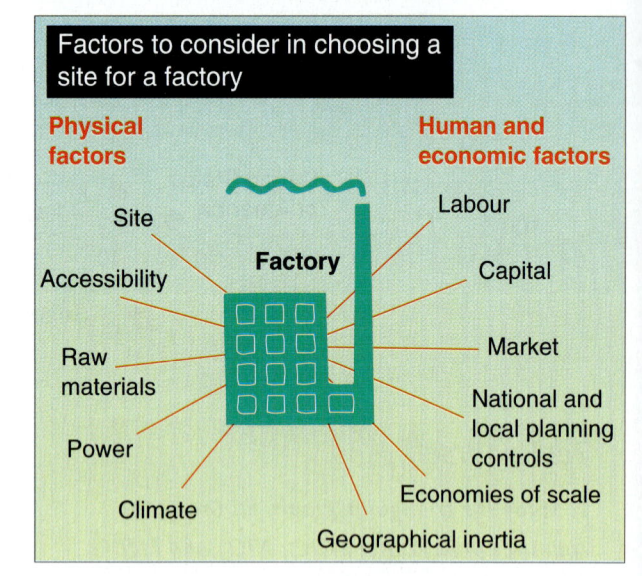

Factors to consider in choosing a site for a factory

Physical factors
- Site
- Accessibility
- Raw materials
- Power
- Climate

Human and economic factors
- Labour
- Capital
- Market
- National and local planning controls
- Economies of scale
- Geographical inertia

Industrial location factors

1 Power

Globally, fossil fuels remain dominant, with coal and oil most important. Industries which use large amounts of coal are generally located on coalfields because it is bulky, heavy and expensive to transport – except by water. Greater London, for example, the largest single industrial area in Britain, developed industrially a long way from a major coalfield, by obtaining cheap coal from North-East England, by sea.

Today, power sources are more flexible because electricity can be transmitted considerable distances, comparatively cheaply, via the National Grid.

2 Raw materials

If an industry uses large amounts of raw materials then it remains advantageous to locate close to their source. However, transport developments in rail, road and bulk sea transport have changed the pattern. Coastal sites at ports facilitate import from world-wide sources, and provide export advantages too.

3 Labour

A large new factory built in an agricultural area would have difficulty in obtaining suitable workers (with industrial skills). New factories, therefore, tend to be built in existing industrial areas – so perpetuating their growth.

4 Markets

Industry must be able to sell its goods, whether they are finished products for customers or components for other factories. An accessible market reduces transport costs. The biggest markets are the existing densely populated urban industrial areas. These, therefore, attract further industrial development until or unless disadvantaged by congestion, land price inflation and environmental deterioration.

5 Transport

Due to the improvements referred to earlier, transport costs tend to represent only a small proportion of total production costs. Transport is, therefore, of little significance except in those industries using bulky raw materials, or producing low value goods.

6 Capital (finance)

Working capital is the money invested in setting up and running a business. It is raised from investors, shareholders and bank loans. **Fixed capital** refers to buildings, equipment and stock. The immobility of fixed capital often results in geographical (industrial) inertia.

Geographical inertia describes the situation where industry remains in its outdated location after the original advantages of that site have become irrelevant. This is because it is often cheaper to pay transport costs than to relocate and build a new factory elsewhere.

7 Government intervention

In Britain, successive governments since World War II have used a 'carrot and stick' approach to influence industrial location.

Tax allowances, loans (at low interest rates), grants, subsidies – even ready-built factories – have all been used as tempting 'carrots' to attract new industries to 'Assisted Areas' where unemployment is high.

Strict planning restrictions in congested, prosperous areas have been used as a 'stick' to direct companies away. For example, the development of Ford's engine plant at Bridgend in South Wales is an excellent example of government intervention to influence location.

Test yourself

1. Which of the following is not an industrial input?
A Capital. B Labour. C Power. D Waste. E Water.

2. Which of the industrial location factors above are: (a) physical (b) human?

Stretch yourself

List the industrial location factors relevant to a named industry you have studied.

Industrial location at global, national and local scales

Key points

▶ At a global scale, major industry is closely associated with middle temperate latitudes.

▶ Major industrialisation is relatively rare in tropical latitudes.

▶ Industry's association with coalfields is notable at both global and national scales.

▶ Industrial decentralisation is found frequently in contemporary EMDC urban areas.

The global distribution of industry demonstrates a concentration in the middle (especially northern) temperate latitudes – particularly in parts of western Europe, north-eastern USA and European Russia. Secondary concentrations in south-eastern Brazil, the Damodar Basin of India, and south-eastern Australia are also important. Major industry is closely associated with coalfields and areas of European influence and there is a sparsity of large-scale industrialisation within the tropics.

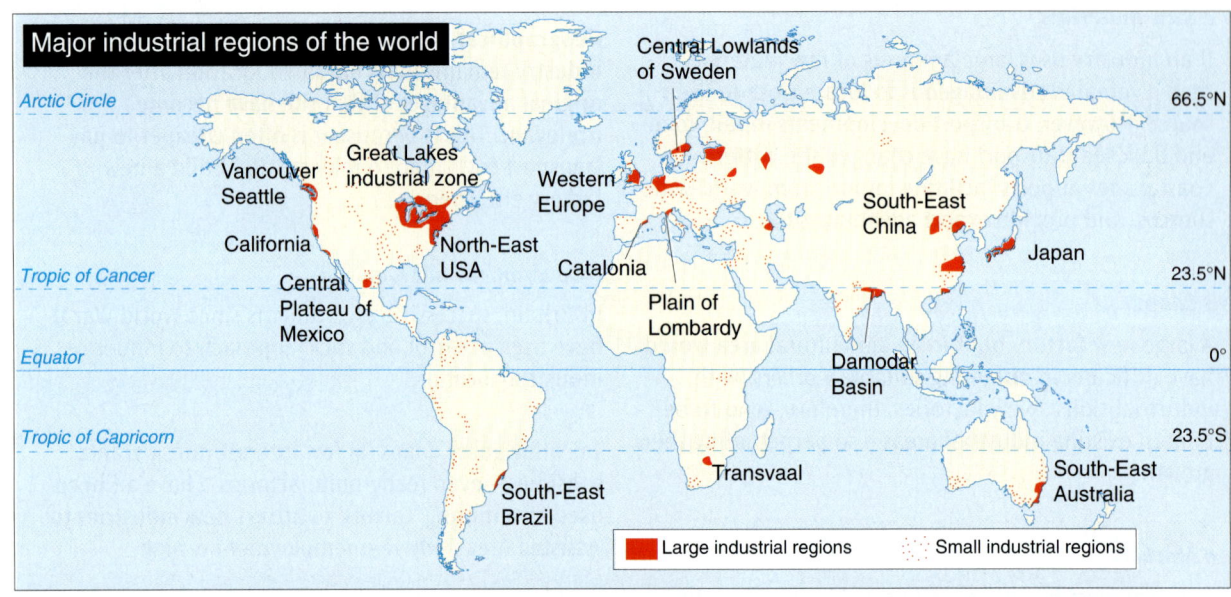

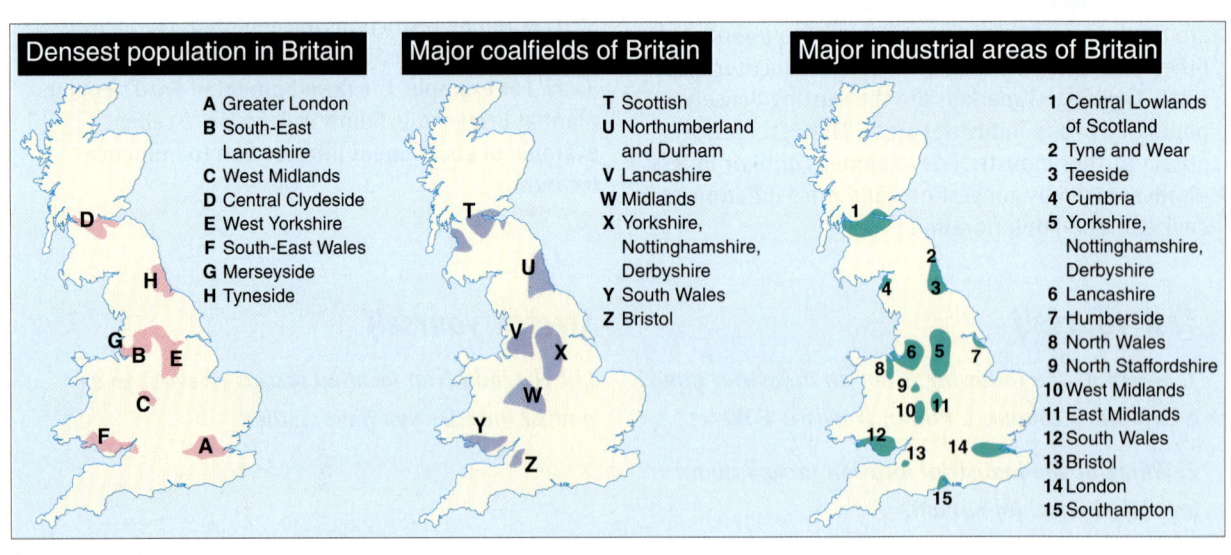

Major industrial regions of the world

- Central Lowlands of Sweden
- Vancouver / Seattle
- Great Lakes industrial zone
- Western Europe
- South-East China
- Japan
- California
- North-East USA
- Catalonia
- Central Plateau of Mexico
- Plain of Lombardy
- Damodar Basin
- South-East Brazil
- Transvaal
- South-East Australia

Large industrial regions / Small industrial regions

Densest population in Britain

- A Greater London
- B South-East Lancashire
- C West Midlands
- D Central Clydeside
- E West Yorkshire
- F South-East Wales
- G Merseyside
- H Tyneside

Major coalfields of Britain

- T Scottish
- U Northumberland and Durham
- V Lancashire
- W Midlands
- X Yorkshire, Nottinghamshire, Derbyshire
- Y South Wales
- Z Bristol

Major industrial areas of Britain

1. Central Lowlands of Scotland
2. Tyne and Wear
3. Teeside
4. Cumbria
5. Yorkshire, Nottinghamshire, Derbyshire
6. Lancashire
7. Humberside
8. North Wales
9. North Staffordshire
10. West Midlands
11. East Midlands
12. South Wales
13. Bristol
14. London
15. Southampton

ECONOMIC THEMES • INDUSTRY

Industrial location at the national scale is well illustrated by Britain – one of the first countries in the world to industrialise. From the late 18th century to the early 20th century (the so-called Industrial Revolution), industry (and therefore population) expanded on the coalfield areas. This was because machinery was driven by coal-fired steam engines.

Today, steam engines are no longer used, but the major urban areas remain as a ready supply of industrial workers, and a large potential market for products. With established **infrastructure** (eg. transport, power and water supplies, industrial services) they remain as industrial areas. However, whilst some have prospered, others are in serious decline. Indeed, many consider Britain economically as 'two nations' (see page 78).

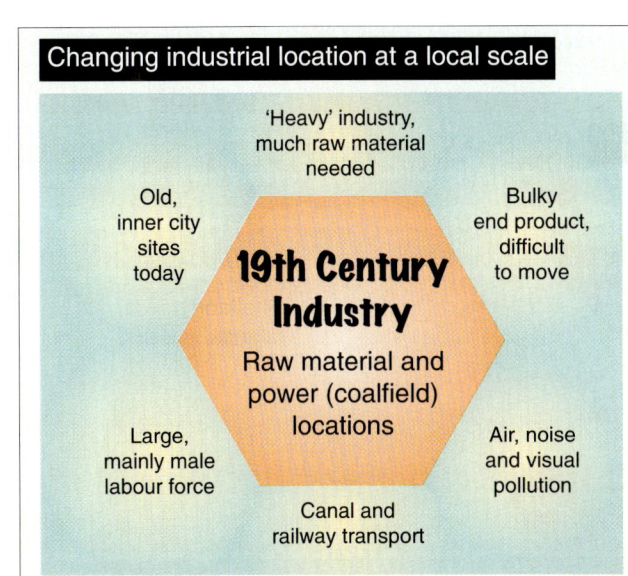

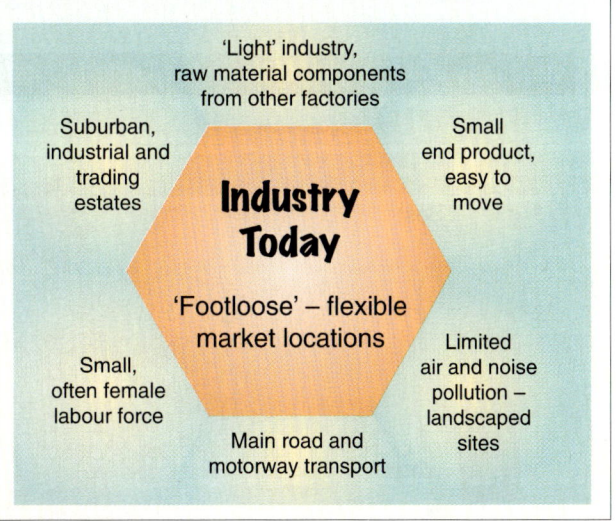

Changing industrial location at a local scale

19th Century Industry
Raw material and power (coalfield) locations
- 'Heavy' industry, much raw material needed
- Old, inner city sites today
- Bulky end product, difficult to move
- Large, mainly male labour force
- Air, noise and visual pollution
- Canal and railway transport

Industry Today
'Footloose' – flexible market locations
- 'Light' industry, raw material components from other factories
- Suburban, industrial and trading estates
- Small end product, easy to move
- Small, often female labour force
- Limited air and noise pollution – landscaped sites
- Main road and motorway transport

The reasons for industrial decentralisation

Push factors from old inner city areas

- cramped sites, with limited room for expansion
- high land prices due to commercial competition
- out-dated buildings and infrastructure
- traffic congestion
- scarce skilled labour (as people move to suburbs)

Pull factors to suburban industrial and trading estates

- space for large buildings and future expansion
- lower land prices due to less competition
- modern buildings and infrastructure
- transport easy, with motorway access
- skilled labour, both manual and managerial, from suburbs and commuter settlements

Test yourself

1. Copy and complete the following sentence selecting from the alternatives given:

Modern industrial estates are usually located in/away from town centres because of their high/low land values and traffic congestion.

2. Explain the term 'infrastructure'.

Stretch yourself

Explain briefly the association of major industry, at a global scale and especially in areas of European influence, with coalfields.

ECONOMIC THEMES • INDUSTRY

Two nations?

The Industrial Revolution saw the beginnings of a North-South divide (then favouring the North). The 20th century has seen a reinforcement of this two nation theory – today with numerous economic and social indicators favouring the South.

The Industrial Revolution saw Britain change from an agricultural to an industrial-based economy; the nation became the 'workshop of the world'. Northern cities grew and prospered on the coalfields, whilst the South (excepting the capital, London) relatively declined.

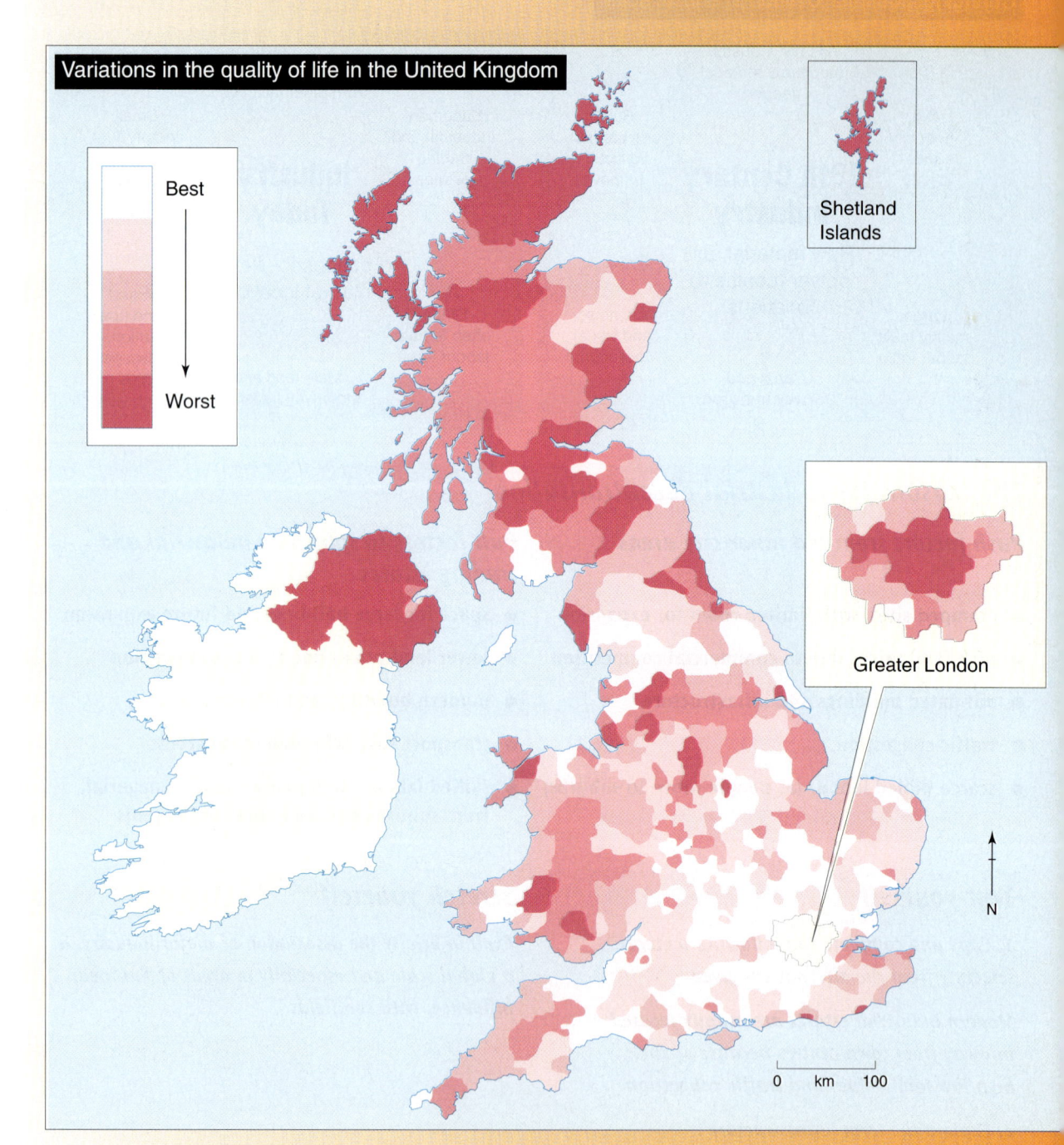

Variations in the quality of life in the United Kingdom

Best → Worst

Shetland Islands

Greater London

ECONOMIC THEMES • INDUSTRY

The 20th century saw a reversal of fortunes. The South started to prosper with a greater variety of lighter industry, and increased emphasis on service occupations – such as finance and marketing. The North declined, suffering **de-industrialisation**. Heavy industry, for example, started to face competition from overseas, and old fashioned working practices and plant (eg. machinery) could no longer compete with low-wage economies elsewhere.

The maps offer a generalised measure of the quality of life and economic prosperity (in terms of Gross Domestic Product) throughout Britain. But such average indicators hide great variations within regions and their interpretation can be a matter of personal judgement. Increasing prosperity in the South during the 1980s was accompanied by congestion, land price inflation and overcrowded services; many would argue these factors reduced, rather than enhanced, the quality of life. Should governments stand by and allow whole areas to decline into environmental degradation and no hope? This is both a political and moral question.

Index of GDP per head

UK average 100
- 100+
- 95+
- 90+
- under 90

- Scotland 93.5
- North-West 93.5
- Northern Ireland 69.5
- Wales 85.7
- West Midlands 90.8
- South-West 96.1
- North 91.9
- Yorks and Humber 93.2
- East Midlands 96.1
- East Anglia 100.8
- Greater London 124.6
- South-East 117.5

Certainly, since the Great Depression of the late 1920s to early 1930s, governments of all political parties – Labour, Conservative, even coalition (politicians working together) during World War II – have addressed the economic, social and environmental problems resulting from northern de-industrialisation and a population 'drift to the South'. The general theme has been how to encourage new industrial development in the North whilst preventing the South from becoming too congested. Until the Thatcher administrations of the 1980s, variations on the so-called 'stick-and-carrot' approach were used.

The **sticks** included planning controls. For example, in the South, compulsory Industrial Development Certificates (IDCs) and Office Development Permits (ODPs) were often refused, but subsequently offered in parts of the declining North. The **carrots** offered as incentives to move north included tax allowances, low interest loans, grants, subsidies and even ready-built factories.

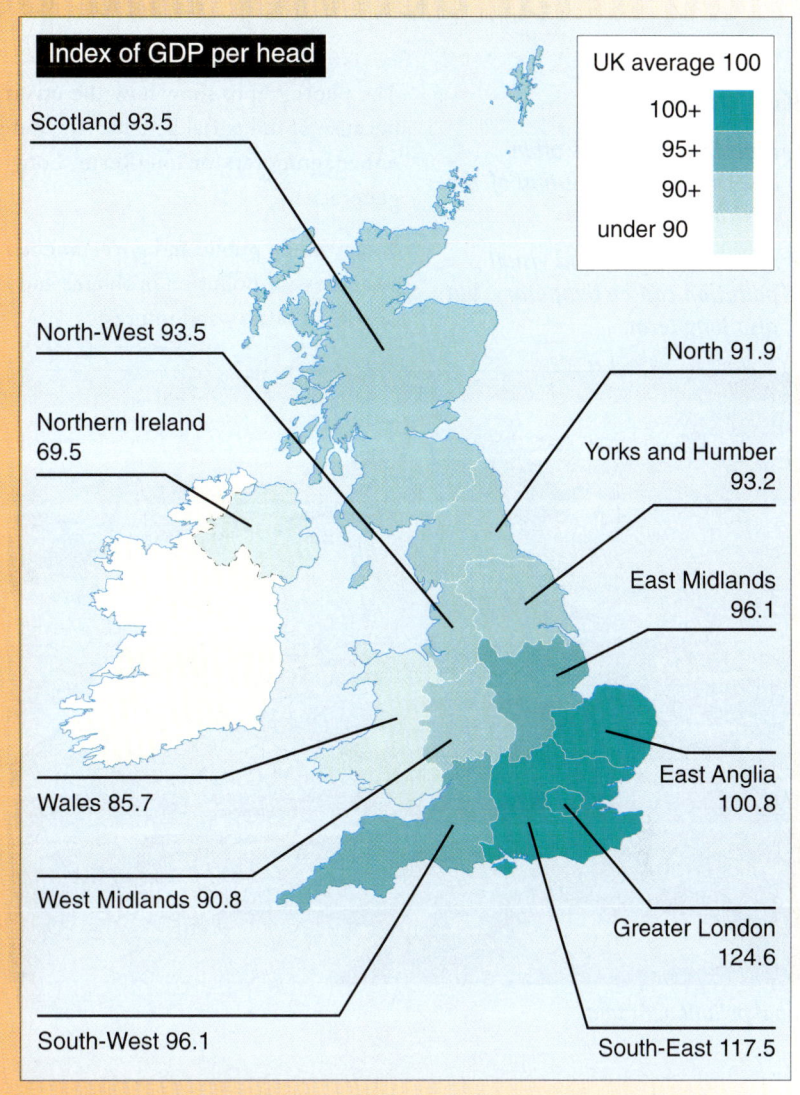

The 1980s, however, saw a distinct change in emphasis. The stick was progressively removed, with eventual abolition of the IDC and ODP (so as not to hinder further development in the South). The carrots were made far more selective, with fewer and smaller Assisted Areas. Most help was focused on individual towns with acute problems, such as Scunthorpe. Areas were designated Enterprise Zones and helped until sufficient prosperity was assured through a new, diversified industrial base.

ECONOMIC THEMES • INDUSTRY

Industrial activity and pollution

Key points

▶ Industrial activity is often associated with pollution of the environment.

▶ Air, water, noise, and visual pollution can be temporary, but also long-term.

The photographs show how the **environment** can be polluted – often because of industrial activity. Air, water, noise and visual **pollution** can be either temporary or long-term. Long-term pollution can affect future generations.

Today, much public and governmental attention is directed towards an awareness of pollution problems and strategies for conserving environments of special beauty and interest.

Canal pollution, Britain.

In Britain, for example, numbers of initiatives have been tried:

- National Parks (see page 102), Nature Reserves and Heritage Coastlines have been created to protect areas of outstanding landscape and scientific interest

- old railway lines have been turned into footpaths and cycleways

- derelict land has been levelled and landscaped

- abandoned quarries and gravel pits have been cleared and flooded for lakes, and rivers are increasingly protected by the Environment Agency

- domestic sewage and industrial effluent is normally treated

- factory noise, smell, and effluent have been controlled

- air quality has been improved since the Clean Air Act (1956)

- waste is increasingly recycled as supermarket bottle, paper, and aluminium can 'banks' become commonplace.

De-industrialisation (industrial decline) is particularly associated with pollution problems, but with enough effort and investment the resulting environmental blight can be addressed. One model approach is the transformation of the Lower Swansea Valley in South Wales.

Air and visual pollution: a wood processing factory in Africa.

80 ECONOMIC THEMES • INDUSTRY

The Lower Swansea Valley

During the Industrial Revolution, the Lower Swansea Valley became one of the most densely industrialised regions of Britain. Coalmining formed the basis of heavy industry, including iron and steel production, copper, zinc and tin smelting. However, 20th century de-industrialisation, stimulated primarily by foreign competition, left the area infamously described as an 'industrial desert' in the early 1960s. Abandoned factories, canals and railways punctuated a landscape of slag heaps and derelict, poisoned land. High unemployment emphasised the need for both economic and environmental regeneration.

The Welsh Development Agency, Swansea County and City Councils and even University College Swansea worked together over a period of two decades to transform the area. Key activities included:

- the demolition of derelict factories and the removal or levelling of slag heaps
- the removal of a massive copper waste tip in the Hafod district (a new school eventually opened on the site)
- the cleaning of the River Tawe – fresh topsoil was laid and grass, shrubs and trees planted to create a landscaped industrial estate and a forested park with sports and recreation facilities
- Swansea Enterprise Park was designated on reclaimed land
- factory units were provided to attract new manufacturing jobs, with retail and warehouse developments too.

The results of this reclamation are now very evident. Birds and fish thrive where previously smelting fumes and effluent destroyed them. Mature vegetation enhances what was wasteland. Employment prospects, housing and social opportunities are much improved.

Mine water pollution – now much improved.

But some worries associated with this, and similar initiatives, still remain. There is the suspicion that their great cost denies other areas of need. People question the benefit of replacing manufacturing jobs by those in services. Finally, does such localised assistance cause employment relocation rather than new job creation?

Test yourself

1. (a) List the four categories of pollution discussed in this section.

    (b) What were the causes of each category in the Lower Swansea Valley before its reclamation?

Stretch yourself

Consider the pollution issues evident in your home area. A useful approach would be to make summary checklists under the following headings: Problems; Responses adopted; Responses needed.

The iron and steel industry: development and change

Key points

▶ Steel production is an example of a heavy manufacturing industry.

▶ Raw material locations have changed to coastal port 'break-of-bulk' sites.

▶ Global overproduction has resulted in fewer, integrated works.

Historical background

Before 1700
Iron smelting, located in forested areas (for charcoal), where rich deposits of iron ore were found. England's Forest of Dean, and the Don Valley near Sheffield, are good examples.

Early 18th century
Coke first used to smelt iron at Coalbrookdale in Shropshire. Hence a coalfield location became advantageous.

Mid-19th century
Bessemer invented a steel converter (1856) allowing better quality steel to be made in larger quantities. Sheffield had the necessary black band iron ore found in the coal measures.

Late 19th century
Thomas and Gilchrist invented a process (1878) allowing poorer quality phosphoric iron ore to be used – hence development at Scunthorpe. British supplies of high grade iron ore started to run out – hence imports starting.

20th century
New iron and steel works located on the coast, in order to allow iron ore imports. These were integrated works, such as Port Talbot in South Wales, where blast furnaces, converters and rolling mills were found together. Molten iron could be taken direct from the blast furnace to the steel mill – therefore requiring no expensive re-heating.

Steel is central to any industrial economy. It is used in construction, transport, and manufacturing – from domestic appliances to ocean liners. The location requirements for an integrated steel works are:

- availability of **raw materials** (most important)
- **power supply**
- **water supply** (millions of gallons per day required for cooling)
- **skilled labour**
- large area of **flat land** (with firm foundations)
- **transport** (bulky raw materials – hence water or rail)
- **accessibility** – vast quantities of iron ore, coal and limestone are needed; the main bulk of this is reduced in making steel so it is cheaper to transport the finished product.

Note: The area around the integrated iron and steel works at Port Talbot in South Wales has been selected for you to test your Ordnance Survey (OS) map skills. See pages 84 and 85.

Steel production at Port Talbot.

Steel making in Scunthorpe

Availability of raw materials and power
Steel industry can be located where raw materials and power are available. Vast quantities of coal (for coke), iron ore and limestone (as a catalyst) are needed. During the last century, low grade phosphoric iron ore had been found in Jurassic limestone deposits at Dragonby. By 1878 Thomas and Gilchrist had invented a method for using this. Consequently, steelworks could develop at Scunthorpe once a railway had been built from South Yorkshire to transport the coal. (Note: Today it is more economical to import high grade ore from Sweden and Brazil, via Immingham, than to use the local Dragonby deposits. Scunthorpe, therefore, is now demonstrating geographical inertia.)

Water supply
Millions of gallons of fresh water, from the River Trent, are required every day for cooling.

Skilled labour
At the turn of the century Scunthorpe was a 'greenfield site'. Consequently, workers had to be attracted to the area from established iron and steel making districts. Many were attracted from Scotland.

Large area of flat land
A vast site with firm foundations was needed. The farmland in the area was marshy, and therefore cheap. Once drained, however, the flat land was ideal.

Accessibility and transport
The site was readily accessible once railways were built to transport coal from South Yorkshire. (This made more sense than transporting the iron ore – with its high proportion of waste – to existing steel plants in Sheffield's Don Valley.) Today, 'merry-go-round' trains, linked to the coastal bulk terminal at Immingham, move both raw materials and finished steel for export. The M180 motorway, completed in the 1980s, has improved Scunthorpe's accessibility further.

Recent trends
Rationalisation during recent decades has closed three of four works in the town. This was due to global economic recession and overproduction. There has been less demand for goods made out of steel, and competition from other metals has increased. Drink cans, for example, are now made from aluminium, and less steel is used in car bodies because better fuel economy is gained from thinner body panels. World capacity for steel production is greater than needed – hence the plants are working at less than full capacity.

Scunthorpe lost thousands of jobs, resulting in 35% male unemployment. The area was designated an Enterprise Zone which attracted many new companies. This status has now ended.

British Steel at Appleby Frodingham, the remaining 'integrated' plant in Scunthorpe, is now highly productive and very profitable – with methods and efficiency respected throughout the industry.

Test yourself

1. The location requirements for an integrated steel works are very similar to any major manufacturing or processing industry – such as a car assembly plant or an oil refinery. For the named major industry you have studied, list its location requirements.

2. Rationalisation is an easy word to confuse, at a glance, with nationalisation. Explain briefly the meaning of both.

Stretch yourself

Consider the most likely cost-effective 'green' approach to reducing iron ore consumption in modern steel production.

OS map skills

All OS maps are covered by a series of 1 kilometre grid squares. This extract shows Port Talbot in South Wales between northings 86 and 96, and eastings 69 and 81.

You should be able to

- use 4 and 6 figure grid references
- determine direction using a 16 point compass
- calculate distances and areas
- convert scales and recognise symbols
- understand contours, gradient and aspect
- describe and interpret relief and drainage
- analyse settlement situation, site and function
- analyse communication and vegetation patterns.

Remember:

Northings identify latitude. They are grid lines which run from west to east – across a map – but are numbered northwards. They are the numbers running up the left hand side of the map and are always quoted first in a grid reference.

Eastings identify longitude. The lines run from north to south – up and down – a map and are numbered from left to right across the top of the map.

Extract from:
OS Landranger 170,
Vale of Glamorgan, Rhonda & Porthcawl, Bro Morgannwg.
1:50,000 Series, 1996.

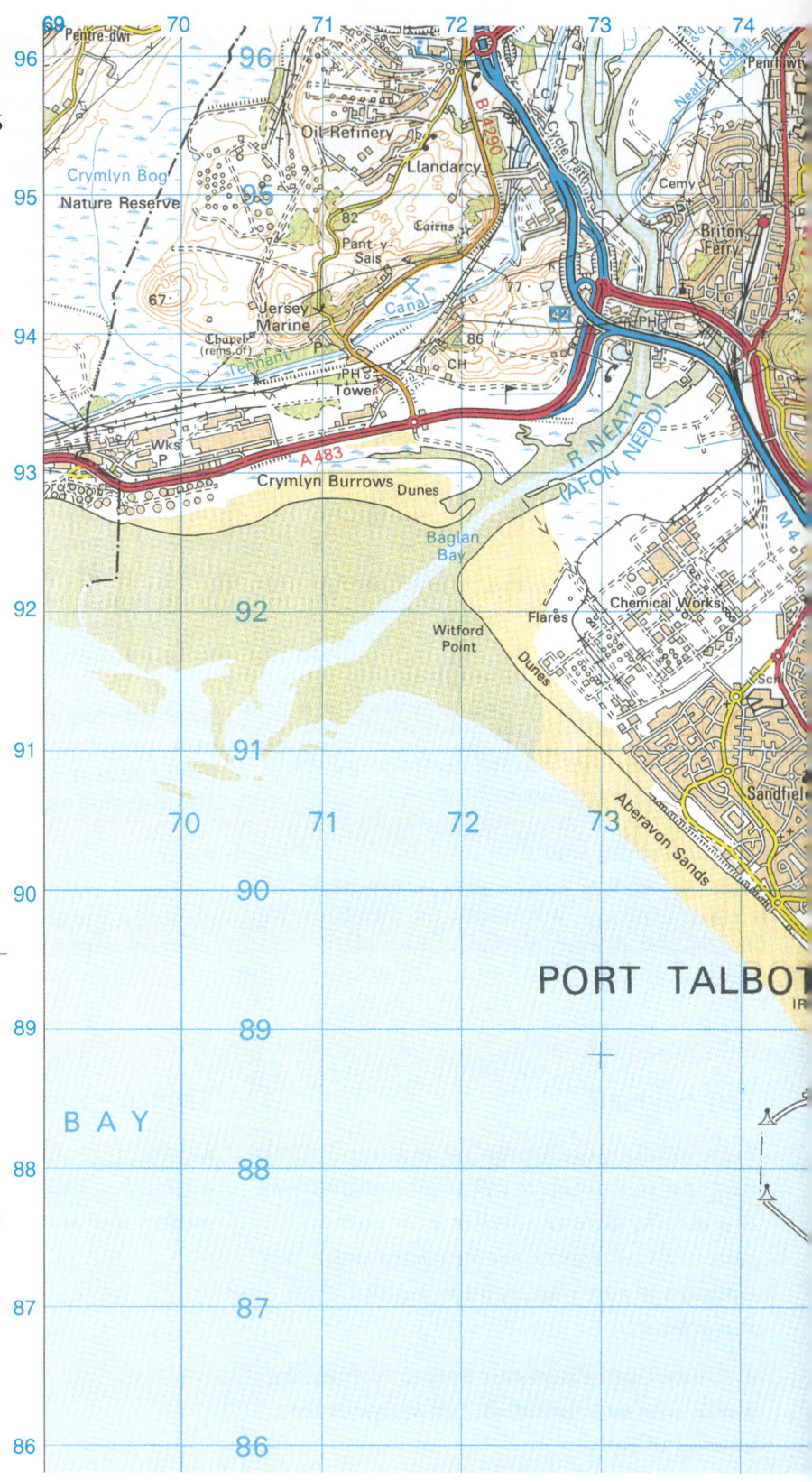

ECONOMIC THEMES • INDUSTRY

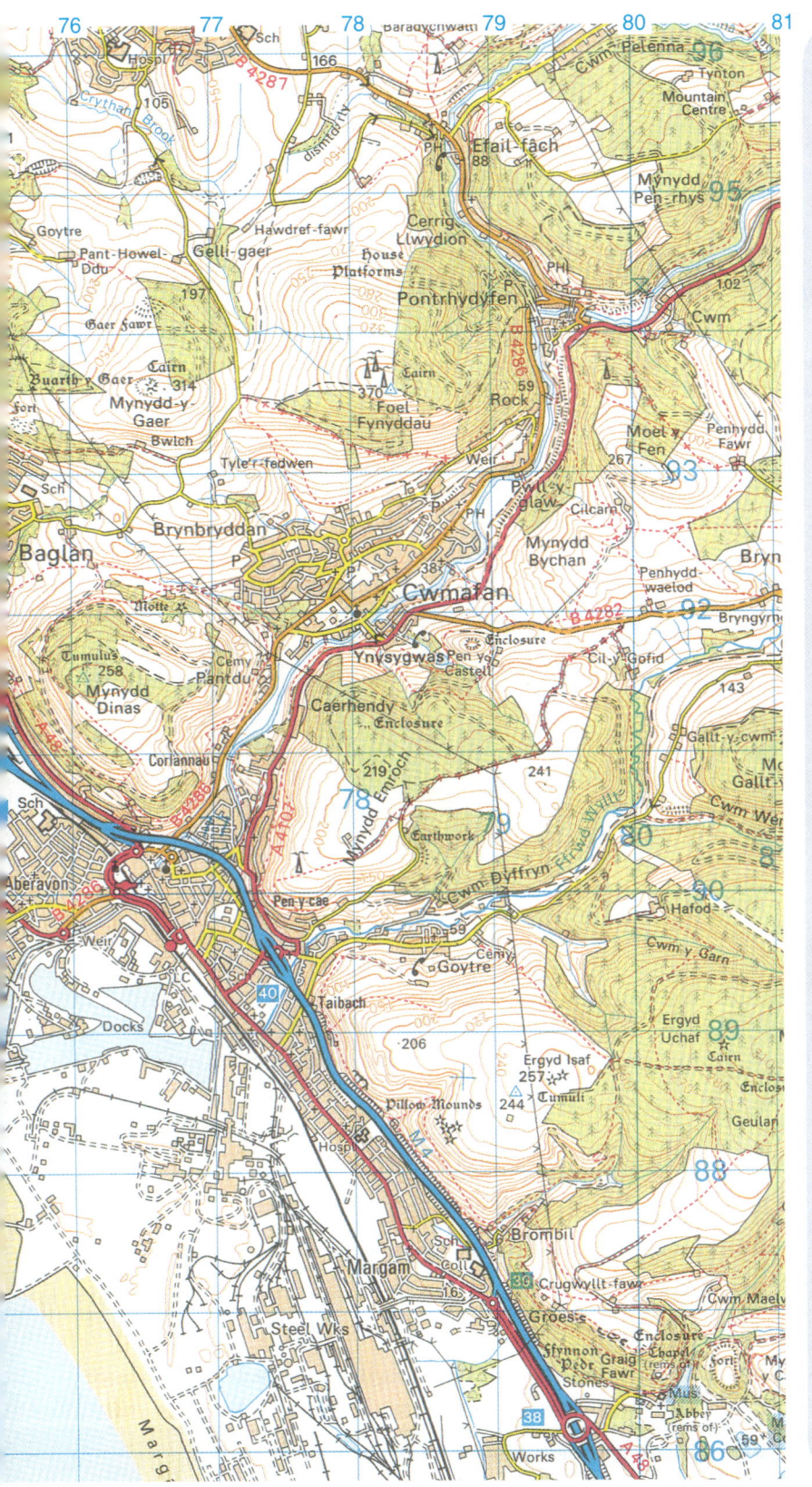

Test yourself

1. What is the land-use in grid square 74 90?

2. What is built at 795 862?

3. What is the total area of the extract?

4. Comment on the distance to, and direction of, the nearest beacon from the one at 742 883.

5. If a sketch of this map was drawn to a scale of 1:100,000, what would be the map distance between grid lines?

6. Comment on the gradient and aspect of the slope from 778 889 to 790 889.

Stretch yourself

(a) Compare and contrast the relief and drainage in grid squares 80 93 and 78 86.

(b) Comment on the settlement situation, site and probable function of Margam (78 87).

(c) Compare and contrast the industrial location factors relevant to the Margam steel works (77 86) and the Llandarcy oil refinery (71 95).

(d) Comment on the principal communications across this extract.

(e) What is the most common hill top land-use south of northing 90?

ECONOMIC THEMES • INDUSTRY

The micro-electronics industry: Silicon Glen and science parks

Key points

▶ The micro-electronics industry typifies 'high tech' growth industries of recent decades.

▶ The industry demands a highly skilled, motivated, intelligent and inventive workforce.

▶ Although footloose, the industry is drawn to accessible, attractive environments.

Micro-electronics is seen as a 'boom', high technology industry for today and the future. Britain's strength in micro-electronics was originally regarded as inventiveness, but product development is less notable today. The Japanese have long been, and remain, more cost-effective in production.

The USA, however, continues to dominate the industry. Its strength lies in the speedy response to changes in the industry. Manufacturing of computers, for example, is controlled by a relatively few major companies, such as **IBM**, who assemble machines world-wide. Similarly, software production is increasingly dominated by **Microsoft**, again in the USA.

Britain's micro-electronics industry is **footloose** (with a relatively free choice of location), but manufacturing is concentrated into two main areas – 'Sunrise Strip', along the M4 corridor, west of London, and 'Silicon Glen' in central Scotland.

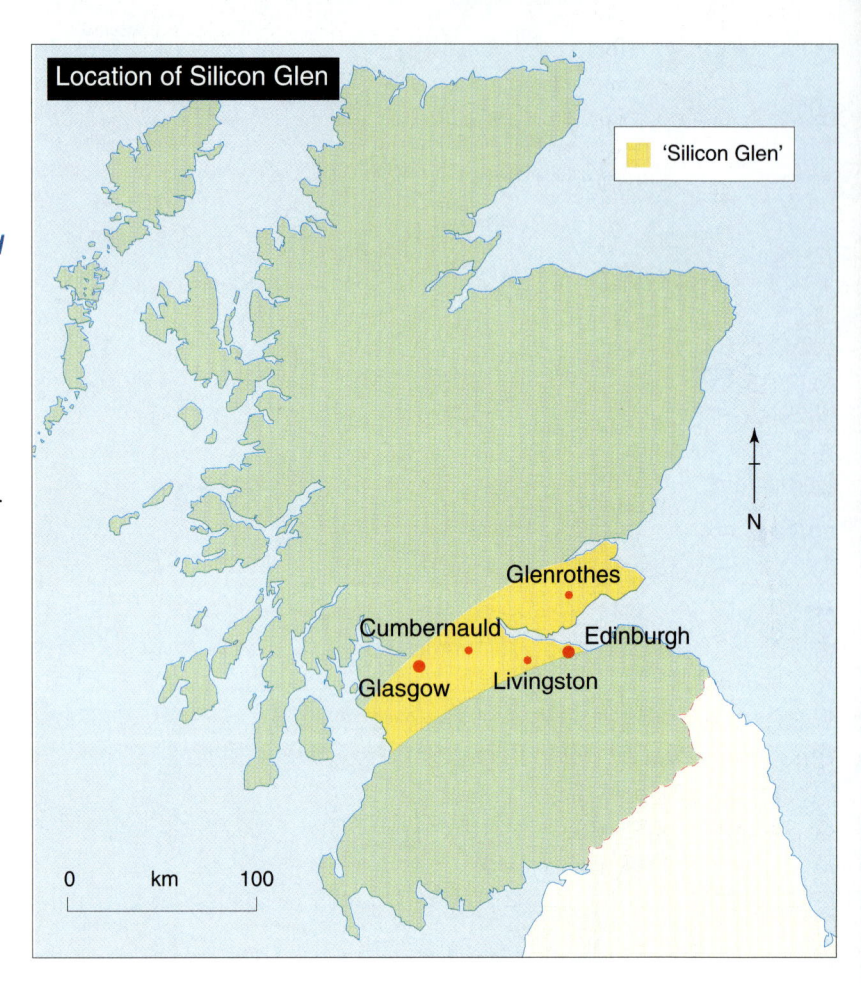

Location of Silicon Glen

Why is Silicon Glen such an advantageous location?

- electronics manufacturing was already established in the area
- skilled labour was readily available
- high productivity, low absenteeism and good labour relations existed
- motorway, rail, air, and sea communications existed
- government intervention made Assisted Area benefits available
- nearby universities, such as Herriot Watt in Edinburgh, specialised in high technology disciplines
- new towns, such as Glenrothes, Livingston and Cumbernauld offered attractive housing and services
- beautiful countryside could be easily reached.

Silicon Glen is a very successful area in this field, but critics have suggested in recent years that it could fail to keep up with others, in Britain and abroad, because of its northerly location. Competition, especially from California, has forced it more and more into assembly rather than product development. However, flexible management and working practices have allowed both established and new firms to prosper.

Much software development in Britain is associated with specialist **Science Parks**. These are similar to out-of-town Business Parks with modern buildings, landscaped surroundings and ample car parking. The main difference is their links with university research facilities.

Cambridge Science Park is typical and occupies a **greenfield** site on the northern by-pass. High tech companies, including software, electronics, scientific instruments and pharmaceuticals, benefit from locating together. They can share infrastructure and specialist support services and build up a pool of suitably skilled (often female) labour.

The Napp Building, Cambridge Science Park.

Test yourself

1. What is meant by the term: footloose industry?

2. Copy and complete the following sentences selecting from the alternatives given:

Raw materials/Skilled workers represent the most important location factor in high tech industries. Good transport, waste disposal/research facilities and attractive inner city/out-of-town locations are also important.

3. Find out the meaning of a greenfield site.

Stretch yourself

Comment on the following disadvantages of high tech companies locating together: land value inflation; salary inflation; labour 'poaching'; overproduction; consequences of recession.

Manufacturing industry in ELDCs

Key points

▶ ELDC manufacturing industry can be classified into modern and traditional sectors.

▶ Modern industry is rarely high tech, but mechanised and often run by multinationals.

▶ Traditional industry is more 'cottage' style, often adopting appropriate technology.

Reasons for the lack of industrial development in ELDCs

Labour
A labour force must be educated, skilled and healthy. Lethargy due to inadequate diets and debilitating diseases – along with a lack of even basic education is all too common.

Raw materials
These are often agricultural products and wood. If these are exported, it is usually without processing, and so domestic (home) industry is not helped. Mineral resources are often exploited by foreign countries (frequently former colonial powers) who provide the capital – but reap the benefits.

Markets
The domestic market is limited by lack of money. Overseas markets are hard to compete with. Remember, EMDCs control world trade prices.

Power
Despite the potential for HEP, particularly in Africa, it is often too expensive to develop in remote areas. Coal and oil are very expensive to import.

Transport
Networks are often crude. Difficulties of relief, clearing forests, costs, building and maintaining bridges, and so on, limit rapid development.

Capital
It is very difficult to generate wealth for industrialisation given the problems above. Foreign countries often give aid, or lend money at favourable interest rates – but in reality it is often difficult to repay the loans.

In ELDCs manufacturing industry consists of both the **modern** and the **traditional** – but collectively employs a minority of the total workforce.

The modern sector is not unlike EMDCs, with skilled workers employed in highly efficient factories, usually in the major cities. Often these are branches of multinational companies (see page 90).

The traditional sector, by contrast, employs more workers and could best be described as '**cottage industry**'. Craft skills, centred on **appropriate (intermediate) technology**, are associated with the villages and small towns of rural areas.

Using traditional skills ...

... Women weave baskets in Bangladesh.

... Men cast bronze in Nigeria.

88 ECONOMIC THEMES • INDUSTRY

Examples of industries likely to develop in ELDCs

- food processing using local 'raw' agricultural products
- wood-based industries, such as furniture and simple tools
- craft produce using local raw materials
- industry using local minerals – eg. bricks, tiles and pottery from clay
- assembly industries, such as bicycles, using imported component parts or machine tools from discontinued product ranges in EMDCs
- consumer products for the local market, such as cheap clothing, soap, sweets and cigarettes, drugs and medicine.

The main advantage in ELDCs is the cheap labour. Providing **appropriate technology** is adopted, successful industrialisation is possible.

Large-scale production based on local raw materials, and requiring simple skills, may be less glamorous than high technology manufacturing, but is far more likely to succeed.

Industrialisation in ELDCs is usually one aspect of wide-ranging governmental plans for general development of agriculture, transport, education, health care and tourism.

Development plans, covering five to ten-year periods, are common, setting targets for employment, output and growth.

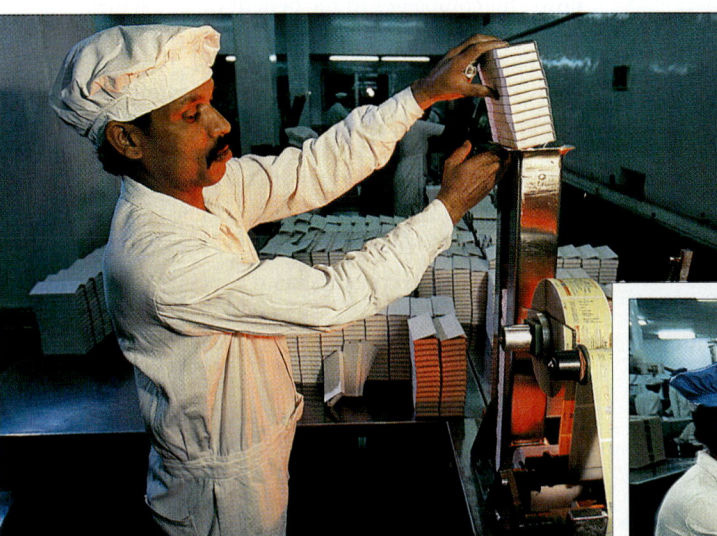

Pill-packaging in Bombay, India.
Note that production is 'mechanised' (done by machinery) but not 'automated' (tasks are done by separate machines and people are needed to set up and control the various processes).

Test yourself

1. What is meant by the industrial terms:
(a) modern sector (b) traditional sector?

2. Which of the following is an industry most likely to be found in an ELDC?

A Computer manufacture. B Paper making.
C Bicycle assembly. D Petrochemicals.
E Shipbuilding.

Stretch yourself

The encouragement of small-scale, labour intensive, traditional industries, particularly in ELDC rural areas, is much favoured by charitable organisations such as Intermediate Technology.
Why is this approach so appropriate? (You should refer to capital availability, the cost of imported fuel and raw materials, type of labour and technical knowledge.)

ECONOMIC THEMES • INDUSTRY

Multinational companies and aid

Key points

▶ Multinationals are usually run from EMDCs, but have branch factories worldwide.

▶ The largest multinationals can be wealthier than the ELDCs they operate in!

▶ The value of multinationals and government aid in ELDCs is the subject of debate.

The influence of **multinational (transnational) companies** is enormous. In ELDCs they talk of 'Coca-Colanisation'. Many of these multinationals are American owned, but most EMDCs have one or two. They produce the world's main brand-name goods, and are massive employers. It is thought that the top 100 now account for around one-half of all world trade! However, their value, especially regarding the process of much needed economic growth in ELDCs, is debatable. It is the same with aid from EMDCs.

Multinational **globalisation** of industrial production is increasingly common. The process clearly has both advantages and disadvantages – to both host countries and consumers alike. But is it colonialism under a corporate rather than national flag?

Multinational companies in EMDCs

High levels of investment and expertise allow new products to be developed, and existing ones to be improved – so creating jobs. Mass production keeps the products relatively cheap – so benefiting the consumer while ensuring high profits.

However, cost-effective production may be highly mechanised, or prove cheaper, in low wage economies elsewhere – so costing jobs. Ultimately, the consumer can suffer if more and more products are produced by a limited range of companies, especially if the profits ultimately return to the headquarter's country.

Multinational companies in ELDCs

Their investment may be especially welcome in poor countries, less able to afford industrialisation without outside help. Local raw materials may be bought, plus a workforce trained in new skills. Taxation revenues may be reinvested to the benefit of all, as new infrastructure is developed.

However, local resources extracted are lost for ever, and may have no value added. The wages paid may be so low as to give locals little purchasing power to stimulate other industries. Ultimately, the multinational company 'calls the tune' and takes the profits. They can always go elsewhere!

Or is it possible, through sensible planning and licence negotiation, for host countries to work with these powerful companies to the benefit of all parties?

Like multinationals, the value of aid is under debate. Does aid money help develop the economies of ELDCs and improve the quality of life of their populations?

Aid should, in theory, support ELDCs on the path to development by, for example, providing capital for investment. By increasing the ELDC's spending power, both recipient and donor should benefit from international trade.

Western advisor supports local industry, Bolivia.

Many ELDCs have come to rely on aid, which can be:

- **bilateral** – strictly between two countries
- **multilateral** – to ELDCs via international organisations such as the World Bank
- **voluntary** – from charities such as Oxfam.

But too often the aid is offered with strings attached. The 'strings' may be trade agreements or, at worst, an armaments deal.

Voluntary aid: water for Eritrean refugees, Ethiopia, 1984.

Who does this benefit? Volkswagen car production, China.

Selling Brazilian-made Avon cosmetics, Amazonia.

Test yourself

1. State five characteristics of a multinational company.

2. Examples of multinational companies include: IBM (USA); Nissan (Japan); Colgate-Palmolive (USA); Sony (Japan); Electrolux (Sweden); Kelloggs (USA). Check your household for products from these and other multinational companies.

3. What is aid?

Stretch yourself

Positive reasons for giving aid include a genuine wish to help ELDCs face short-term disasters, such as famines, and encouraging long-term self-help. Positive results include agricultural reform, the provision of clean water, and the introduction of appropriate technology. However, detailed investigation of the arguments for and against aid will also reveal questionable motives and negative results.

For a named aid project you have studied, summarise its positive and negative results.

World development characteristics

Key points

▶ Wealth, economic growth and employment structure provide clear indications of development.

▶ Education, health and social characteristics give a fuller development picture.

▶ Rostow's model suggests a country follows five stages to become economically developed.

Throughout this book differences have been described between the economically developed countries (EMDCs) of the North and the less economically developed countries (ELDCs) of the South (see map). This is one way of grouping countries, but perhaps it is too simple. This method suggests that economic growth, employment structure (see page 72) and wealth best indicate development.

The most common measure of comparative wealth is **gross national product (GNP) per capita**. This is the value of all goods and services produced by a country in a year, including earnings abroad, divided by the number of people living there. True, the creation of wealth is central to many theories trying to explain a development process.

W.W. Rostow's model of economic growth has been particularly influential. It suggests that all countries have the potential to pass through distinct stages to develop economically through industrialisation.

Whether or not all countries could progress in this way is open to debate. Some countries are unlikely to ever become economically developed due to rapid population growth, limited raw materials and insufficient capital for investment (even with aid – see page 90). Wealth generated through industrialisation is the most important indication of development – but there are others. Education, health and social indications are just as informative, as the table shows.

W.W. Rostow's model of economic growth

Stage 1
A subsistence economy based on farming. There is limited capital (money) and technology available to use resources and so develop industry.

Stage 2
Resources are developed and improvements to agriculture start – often with overseas help. The beginnings of a transport network allows both resources and farm products to be exported.

Stage 3
Increasing use of resources, plus investment in agriculture, transport and services. This sees the start of modern industrialisation in some core regions such as around the capital city.

Stage 4
Economic growth spreads more widely as technology and transport improve. There is likely to be rapid urbanisation and more mechanisation in farming.

Stage 5
Rapid expansion of service industries as manufacturing declines. Social services support the less advantaged.

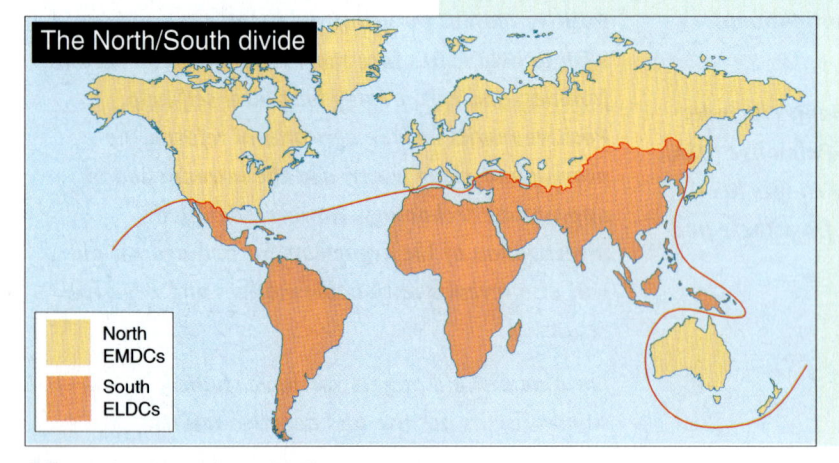

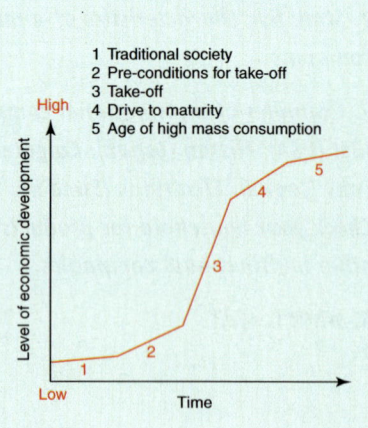

The North/South divide

- North EMDCs
- South ELDCs

1 Traditional society
2 Pre-conditions for take-off
3 Take-off
4 Drive to maturity
5 Age of high mass consumption

	Economically more developed countries	*Economically less developed countries*
Wealth	High GNP per capita; 85% of the world's income	Low GNP per capita; 15% of the world's income
Employment	Secondary (manufacturing) and particularly tertiary (service) jobs dominate	Primary (especially farming) jobs dominate
Trade	High volume (85% of world total) and value (especially manufactured goods)	Low volume (15% of world total) and value (primary products dominant)
Communications	Efficient, road, rail and air transport networks plus widespread telecommunications	Efficient transport networks and telecommunications tend to be restricted to urban areas
Energy	80% of world total; high consumption of oil and coal, plus nuclear and HEP	20% of world total; low consumption mainly of fossil fuels, with wood still important
Housing	High standard of permanent housing with amenities such as power, water and sewerage	Low standard of often temporary housing with few, if any, amenities
Population	Low fluctuating birth rate; low steady death rate; long life expectancy; low infant mortality; relatively low dependency ratio; slow population growth; high percentage urban	High but falling birth rate; relatively high but falling death rate; short but increasing life expectancy; relatively high but falling infant mortality; relatively high dependency ratio; rapid population growth; low but rapidly rising percentage urban
Health	Very good health care, staff and facilities; hundreds of patients per doctor	Relatively poor health care, staff and facilities, especially in rural areas; thousands of patients per doctor
Diet	Balanced, high protein diet; several meals per day	Unbalanced, low protein diet; malnutrition common
Education	High literacy; most have access to full-time primary and secondary schooling	Relatively low literacy, especially amongst women; schooling a privilege

Test yourself

1. Study the map of the North/South divide and name three continents in the North and three in the South.

2. Match the following regions/countries to likely stages in Rostow's model: Bangladesh; Portugal; Amazonia; UK; India.

Stretch yourself

State and justify the characteristics you would adopt to describe development.

World development measures

Key points

► There are clear relationships between wealth and other characteristics of development.

► Relationships between two variables are known as correlations.

► Correlations can be shown visually on scattergraphs and/or tested statistically.

► The Human Development Index measures development using economic, social and welfare indicators.

Wealth is the most important of many development characteristics. Indeed there are often close relationships between wealth and education, health and other social indicators (see page 93).

Such a relationship is called a **correlation**. A correlation can be shown visually on a **scattergraph**. A **line of best fit (trend line)** may then be plotted to show the relationship.

The example shows the correlation between GNP (a measure of wealth) and the rate of infant mortality (indicator of poverty), ie. the richer a country (one variable), the lower the rate of infant mortality (the other variable). This is because richer countries collect more taxes to pay for high quality health care for mothers and babies.

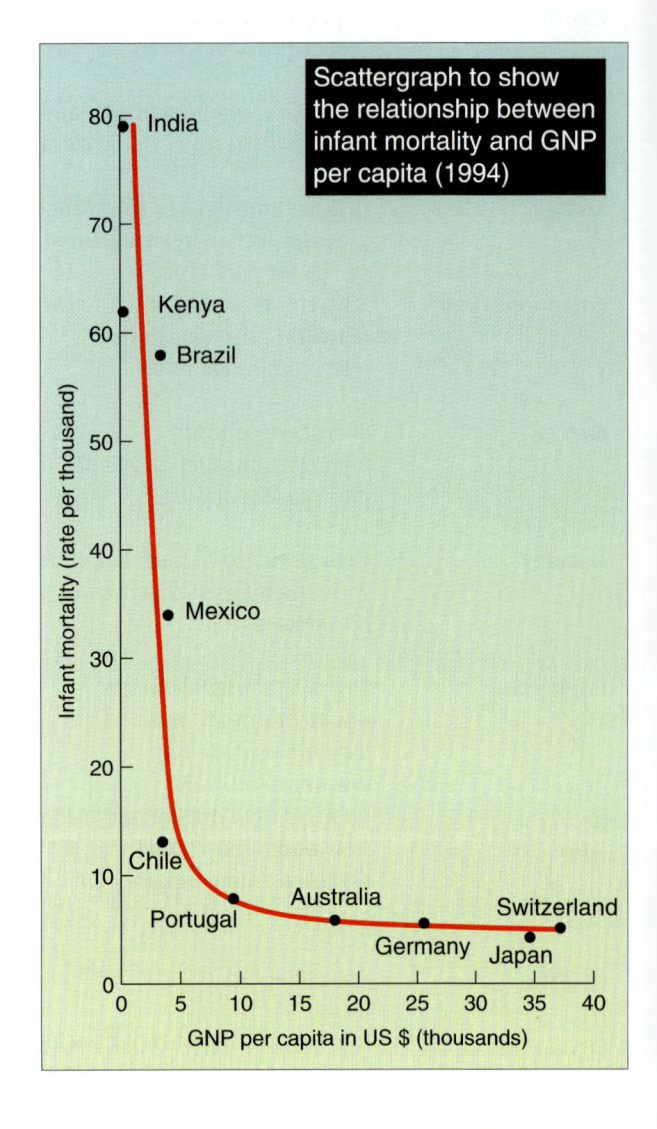

Scattergraph to show the relationship between infant mortality and GNP per capita (1994)

Types of correlation

A relationship between two variables is called a correlation. Correlations can be shown visually on scattergraphs and/or tested statistically to see if the relationship is real or accidental. Occasionally a point may lie a long way from the line of best fit. These points are called **anomalies** and have to be explained separately.

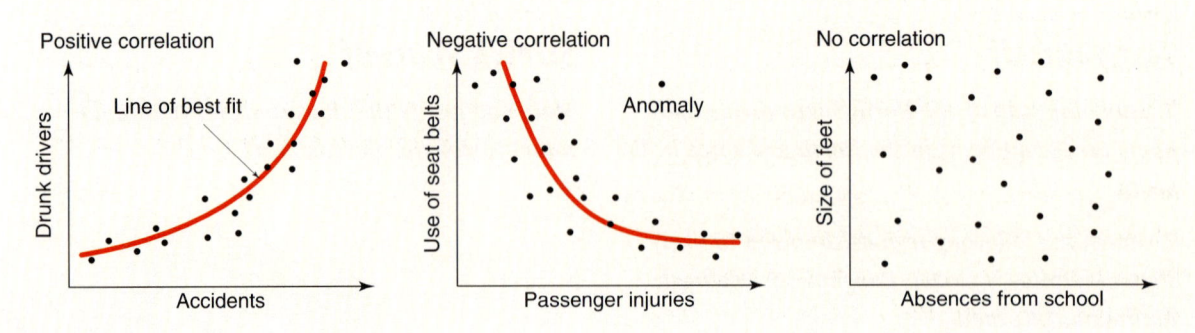

Positive correlation

Negative correlation

No correlation

ECONOMIC THEMES • DEVELOPMENT

Other measures of development

Whilst wealth is clearly an important indication of development it does suggest that income alone determines standard of living. However, people's quality of life involves other considerations too. In the 1980s, the Overseas Development Council introduced a **Physical Quality of Life Index (PQLI)** as an alternative measure of development to GNP per capita.

The PQLI was a social rather than economic measure averaging literacy, life expectancy and infant mortality rates. However, by excluding wealth directly, the PQLI was limited in its application. In the 1990s the UN suggested a much improved alternative. Their **Human Development Index (HDI)** scores each country or region on income, life expectancy and education. By adjusting wealth to **purchasing power** the real value of income is accounted for. **Life expectancy** measures both health care and safety. **Education** combines adult literacy with years of schooling, so accounting for attainment beyond basic literacy.

In the HDI each indicator is given a score ranging from 1 (the best) to 0 (the worst). Average scores of these variables for whole countries or regions within them can then be used to make comparisons. You can see strong similarities between the PQLI and the HDI and, when mapped, with the simple North/South map (see page 92). The highest PQLIs and HDIs, for example, are found in EMDCs of the North.

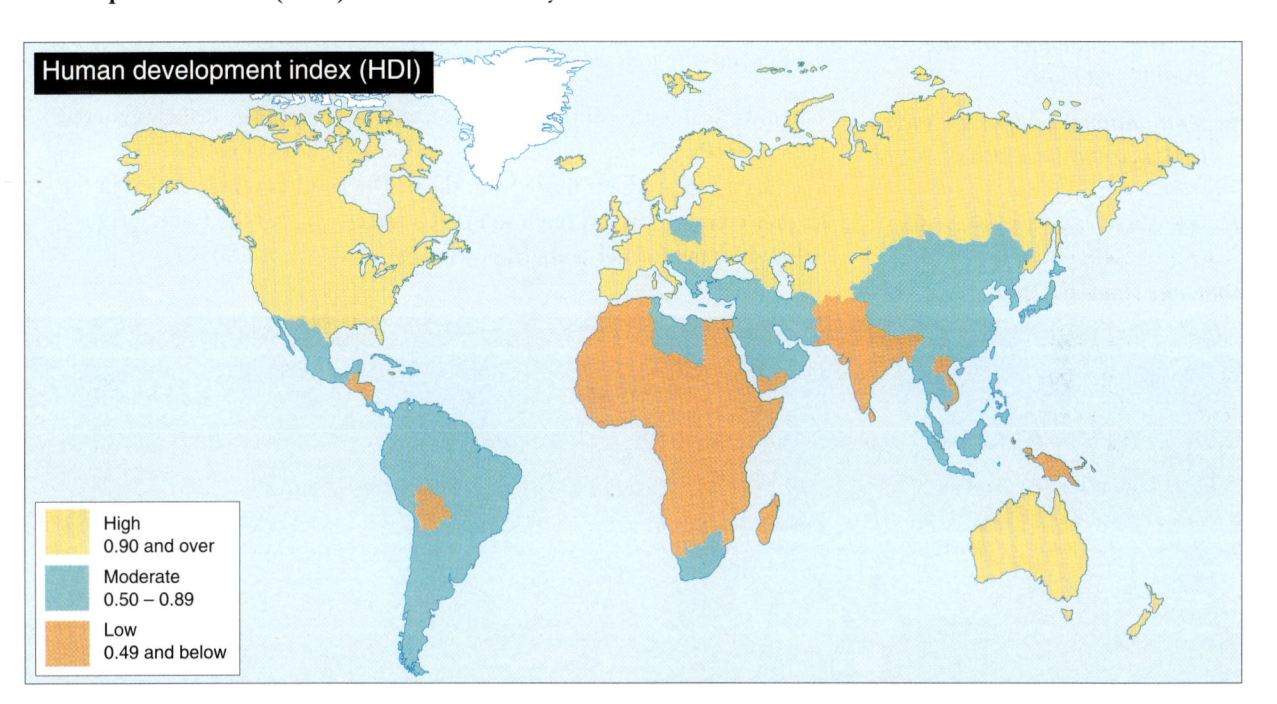

Human development index (HDI)

Legend:
- High 0.90 and over
- Moderate 0.50 – 0.89
- Low 0.49 and below

Test yourself

1. Study the main scattergraph. Is the correlation between GNP per capita and infant mortality positive or negative?

2. Copy and complete the following sentence selecting from the alternatives given:

Poorer ELDCs are associated with higher/lower infant mortality, greater/fewer numbers of patients per doctor, high/low rates of adult literacy, high/low industrial energy consumption and many/few newspapers sold per thousand people.

Stretch yourself

Consider the number of newspapers sold per thousand people as an indication of relative levels of development.

Why might this be a more sophisticated measure than infant mortality and adult literacy rates, energy consumption and/or patient:doctor ratios?

World trade

Key points

▶ Trade represents the flow of goods from producers to consumers.

▶ Manufactured goods are worth much more than the raw materials that make them.

▶ EMDCs effectively control world trade by 'fixing' the prices of ELDC exports.

▶ Pacific Rim countries have fast growing economies and are trading vigorously.

▶ Multinational companies, such as IBM, account for much of world trade.

All countries must trade, because no country can provide all the food, raw materials, energy resources, and manufactured goods it needs. Two states exist:

- Countries that sell (**export**) more commodities to other countries than they buy (**import**) will have a **trade surplus** – making them richer.

- Countries that buy more than they sell will have a **trade deficit** – making them poorer.

International trading, on a large scale, began in the 19th century. The Industrial Revolution saw many European countries establish colonies throughout the South. Trade often involved the European colonial powers importing food and raw materials from the colonies and exporting manufactured goods to them in return.

The historical legacy of this period can still be seen today. Primary goods, such as foodstuffs and raw materials, are worth far less than the manufactured products made from them. The resulting trade deficit in the former colonies has left them as ELDCs today – just as the trade surplus enjoyed by the former colonial powers has made them EMDCs.

Container terminal, Cyprus.

There are numerous trading difficulties facing ELDCs.

Sadly, too many ELDCs have become overdependent on the export of a limited range of primary goods – sometimes only one or two foodstuffs or raw materials. Foodstuffs and raw material prices are badly affected by changes in supply and demand.

If demand is great, then prices should be high, although most prices are fixed by EMDCs, so the exporting ELDC's don't reap the benefit. If demand is low then the price can collapse. Overproduction has the same effect.

Crop failures, or more competition in the market, affect the economy of ELDCs. Most are trapped in situations of increasing debt as the **trade gap** – between the value of their exports and imports – gets ever wider. Such is this debt that ELDCs are buying less, and the volume of world trade is declining.

Trade still represents, however, a good way for countries to increase wealth and raise living standards. Consequently, many countries have joined together to encourage trade between them. These **trading blocs (common markets)** include the EU which accounts for more than one-third of world trade.

Within such groups goods can be sold cheaper by eliminating import duties (**tariffs**) previously paid every time goods crossed a national border. This stimulates demand, and secures jobs. Furthermore, cheaper goods compete better with imports from beyond the trading bloc, especially if the latter are kept relatively more expensive by tariffs, or limited in volume by **quotas**.

Today 85% of world trade still involves EMDCs – which is one reason why the development gap between North and South is so great. However the NICs of SE Asia, such as South Korea, Singapore, and Taiwan are accounting for more and more trade. Indeed, trade amongst the so-called **Pacific Rim** countries (the USA and eastern Asia) now exceeds that of the previously dominant North Atlantic (USA and EU).

GATT and WTO

General Agreement on Tariffs and Trade (GATT): the World Trade Organisation (WTO)

Free trade means that governments neither restrict nor encourage the movement of goods.

Market forces, (supply and demand, and transport costs) regulate import and export of goods. There are no tariffs or quotas influencing the situation.

Most economists agree in theory that free trade would increase world trade, create industrial jobs and improve living standards.

However, automatic free trade is rare because it can only work if everyone agrees to it. Most countries want to protect their own jobs and industries by controlling imports (using tariffs and/or quotas). Consequently other countries feel the need to protect their interests too, and trade barriers go up everywhere.

In 1948 the first General Agreement on Tariffs and Trade (GATT) came into effect. This removed many global restrictions to trade and had a considerable effect on world trade patterns.

But a new agreement, signed in 1994, proved very difficult to negotiate. Arguments about 'unfair' US agricultural subsidies, and Japan imposing strict tariffs on imports whilst freely exporting high value electrical goods and cars, were of particular note. Inevitably, the richest EMDCs dominated the talks.

The new GATT agreement founded the World Trade Organisation to assist the implementation of its principles. WTO's aim is to help end world economic recession by 'freeing up' global trade, reducing unemployment and enabling poorer ELDCs to develop further.

Test yourself

1. What is meant by the terms: (a) commodity (b) imports (c) exports (d) deficit (e) surplus (f) tariff?

Stretch yourself

(a) What are company cartels? (b) Why are their activities not good for consumers?

Tourism

Key points

▶ Tourism is the world's fastest growing industry and biggest employer.

▶ Tourism brings many economic benefits, but disadvantages too.

▶ Related environmental problems are leading to so-called green 'eco-tourism'.

Package holidays – convenient and relatively inexpensive

Greater awareness of travel opportunities

Longer, paid, holiday allowances

Greater mobility – more car ownership, cheaper air fares, and so on

Greater affluence and more money to spend on longer and more frequent holidays

A study of tourism requires an understanding of the destinations, expectations, needs and consequences of people travelling for leisure and recreation.

Today tourism is the world's most important industry in terms of revenue generated, and people employed. More and more people, primarily in EMDCs, have:

- a higher standard of living with more disposable income

- more leisure time, with shorter working hours and 3 to 4 weeks annual paid holiday

- greater mobility with increased car ownership

- greater travel opportunities with 'package' holidays with cheaper convenient charter flights and accommodation arrangements abroad

- a greater desire to travel due to increased choice and awareness via advertising, education and the media.

Greater prosperity and medical improvements mean that there are ever-increasing numbers of active retired people whose disposable income is not reduced by, for example, economic recession. The growth potential of the tourist industry seems assured.

European countries, such as Spain, take the most visitors. However, relatively cheaper, and quicker long distance flights, using bigger fuel-efficient jets, have 'shrunk' the world. Once remote locations, the domain of professional explorers, are now accessible to ordinary people.

A greater interest in contrasting cultures, fed by extensive film, television and other media coverage, has led increasing numbers of people to seek more ambitious holiday experiences. The tourist industry has responded by providing cultural, historic, and activity holidays in increasingly exotic locations.

An exotic holiday, Antartica.

More and more ELDCs are aware of, and seeking to develop, their tourist potential. But the explosion of tourism, worldwide, has led to considerable concern over the problems caused – especially environmental damage related to erosion, sewage disposal etc. Such problems could eventually destroy the very locations being exploited.

As a result, more examples of sensitive 'green' tourism are found. '**Eco-tourism**' is seen as the way forward. People are encouraged to visit in small groups and blend into their surroundings; camping or staying in local hostels rather than large hotels.

Off the beaten track: eco-tourists following the Inca trail in Peru.

The seasonal nature of tourism

Tourism can generate many new jobs. After initial construction however, many of the jobs tend to be low-paid, part-time and seasonal. It is seasonal fluctuation that creates the biggest problems for areas dependent on the tourist trade. Few holiday resorts in Britain, for example, are able to attract visitors throughout the year. But the season can be extended. Some resorts have built conference centres in order to keep hotels busy. Other initiatives include out-of-season reductions, mini-break 'theme' specials – even specific attractions such as the Blackpool Illuminations.

Some Spanish resorts now let villas, hotel rooms and self-catering apartments to elderly visitors. This is done for the whole winter, at great discounts, rather than leave the rooms empty. But seasonal variations still persist. This leads to greater congestion, pollution and frustration for over-charged, under-appreciated tourists in the high season – yet resort unemployment, reduced services and empty properties in the low season. Tourism is certainly not all glamour and fun!

No sun: no holiday?

Test yourself

1. What is the meaning of the terms: (a) leisure (b) recreation (c) tourism?

2. Which of the following has least helped the growth of tourism? A Greater affluence. B More unemployment. C Greater mobility. D More leisure time. E Greater awareness of different countries.

Stretch yourself

'The world has shrunk and our holiday expectations have risen.'

Examine this statement by asking people you know from different generations about the nature, length and destination of their childhood holidays.

ECONOMIC THEMES • TOURISM

Tourism in an EMDC – Switzerland...

Switzerland is a land of spectacular glaciated mountains, lowland lakes and attractive, historic towns and cities. This has allowed tourism to grow from small mountaineering and skiing origins in the late 19th century to the country's third biggest industry today.

Alpine resorts, with two peak seasons of winter (snow sports) and summer (scenery) might appear to have the best of everything. There are varied attractions for the young, elderly and disabled. There are winter sports, hiking, climbing, skating, swimming and sailing, plus dramatic scenery and clean, fresh air. Yet tourism has changed both the Alpine environment, and the traditional way of life. Consider some of the key factors:

- More than one-third of all jobs now depend on tourism. In typical Alpine valleys, such as in the southern Valais canton (region), this rises to more than half the workforce involved in tourism for some, or all, of their income.

- New roads, car parks, hotels, ski-lifts, cable railways and restaurants – plus other infrastructure, such as water supply and sewerage – all provide employment both during construction, and in their subsequent operation.

- Tourism has resulted in a slowdown of rural depopulation; subsidised agriculture has adapted to preserve some alpine meadows, and grazing cattle, expected by tourists.

- Large resorts, with apartment complexes, built in the 1970s and '80s have, arguably, in some locations blighted the very landscape visitors come to enjoy.

- Alpine footpath, and ski piste erosion is a problem, with the potential for fire, landslide, and avalanche increased (see page 146).

Valley economies may well benefit from improved accessibility, public services and employment opportunities, but locals end up paying inflated prices for their basic needs too. Switzerland now recognises that it has reached 'saturation point' for tourism. Government emphasis is changing, therefore, away from new development to improving existing facilities, and using them more efficiently. They try to attract more visitors during the low seasons of spring and autumn. There is also the 'exclusive' potential of premier resorts, such as Zermatt, which might 'price out' all but the very wealthy, so ensuring tourism revenue, but reducing problems of congestion.

The Matterhorn overlooking Zermatt – in winter

– and in summer.

... and an ELDC – Kenya

Kenya's tourist industry has developed much more recently than Switzerland's – yet in the space of only a few decades, it has grown to be the nation's major source of overseas revenue. Stunning landscapes (coral coastlines, grassland wildlife (game) reserves, glaciated mountains) form the basis of photo-safari, and beach holidays.

There are over ten hot and sunny months each year, during which visitors can relax on fine sand beaches, or enjoy water sports in sheltered lagoons. Kenya's scenery includes the Great African Rift Valley with its unparalleled hikes and botany. But it is the wildlife, conserved (protected) in game reserves and National Parks, that most visitors come to see. Guided photo-safaris, in minibuses, allow access to otherwise endangered species such as the lion, cheetah, elephant, hippo, leopard and black rhino. There are also zebra, giraffe, and wildebeest and numerous species of bird, such as vast flocks of flamingos. All in all, Kenya's wildlife potential adds up to an extraordinary resource.

However the tourist industry, as elsewhere, has both advantages and disadvantages. The provision of tourist facilities, from accommodation to infrastructure, has provided employment, and raised living standards – and the money is needed in this relatively poor ELDC. But investment is only being concentrated into areas with tourist potential. Also, employment, whether making and selling souvenirs, or performing tribal dances, can prove degrading to former nomadic hunter-gatherers, such as the Maasai, moved from their traditional hunting grounds to make way for the game reserves.

The justification for wildlife conservation may be unarguable, but so are calls for stricter controls on photo-safari minibus drivers. Anxious for good tips, many drive so close as to disturb the animals' natural hunting, resting, and mating. Furthermore, soil erosion is made worse by drivers leaving the designated routes. Environmental damage is also causing increasing concern along the coast. Natural vegetation, animal habitats, and established agriculture is destroyed and/or displaced with the building of new hotels. Also coral is a fragile, living organism, easily damaged by swimmers, snorklers, and the anchors of glass bottomed excursion boats.

As in all fragile environments, sensitive planning and careful management has to be a priority if tourism is not to destroy the very resources visitors come to enjoy.

Employment opportunity or degradation?

Kenya: photo safari.

National parks

Key points

- National Parks are beautiful areas, defined by government as deserving protection.
- They allow many recreational opportunities, but also pose conservation challenges.
- Large numbers of visitors leads to road congestion, footpath erosion and litter.
- Conflicts of interest occur – between visitors, farmers, local residents and industry.

The first National Park (Yellowstone in the USA) was created in 1872. Since then other countries have designated large areas of unspoilt scenery as National Parks. The first in Britain was the Peak District (1951). Since then others in England and Wales have been defined as:

'Areas of great natural beauty giving opportunity for open-air recreation, established so that natural beauty can be preserved and enhanced, and so that the enjoyment of the scenery by the public can be promoted.'

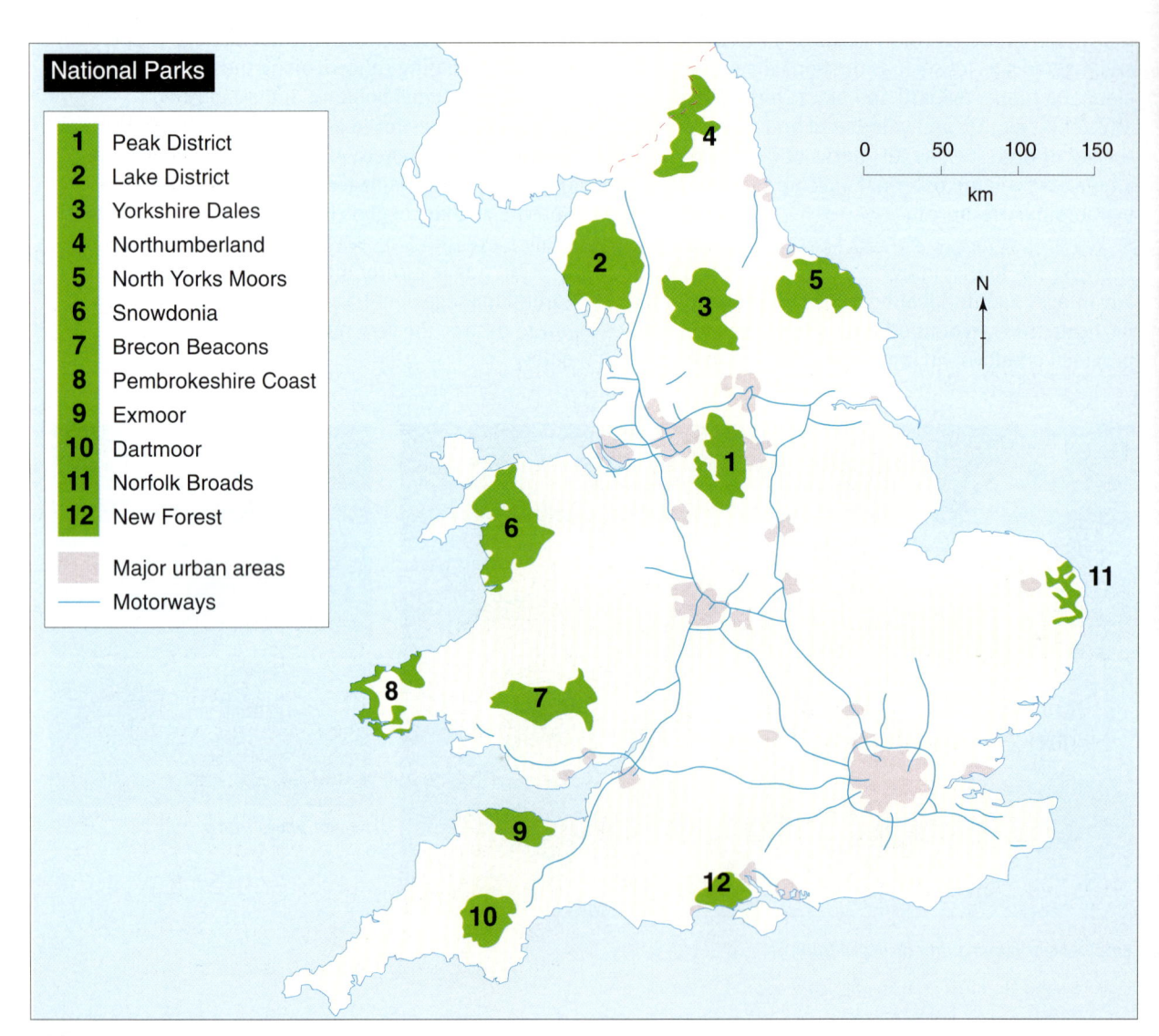

National Parks

1. Peak District
2. Lake District
3. Yorkshire Dales
4. Northumberland
5. North Yorks Moors
6. Snowdonia
7. Brecon Beacons
8. Pembrokeshire Coast
9. Exmoor
10. Dartmoor
11. Norfolk Broads
12. New Forest

- Major urban areas
- Motorways

ENVIRONMENTAL THEMES • RECREATION

People are increasingly mobile and can easily travel from towns and cities to enjoy National Parks. The Parks are a much appreciated contrast to urban pressures and pollution. Millions, for example, now live within a reasonable two to three hour car ride from their nearest National Park – a journey made that much easier by motorways.

The attractions sought vary according to which National Park is visited. But spectacular upland scenery, for example, is common. **Active** recreational activities – hiking, rock climbing, sailing, hang gliding – are very popular; so are **passive** activities such as car rides, sightseeing and picnicking.

However, public enjoyment within the National Parks needs managing. Visitors demand attractive landscapes, facilities and services. For these to be ensured landscape conservation and pollution control have to be effective. There are also the needs of the local communities – their employment opportunities and services – to be met.

There are always going to be **conflicts of interest**. Given that four-fifths of National Park land is owned by farmers, the conflict between their needs and those of others tends to be a prime consideration.

Agricultural use of the land can be affected by:

- water companies needing reservoir sites – often prime (low-lying) agricultural land
- commercial forestry, quarrying and even military training
- wall and crop damage by hikers and stock lost through 'sheep worrying'.

Farming, already likely to be economically precarious in such challenging environments, is under pressure.

Yet it tends to be conflicts between people that demand most attention. Visitors congest roads, buy and rent holiday homes and want souvenir shops rather than supermarkets. Local residents understandably want less traffic, affordable housing and convenience shops. Locals also need employment, likely to be met in primary industries such as quarrying which cause considerable environmental damage and pollution.

Even different groups of visitors have conflicting demands. Water skiing is difficult to reconcile with angling, for example. Add to all this the constant need to conserve the scenery and wildlife, and the considerable challenges of National Parks management start to become appreciated. Indeed, reconciling existing land-uses and conservation with public access has been described as one of the most difficult planning issues of our time.

The increasing number of visitors is certainly causing concern. Narrow roads become jammed with traffic, car parks soon fill up and special beauty spots ('**honeypot**' locations) become overcrowded. National Park authorities have encouraged co-ordination between interested parties, such as the National Trust charity and conservation volunteers, to address these problems. Initiatives include, for example, repairing and re-routing footpaths, and ensuring that visitor services such as caravan/camp sites, are landscaped.

Test yourself

1. Why are especially popular beauty spots called honeypot locations?

2. Which of the pairs (A to E) best represent a conflict of interest in a National Park?

A Adventure centres and water skiing.

B Afforestation and water supply.

C Caravan sites and car parks.

D Farm workers' cottages and holiday homes.

E Sheep farming and hay cultivation.

Stretch yourself

The National Park authorities have a difficult role. They must conserve the environment, ensure visitor access and enjoyment and yet also protect the welfare and needs of the people who live and work there.

Concentrating on the positive will help you to appreciate the difficulties of their task, especially given their acknowledged shortage of funds.

For a named National Park you have studied, consider and summarise its specific problems and the effectiveness of the solutions attempted.

Malham – a typical honeypot location

A 'honeypot' is a leisure or recreation facility prone, because of its popularity, to overcrowding at peak times. Whether an historic building, such as the Tower of London, or an especially attractive coastal bay, such as Lulworth Cove in Dorset, effective management of the honeypot is essential.

Many honeypots are within National Parks. Some of these have been actively promoted by the authorities to concentrate limited amenities – such as car parks, information centres, toilets and picnic areas. Such a policy can ensure that more environmentally sensitive areas within the National Park are less intensively visited, and so remain unspoilt.

Malham, in the Yorkshire Dales, illustrates honeypot management issues well. Attractions such as the Cove (limestone pavement), Janet's Foss (waterfall and

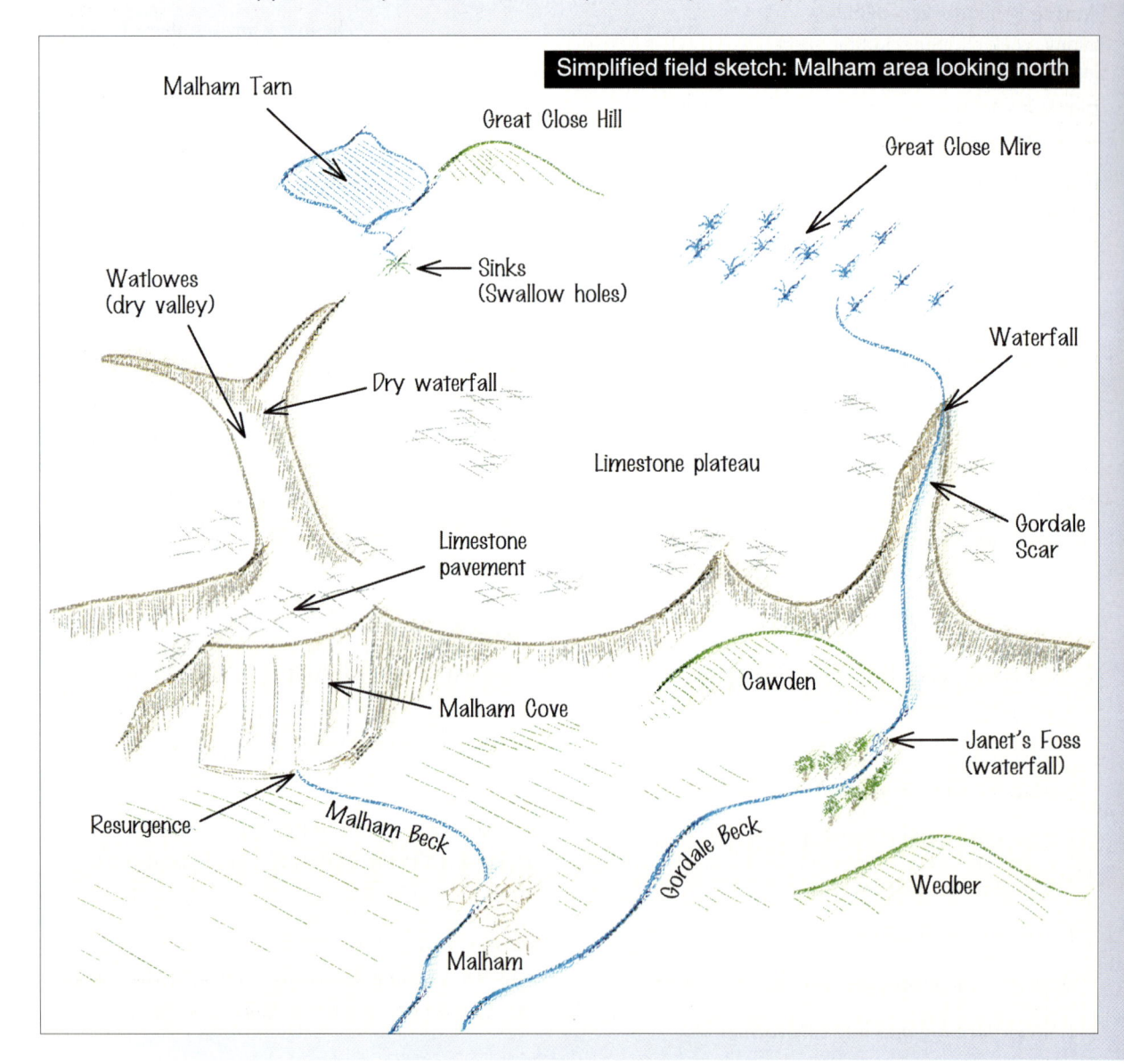

Simplified field sketch: Malham area looking north

Labels: Malham Tarn, Great Close Hill, Great Close Mire, Watlowes (dry valley), Sinks (Swallow holes), Waterfall, Dry waterfall, Limestone plateau, Gordale Scar, Limestone pavement, Malham Cove, Cawden, Janet's Foss (waterfall), Resurgence, Malham Beck, Gordale Beck, Wedber, Malham

plunge pool), Gordale Scar (gorge) and Malham Tarn (moraine dammed lake) account for only 0.5% of the Yorkshire Dale's total area, but cater for at least 12% of its visitors. The price paid, however, has been excessive overcrowding on sunny weekends, notably during school and bank holidays. Footpath erosion has been particularly acute, with wall damage caused by impatient visitors unwilling to queue at stiles, trampling of vegetation, litter accumulation and damage to the limestone rock formations by both walkers and rock climbers.

Even overspill car parks have proved insufficient to cope with the numbers, leading to kerb parking, and so further damage along Malham's access roads. The area's outstanding geological and geographical interest means parties of students studying not only physical features, but also the human problems which they are, in part, contributing to! The resulting management and conservation initiatives at Malham are both typical, and flexible.

The National Trust now owns, and maintains, key locations, such as Janet's Foss, so reducing agricultural conflicts. A progressive programme of footpath repair and maintenance is in operation. Nylon reinforcement sheets, overlayed by crushed limestone, create a hard wearing, and hopefully permanent surface. Timber risers cut along steep sections of path, including the Cove, during the 1970s, have since been replaced by steps made of limestone. Stiles have been doubled over many walls. Disabled access has been improved, in places, by the adoption of 'kissing gates' large enough for wheelchairs.

The National Park information centre offers expert advice, car parking, toilets and a picnic area, plus displays and educational facilities for public and students alike. Footpath signposting, in both cast iron and carved wood, is effective, and environmentally sensitive, and all litter bins have been removed – so encouraging visitors to be responsible and to take their rubbish home. (This brave innovation is proving very effective, but litter persists where easily trapped amongst the limestone pavements.) Rough cut, high limestone curbing has been laid along access roads in order to discourage roadside parking, and some local farmers offer farmyards as overspill car parks – at a price! Yet, sadly, notices throughout the area continue to remind visitors of the occurrences of sheep worrying, vandalism, and car crime. Continued planning and management will be the key to successful futures for National Park, and other honeypots.

Perhaps further commercialisation is as inevitable as increasing access control through roads closed to traffic at peak times, and park and ride schemes to selected viewpoints. Careful planning, design using local materials and landscaping with shrubs and trees, allow visitor amenities to be relatively unobtrusive. Scenic honeypot locations can never be entirely natural, but such an approach allows public access with controlled impact.

Footpath erosion through overuse.

First 'steps' towards solving the problem.

Limestone landforms

Key points

- Carboniferous limestone is a sedimentary rock formed from sea shells and coral.
- Limestone is a hard rock, and chalk a soft rock made of calcium carbonate.
- Limestone is permeable and layered in bedding planes, fractured by joints.
- Water flows along and down these cracks, creating caverns with distinctive features.

All rocks affect the landscape, but Carboniferous limestone forms particularly distinctive scenery, known as **karst**. Limestone is the only common rock that is hard, yet dissolves in water. It is made mainly of calcium carbonate, which is the remains of sea shells and coral, formed millions of years ago on the bed of tropical seas.

Since its uplift from the sea, limestone has been subjected to erosion, particularly chemical weathering. It is soluble in rainwater, which is a weak carbonic acid.

Rainwater flowing over an impermeable surface will, on reaching (permeable) limestone, be able to dissolve the joints into grooves called **grykes**, leaving blocks of limestone in between called **clints**. Exposed clint and gryke surfaces are called **limestone pavements**, such as found on top of Malham Cove in the Yorkshire Dales.

Surface rivers can 'disappear' down joints at a **swallow hole (sink)**. Once underground the water can flow along the bedding planes, and down other joints, dissolving the

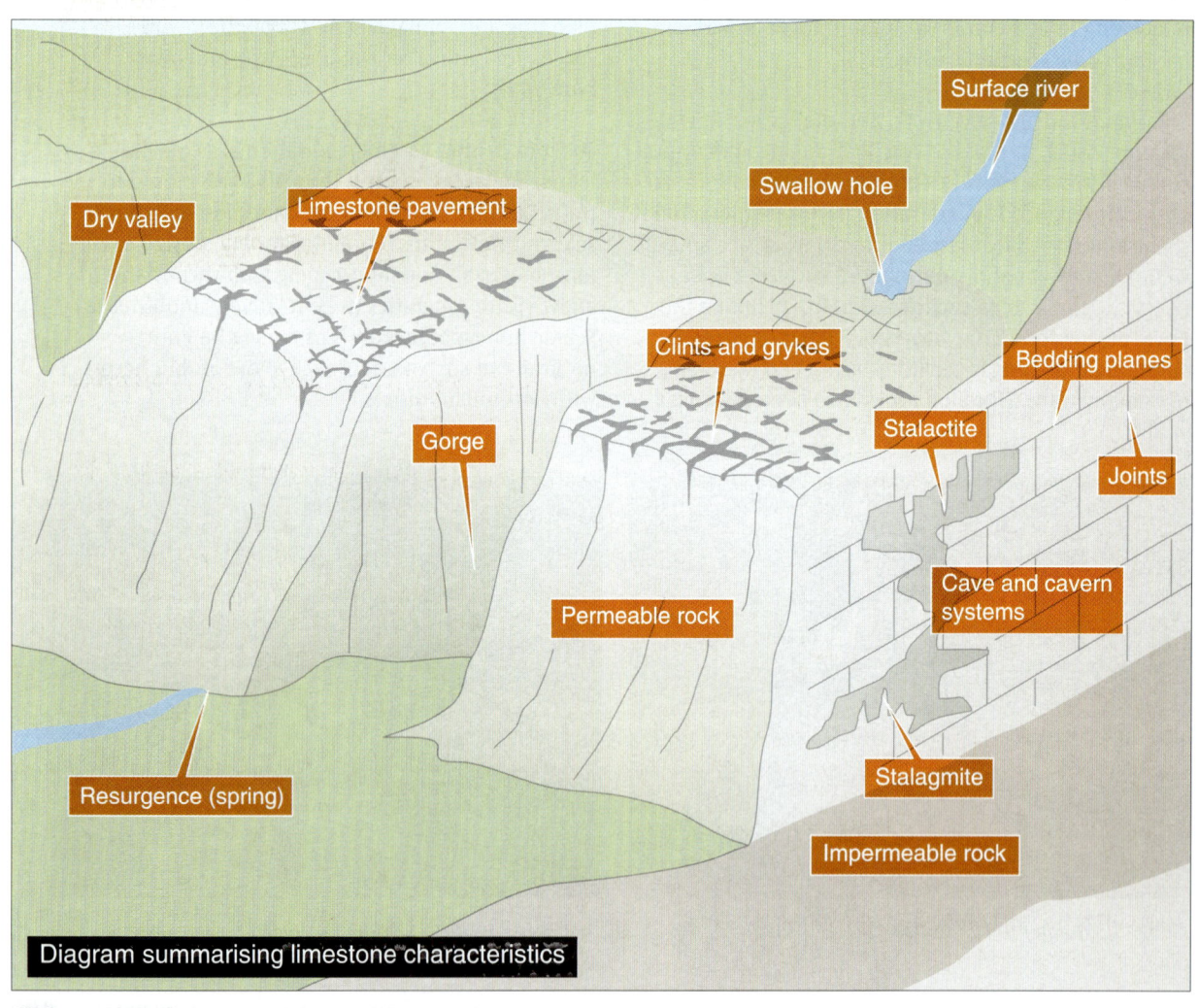

Diagram summarising limestone characteristics

Aptly named 'The Entrails': stalactites, stalagmites and pillars in Box Cave, Somerset.

rock, which is washed away in solution. Over thousands of years the joints and bedding planes can be enlarged into underground cave and cavern systems. Water dripping from the roofs of caves leave microscopic deposits of re-precipitated calcium carbonate; these very slowly grow as icicle-shaped **stalactites**. The drips splash on the cave floor leaving more rounded deposits – **stalagmites**. Should the two join, a **pillar** is formed. Potholers exploring cave systems have also discovered 'curtains' of re-precipitated deposits draped over cavern walls, called **flowstone**. Should, eventually, the underground river reach impermeable rock, it will flow over this until emerging from the surface as a **resurgence (spring)**.

The surface relief of limestone landscapes are characterised by an absence of surface rivers, yet spectacular, steep sided gorges, and dry valleys. **Gorges**, such as at the head of Gordale Scar near Malham, are frequently explained as collapsed underground rivers and caverns. Many **dry valleys** were cut at the end of the last Ice Age, by powerful surface rivers of meltwater which could not flow underground because the land was still frozen. The Watlowes above Malham Cove was formed in this way, and consists of lower and upper dry valleys, separated by a dry waterfall.

Test yourself
Match the following to their descriptions:

1. Limestone cavern
2. Clints
3. Swallow hole (sink)
4. Gorge
5. Resurgence (spring)

(a) Where an underground river meets impermeable rock and reappears at the surface

(b) Steep sided valley usually resulting from a cavern collapsing

(c) Large underground cave with stalactites, stalagmites and pillars

(d) Exposed limestone joint down which a surface river 'disappears'

(e) Blocks on a limestone pavement separated by grooves called grykes

6. What is meant by: (a) permeable rock (b) impermeable rock?

Stretch yourself

What simple fieldwork chemical tests could you perform to prove that an underground river flowed through limestone?

Glacial landforms of erosion

Key points

▶ The last of the earth's many Ice Ages ended about 10,000 years ago.

▶ Ice sheets in high latitudes, and glaciers, also found in cold upland regions, remain.

▶ Glaciers sculpt the landscape – by eroding, transporting and depositing.

▶ Freeze-thaw weathering, and erosion by plucking and abrasion are major glacial processes.

In very cold weather, as in the Ice Ages, snow builds up in any shaded depressions in mountainous regions. The increasing weight of this accumulation compresses the snow into ice. When the depression can hold no more, the ice will flow downwards, through gravity, as a **glacier**. The glacier will usually take 'the line of least resistance' along existing river valleys.

Ice sheets will only be found if there is a major blanket covering of ice, such as at the height of the last Ice Age. Ice sheets spread all over the total landscape, rounding and smoothing the original hills and mountains.

Rock material is added to the glacier or ice sheet by:

- plucking – the ice freezing to rock walls and pulling chunks off
- freeze-thaw weathering (see frost shattering – page 144)
- abrasive action – the ice knocking and grinding loose debris into the ice.

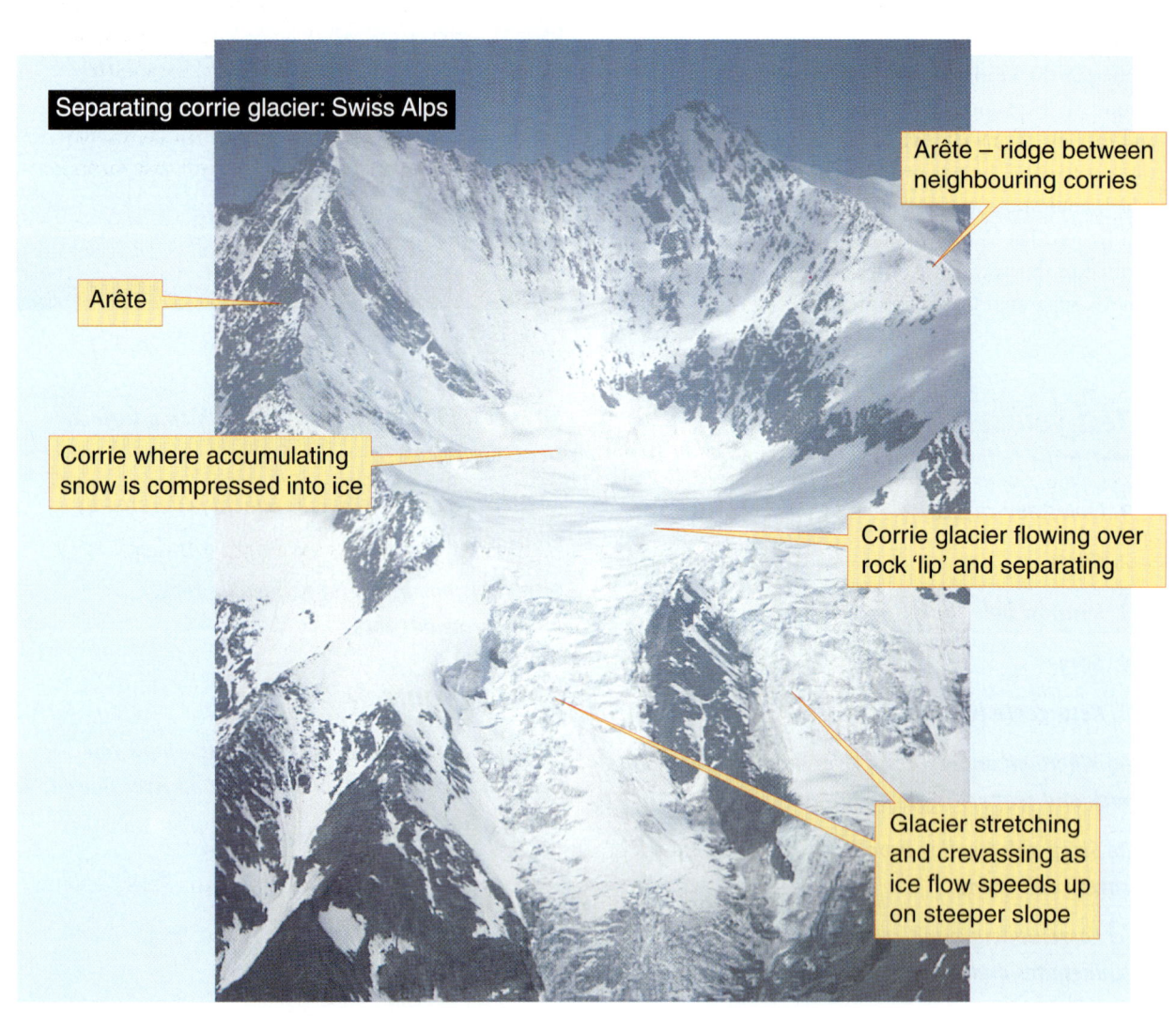

Separating corrie glacier: Swiss Alps

Arête – ridge between neighbouring corries

Arête

Corrie where accumulating snow is compressed into ice

Corrie glacier flowing over rock 'lip' and separating

Glacier stretching and crevassing as ice flow speeds up on steeper slope

108 ENVIRONMENTAL THEMES • LANDFORMS

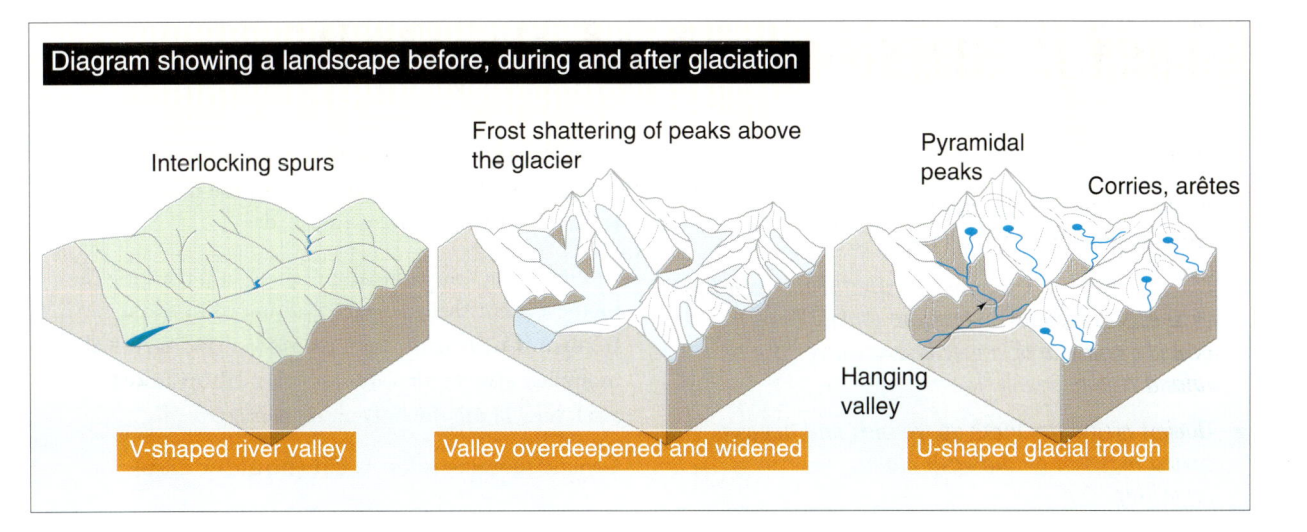

Diagram showing a landscape before, during and after glaciation

- Interlocking spurs — V-shaped river valley
- Frost shattering of peaks above the glacier — Valley overdeepened and widened
- Pyramidal peaks, Corries, arêtes, Hanging valley — U-shaped glacial trough

This makes glaciers very powerful erosive agents, abrading the existing landscape to form the classic features of glacial erosion. Good examples of glacial landscapes are found in the Swiss Alps and Snowdonia, Wales.

Corries, also known as cirques or cwms, are the original mountain depression plucked and steepened into armchair-shaped hollows. They often contain a deep rounded lake called a **tarn**. Corries may be separated by sharp ridges called **arêtes**. Three or more corries cutting back will cause a **pyramidal peak**, such as the famous Matterhorn in Switzerland (see page 100).

U-shaped valleys, also known as **glacial troughs**, are existing river valleys which have been eroded further by advancing glaciers. The glacier overdeepens and straightens the valley – cutting (**truncating**) any **spurs** off. Rivers flowing along these troughs today are likely to seem relatively small – hence the name **misfit streams**. Smaller tributary glaciers which are far less erosive are left as **hanging valleys**. Waterfalls may cascade from these today, often fed by corrie tarns.

Test yourself

Match the following to their descriptions:

1. Glacier
2. Ice sheet
3. Plucking
4. Abrasion
5. Corrie
6. Arête
7. Pyramidal peak
8. Glacial trough
9. Hanging valley
10. Misfit stream

(a) Distinctive pointed mountain created by corries cutting back

(b) Upland armchair-shaped hollow often containing a tarn

(c) Smaller tributary valley left high above the main trough

(d) River valley straightened and overdeepened by glacier into a U-shape

(e) River in glacial trough too small to have eroded such a valley

(f) Ice blanketing an entire landscape

(g) Moving ice freezing onto rock and pulling chunks off

(h) Narrow sharp ridge between neighbouring corries

(i) Ice pulled downhill by gravity

(j) Debris laden moving ice eroding rock by grinding it down.

Stretch yourself

Explain why glacial ice is so dirty.

Glacial landforms of deposition

Key points

▶ Glacial deposition occurs when rising temperatures cause the ice to melt.

▶ Glacial deposits create far less spectacular landforms than those sculpted by erosion. Glacial moraines provide evidence of a glacier's advance, size and retreat.

▶ Glacial meltwater picks up, rounds and deposits sorted material on outwash plains.

Glaciers and ice sheets will carry vast quantities of rock waste – **moraine**:

- lateral moraine along the sides
- medial moraine where two glaciers have joined
- ground moraine at the bottom
- terminal moraine across the snout
- recessional moraines, marking periods when the glacier's retreat was halted.

When the ice melts away the moraines form impressive mounds of material. This debris provides evidence about the behaviour of the glacier.

Recessional moraines mark the position of the glacier's snout during periods when the melting ice has remained stationary for a time.

Parallel to any recessional moraines, and marking the furthest point that the glacier advanced to, is the **terminal moraine**. Both recessional and terminal moraines may dam rivers to form **ribbon lakes** stretching along the bottom of glacial troughs.

Ground moraine is left as **till (boulder clay)**.

Debris may also form in 'swarms' of smooth, elongated hills called **drumlims**. There are also deposited massive rock boulders, called **erratics**. The latter may have been transported by the ice over long distances. By analysing the rock material of an erratic, its origin can be determined and so the direction of the glacier's flow can be confirmed.

Finally, melting ice produces vast quantities of **meltwater** which picks up unsorted glacial debris. The water rounds the material by attrition before depositing it to build up **outwash plains** beyond the terminal moraine. This fluvioglacial material is sorted, with the coarsest material deposited first and the finest last.

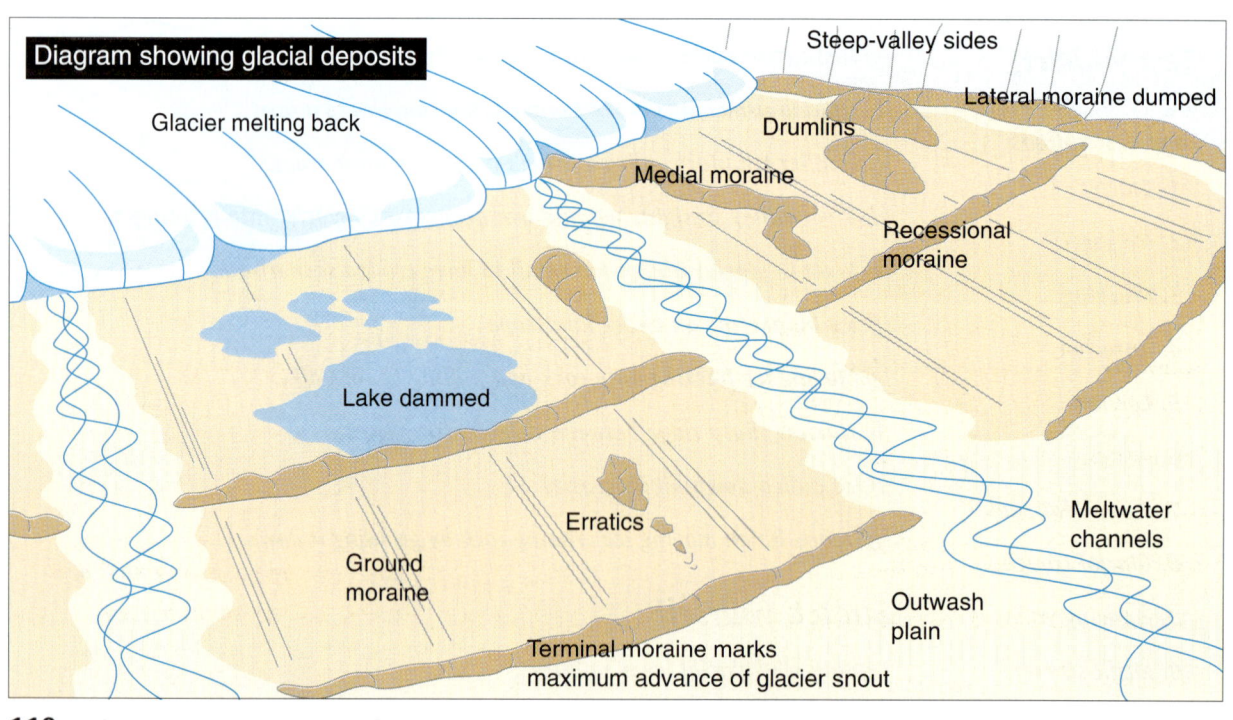

Diagram showing glacial deposits

- Glacier melting back
- Steep-valley sides
- Lateral moraine dumped
- Drumlins
- Medial moraine
- Recessional moraine
- Lake dammed
- Erratics
- Ground moraine
- Meltwater channels
- Outwash plain
- Terminal moraine marks maximum advance of glacier snout

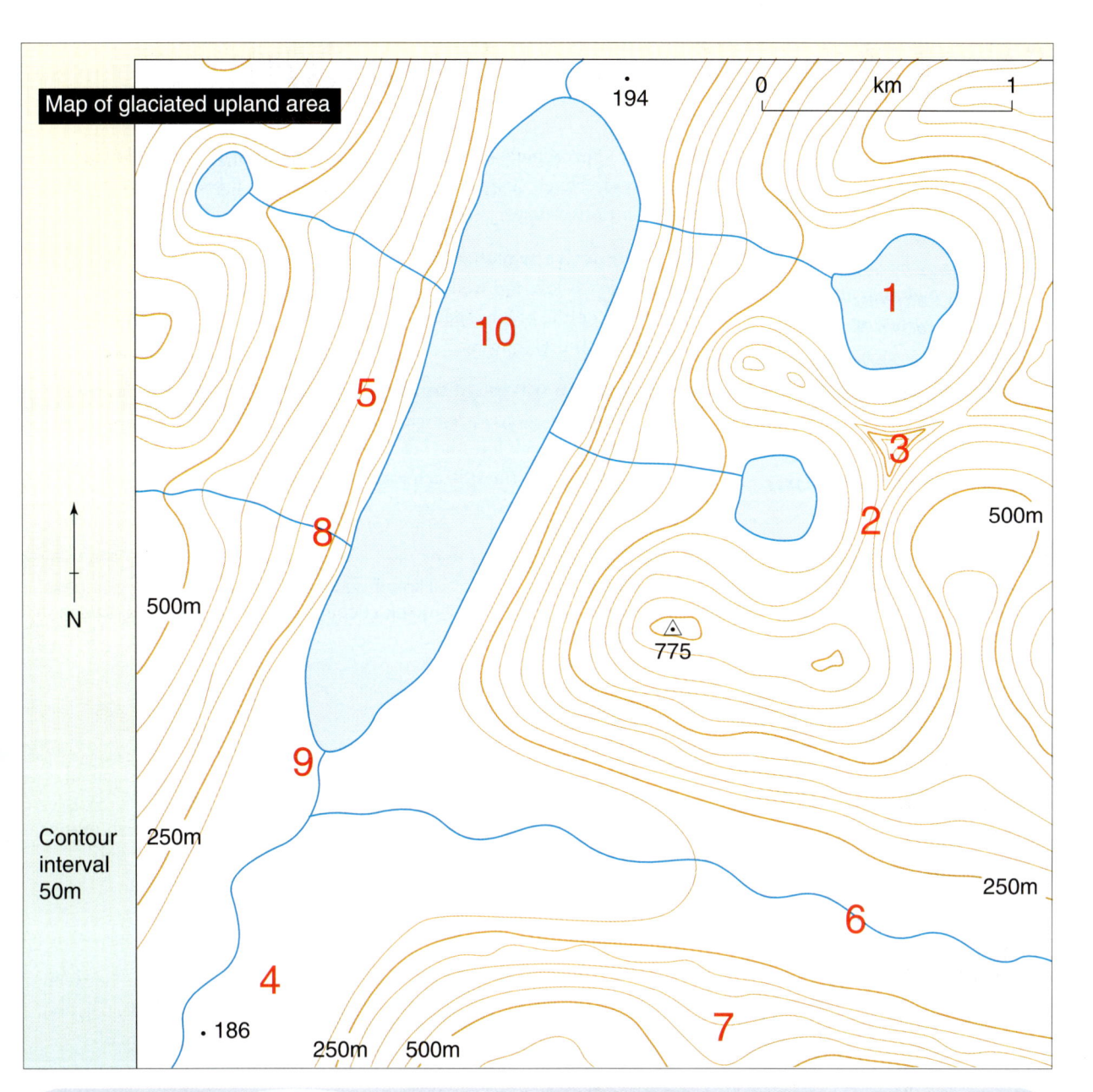

Test yourself

1. Study the 1:25,000 contour map above. It is typical of a glaciated upland area such as Snowdonia or the Lake District. Match the numbered features to the descriptions below:

(a) Waterfall cascading from a hanging valley

(b) Pyramidal peak

(c) WNW facing corrie containing a tarn

(d) Probable site of recessional moraine

(e) Arête

(f) Ribbon lake

(g) Truncated spur

(h) Misfit stream

(i) Glacial trough

(j) Dry hanging valley

Stretch yourself

Using the photographs (on pages 100 and 108) and the map above as a guide, draw an annotated diagram of a pyramidal peak.

ENVIRONMENTAL THEMES • LANDFORMS **111**

Coastal landforms of erosion

Key points

▶ The coast is particularly affected by wave action.

▶ Waves erode by abrasion, attrition, hydraulic action and solution weathering.

▶ Wave attack, concentrated in the inter-tidal zone, creates distinctive features.

▶ Constructive and destructive coastal processes will balance naturally.

Any wave approaching a beach is slowed by friction with the shallowing sea bed. This effectively 'trips the wave up', resulting in it breaking. Waves are divided into two types:

- **Constructive waves** are common in summer, and build beaches up. If each wave is low and well separated, the breaking **swash** will carry material up the beach. The material will be deposited as the returning **backwash** drains away.

- **Destructive waves** are associated with winter storms, and destroy beaches. Where waves are higher, and more frequent, the backwash has less chance to soak into the beach. Each new breaker adds more running water to drag the finest beach material back out to sea.

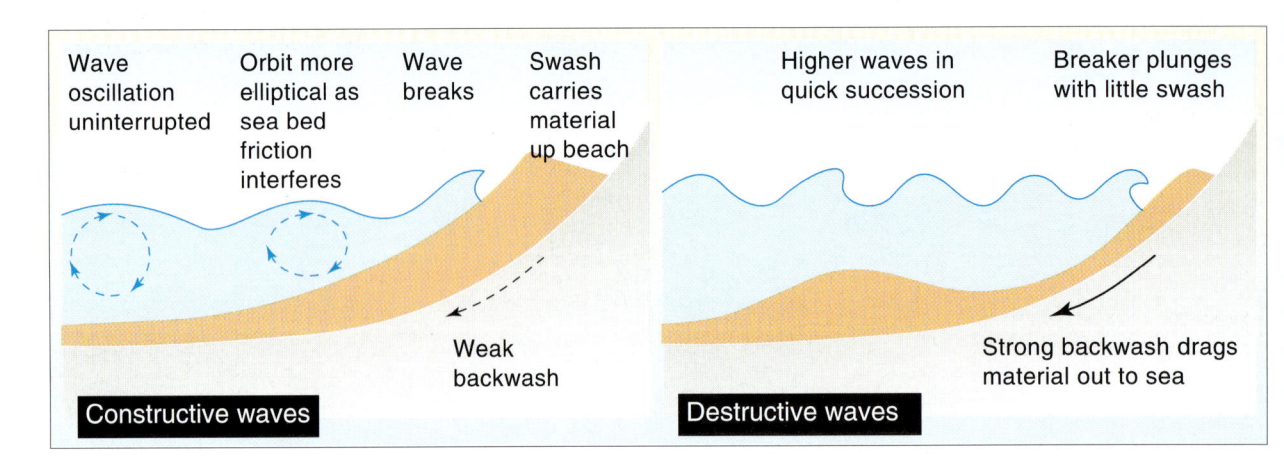

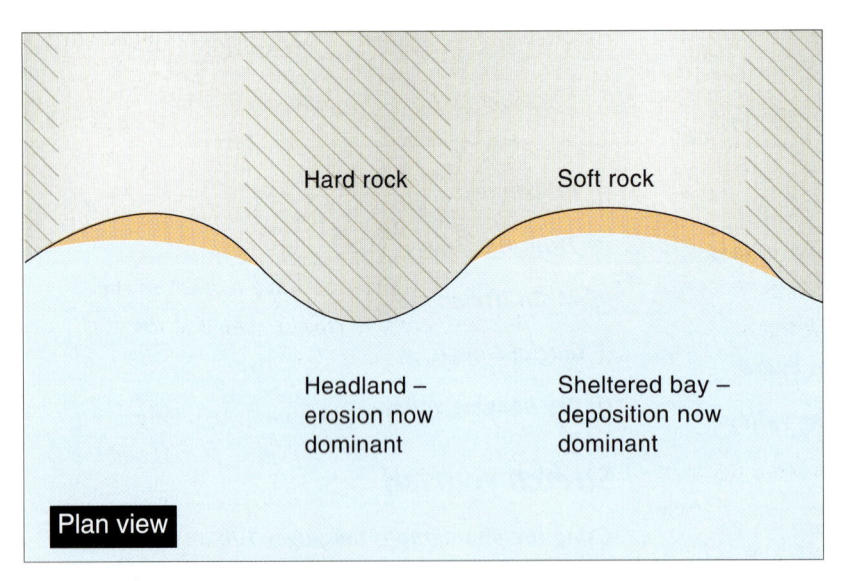

Constructive waves: Wave oscillation uninterrupted — Orbit more elliptical as sea bed friction interferes — Wave breaks — Swash carries material up beach — Weak backwash

Destructive waves: Higher waves in quick succession — Breaker plunges with little swash — Strong backwash drags material out to sea

Plan view: Hard rock — Headland – erosion now dominant; Soft rock — Sheltered bay – deposition now dominant

A natural seasonal balance between beach construction and destruction, is not unusual, unless human activities intervene (see page 115 for details of coastal management using groynes, rock armour and beach nourishment).

Natural balance can also be demonstrated between the erosion of hard rock headlands, and the deposition of the resulting material in adjacent bays, eroded from softer rock structures.

The inter-tidal zone is subject to powerful physical attack. Erosive forces include:

- **chemical weathering** by **solution**, because sea water contains salts and acids which dissolve some rocks
- **corrasion**, with waves pounding against rocky headlands and hurling sea bed material against the cliff
- **attrition** where the loose material itself rubs and rolls together, and so is worn smaller, and smoother
- **hydraulic action** which is a particularly spectacular form of coastal erosion; air, trapped by the breaking wave, is compressed in any cracks in the headland rock, only to be released explosively immediately after.

The weakening, and so erosion, of the rock is remorseless. Holes and cracks get bigger forming **caves**. When these have eroded through the headland, **arches** are formed. Continued wave action widens the arch until the roof can no longer be supported. The resulting **stack** will itself be eroded before collapsing to a **stump**.

Constant undercutting of a cliff will form a **wave cut notch** above which the cliff rock is unsupported. Eventually this collapses, a new notch is started, and the sequence will repeat itself. Progressive retreat of cliffs in this way form a gently sloping **wave cut platform**, exposed at low tide.

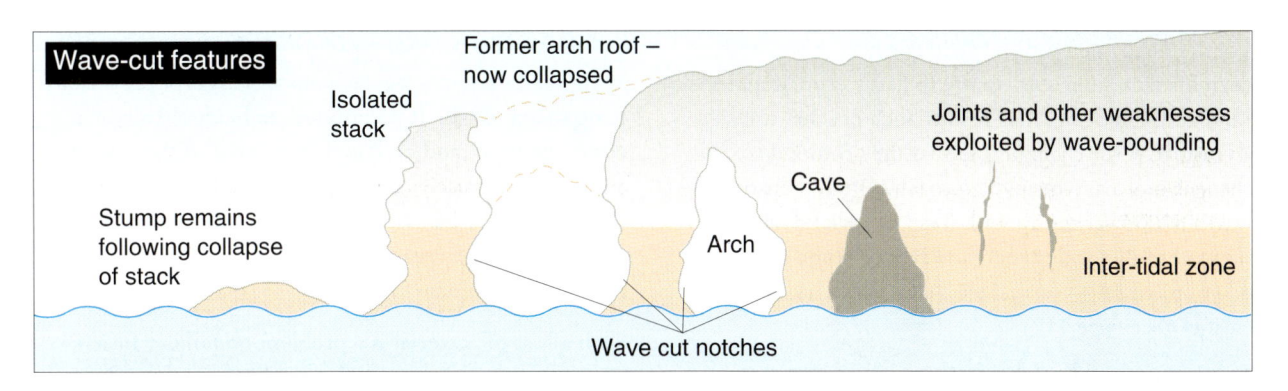

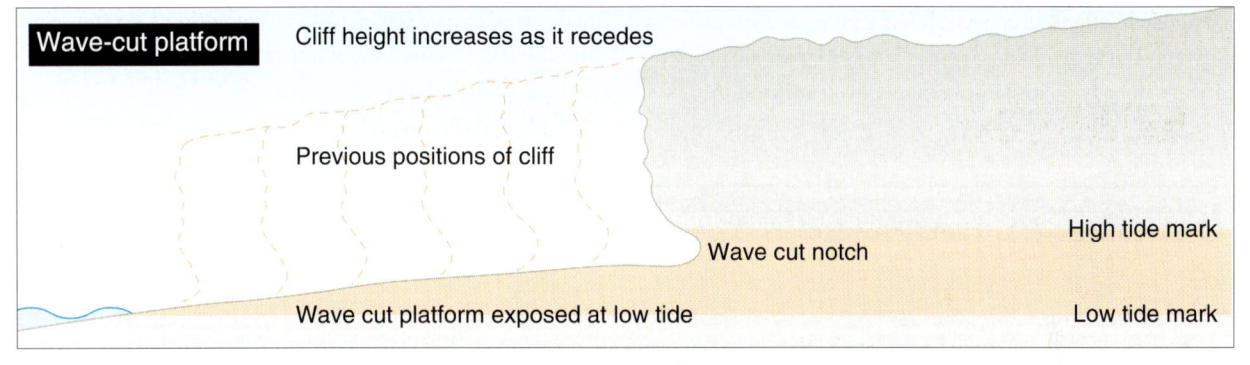

Wave-cut features

- Former arch roof – now collapsed
- Isolated stack
- Joints and other weaknesses exploited by wave-pounding
- Cave
- Stump remains following collapse of stack
- Arch
- Inter-tidal zone
- Wave cut notches

Wave-cut platform

- Cliff height increases as it recedes
- Previous positions of cliff
- High tide mark
- Wave cut notch
- Wave cut platform exposed at low tide
- Low tide mark

Test yourself

1. Explain briefly the terms: (a) swash (b) backwash (c) constructive waves (d) destructive waves.

2. State four processes by which waves erode the coast.

3. Assume wave pounding of an exposed hard rock headland joint in the inter-tidal zone. Complete the sequence of coastal landforms leading to a stump:

Joint _____ _____ _____ Stump

Stretch yourself

Study the diagram showing wave erosion in the inter-tidal zone causing cliff retreat and the formation of a wave cut platform.

Could such a sequence continue indefinitely? If not, why not?

ENVIRONMENTAL THEMES • LANDFORMS

Coastal landforms of deposition

Key points

▶ Waves erode and transport material before depositing it in sheltered water.

▶ Beaches are dynamic stores of material which protect the coast.

▶ Longshore drift carries material along a beach, unless checked by groynes.

▶ Defending one stretch of coast may, unintentionally, intensify erosion further along.

Coastal deposition can only occur where waves and currents lack sufficient energy to carry eroded material. Sand and shingle beaches result. Such beaches are **dynamic** (ever changing) in that they respond to changes in wave type and approach. Often, constructive waves build beaches up with fresh material during the summer, only for destructive waves to comb it back down in winter – a sequence that ensures an overall balance (see page 112).

The variety and flexibility of beach material is a particularly effective coastal defence; the air spaces between the individual particles act as a great absorber of wave energy. (This simple principle is utilised by emergency run-away vehicle sand traps at the bottom of steep hills, and gravel traps at motor racing circuits. Energy, from the momentum of the impacting vehicle, is dissipated throughout the adjusting particles, and millions of flexible pore spaces.)

Waves, as we know, approach the beach according to the wind direction that created them. Only occasionally will this be at right angles. The swash, consequently, will often carry its material up the beach at an oblique angle. The returning backwash, however, is dependent on gravity, and so will return at right angles. Each swash and backwash, therefore, progressively moves material along the beach in a zig-zag course. This process is called **longshore drift**. If it continues unhindered along a coast, **spits** of sand or shingle can build. If these stretch across river estuaries they can trap a **salt marsh** in the sheltered water behind. Spits occasionally extend all the way across a bay, creating a **bar**. Slapton Sands in Devon may have been formed this way.

Such a loss of material is a problem on holiday beaches. Consequently, many are defended by sequences of breakwater fences (**groynes**) running down to the sea. Sand piled up against the windward side of each groyne can be redistributed if necessary.

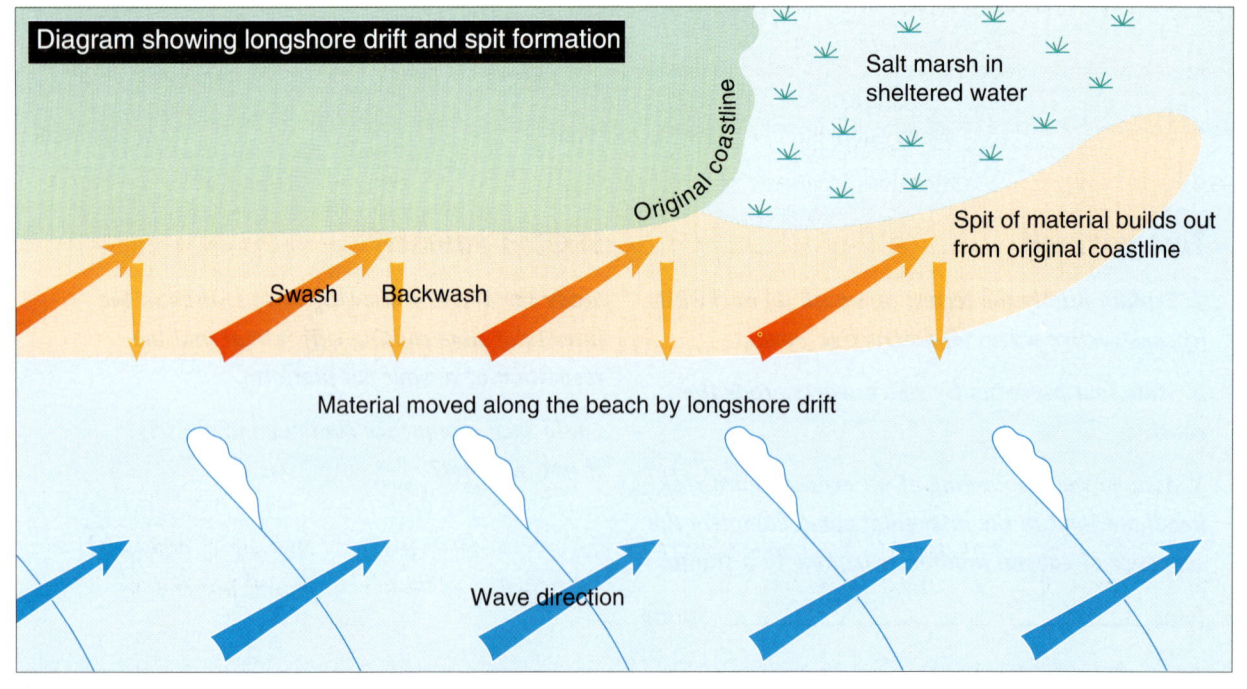

Diagram showing longshore drift and spit formation

Coastal management

The use of groynes is a common example of coastal management – in this case to protect a beach. Such is the power of the sea that coastal settlements, such as holiday resorts, are often traditionally defended by concrete walls supporting promenades.

This **hard engineering** is less in favour today – partly due to the high cost of construction and maintenance. By deflecting waves, rather than dissipating their energy, concrete sea walls are prone to relatively rapid erosion. Modern sea defences tend to be cheaper, yet more effective. Piles of granite blocks, for example, known as **rock armour**, dissipate wave energy very effectively. The promenade at Hornsea, and the village of Mappleton further down this vulnerable, soft, boulder clay Holderness coast, are now protected by it.

Soft engineering is seen as the way forward in most cases. The Environment Agency (EA), responsible for coastal protection in England and Wales, has chosen **beach nourishment** to defend vulnerable stretches of England's east coast in future. This effectively means rebuilding beaches using sand dredged from offshore, and pumped onto the beach!

A key point to consider is that, even using the cheapest methods of defence, controversial political decisions are inevitable. Which coast do we save, and which do we abandon? Furthermore, defending one stretch of coast may accelerate erosion elsewhere, especially if the area further along is dependent for its protection on a supply of material carried by longshore drift. Severe erosion to the immediate south of both Hornsea and Mappleton illustrate this particularly dramatically.

Diagram showing use of groynes
Material builds up against the groynes
Wave direction

Test yourself

1. Explain briefly the following terms: (a) longshore drift (b) groynes (c) rock armour (d) beach nourishment.

Stretch yourself

Explain the differences between 'hard' and 'soft' engineering approaches to coastal protection.

ENVIRONMENTAL THEMES • LANDFORMS

River landforms

Key points

▶ Rivers should be thought of as transport systems of water and sediment.
▶ Rivers can pick up weathered material, transport it, cause erosion and deposit it.
▶ Near its upland source a river will erode a narrow, steep-sided, V-shaped valley.
▶ Nearer its mouth the river meanders across a flood plain within a wide, gentle valley.

A river can transport its sediment **load** in different ways. It can be:

- rolled (**traction**)
- bounced (**saltation**)
- carried, if fine enough (**suspension**)
- dissolved and then moved (**solution**).

Excess energy river in spate in Norway.

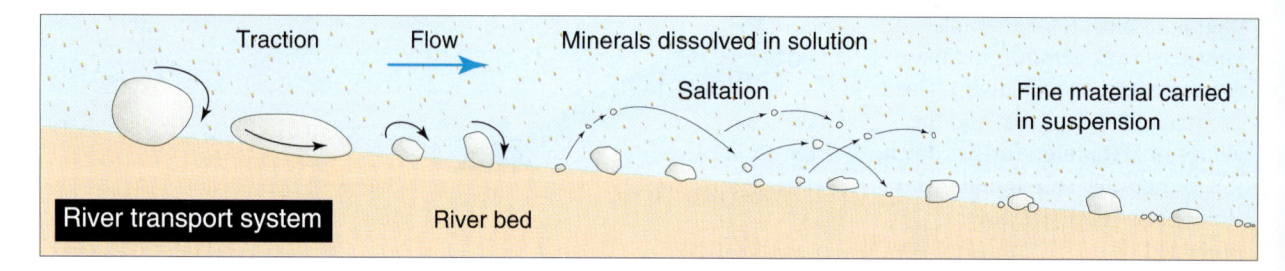

River transport system — Traction, Flow, Minerals dissolved in solution, Saltation, Fine material carried in suspension, River bed

Should the river have extra energy, such as when in flood, the transported load will **erode** (wear away) its course by:

- **abrasion (corrasion)**
- **hydraulic action**
- **solution.**

The river's bedload breaks up through **attrition** (see page 113).

Near the river's source, in hilly or mountainous areas, gradients are steep. This gives the river extra energy enabling larger material, such as pebbles, and occasionally boulders to be carried along the bed. These erode downwards, cutting a steep-sided **V-shaped valley**. This winds its way round hillsides which stand out as **interlocking spurs**. Should the river meet a band of softer rock, then this will be eroded even more rapidly, quickly forming a marked drop known as a **waterfall**. In time the harder rock will be undercut and

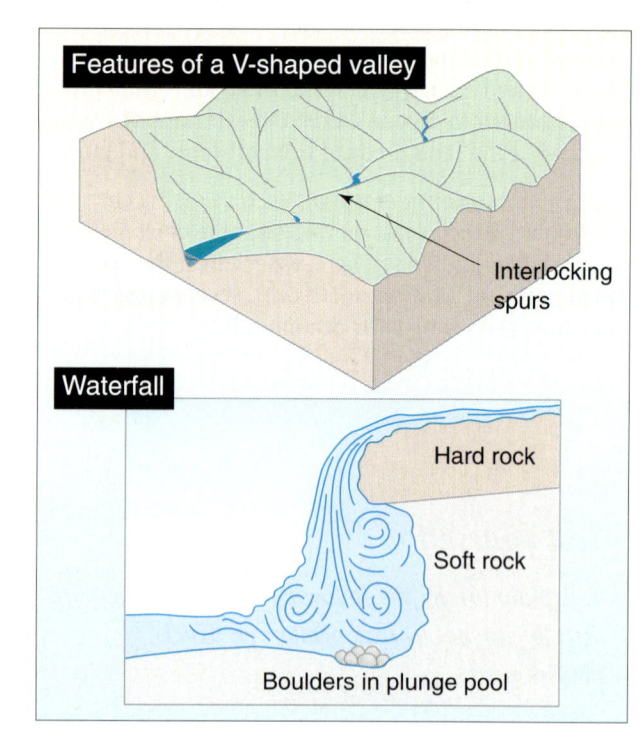

Features of a V-shaped valley — Interlocking spurs

Waterfall — Hard rock, Soft rock, Boulders in plunge pool

116 ENVIRONMENTAL THEMES • LANDFORMS

eventually collapse into the swirling water beneath, where hydraulic action and abrasion will enlarge the **plunge pool**. The repeating sequence of undercutting and collapse will cause the waterfall to cut back (retreat or **recede**) leaving a steep-sided **gorge**. Thinner layers of soft and hard rock will erode unevenly to create **rapids**.

As rivers approach their mouths they develop increasingly large bends called **meanders**. The gradient on this lower stretch of river will be less, and the valley much wider, with gentle slopes. During its course the river will have collected more and more water. The channel will be much bigger, therefore, and capable of carrying more, but finer, sediment.

Sideways **(lateral) erosion** of the banks, rather than the vertical downcutting noted upstream, dominates. This means that the current swinging to each outside bend can undercut it by abrasion and hydraulic action, whilst sediment will be deposited from the slow moving water on the inside bend. The effect over time is to exaggerate the meanders, and widen the valley further. The neck between meander loops can be eroded so narrow that eventually the river cuts right through. The main current will now take the shortest route, straight through the cut, and so no longer be swung out to continue eroding the banks. Consequently, water nearest the banks will be slowed by friction, allowing deposition to build up sediments which block off the old meander. This will leave a crescent shaped **ox-bow lake** which will eventually dry up unless temporarily filled after heavy rain, or a flood.

Flood conditions account for the other distinctive features of this lower river course landscape. A river about to overflow its banks will be moving quickly, and carrying far more sediment. When it floods, the coarsest, heaviest material is deposited first, building **levées**. The finer silt is carried further, however, only settling once the spreading waters slow to a halt. Each successive flood builds the levées more, and adds another layer of **alluvium** to the surrounding **flood plain**.

Finally, on reaching the mouth, the river current is abruptly slowed. This can cause much of the sediment load to be deposited. Should the mouth be a sea with few currents, or little tidal range, or even a lake, then these deposits may build up to form a **delta**.

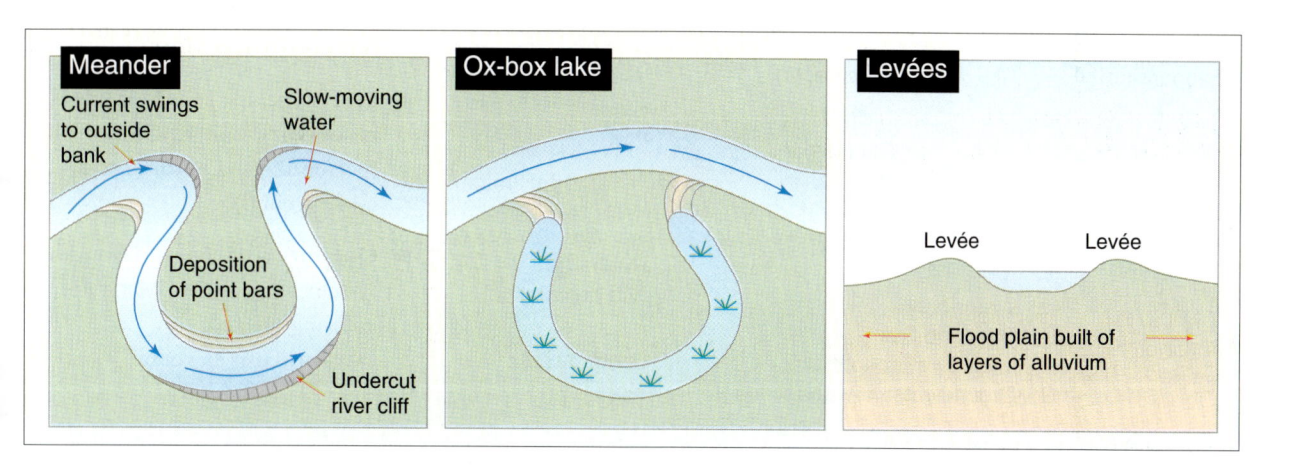

Meander
Current swings to outside bank
Slow-moving water
Deposition of point bars
Undercut river cliff

Ox-box lake

Levées
Levée Levée
Flood plain built of layers of alluvium

Test yourself

1. Copy and complete the following sentences selecting from the alternatives given: Rivers near their source flow down gentle/steep gradients eroding V-/U-shaped valleys. Nearer the river mouth, however, gradients are gentler/steeper. The river contains less/more water and sediment and meanders over a wide flood plain of deposited material called alluvium/levées.

Stretch yourself

Human interference to the channel is going to be much more in evidence along the lower course of a river because far more people settle there. List as many river channel alterations you can find examples of and summarise the reasons for them.

ENVIRONMENTAL THEMES • LANDFORMS

Drainage basins and storm hydrographs

Key points

- A drainage (river) basin, bordered by watersheds, is the land area drained by a river.
- The drainage basin is an open system, whereas the hydrological cycle is closed.
- Storm (flood) hydrographs show the relationship between precipitation and discharge.

A **drainage (river) basin** is an area of land from which one river and its tributaries, collects its water. A **watershed** or **drainage divide** separates one drainage basin from another – rather like the ridge tiles along a roof.

Think of drainage basins as **open systems** with inputs, transfers, stores and outputs.

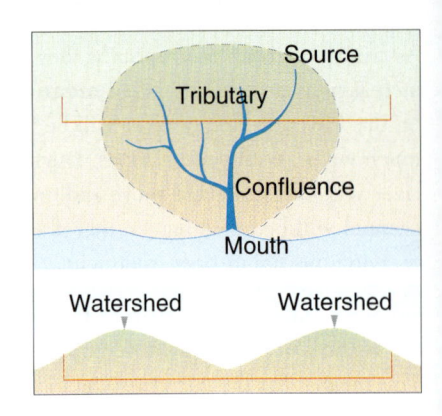

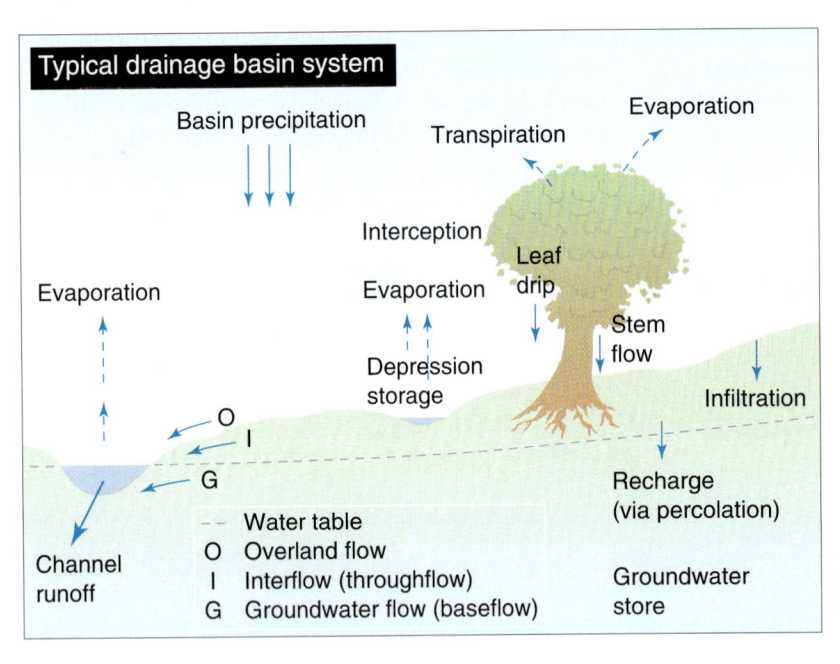

- The **input** is **precipitation**, such as rain and snow.
- **Transfers** (flows) move the water, either on the surface as **runoff**, or through the soil (**throughflow**), or ground (**groundwater flow**).
- **Stores** include surface **lakes** and **reservoirs**, and **aquifers** (permeable and porous rocks underground).
- **Outputs** are the losses from the system, such as the river water entering the **sea**, or **evaporating** en route.

Typical drainage basin system

- -- Water table
- O Overland flow
- I Interflow (throughflow)
- G Groundwater flow (baseflow)

The hydrological (water) cycle

The hydrological cycle represents the continuous transfer of water from the oceans into the atmosphere, then on to the land, and back to the oceans. At any one time 99% of the world's water is being stored – either in the oceans (97%), or as ice (2%). This leaves a mere 1% in the process of transfer – either as vapour in the atmosphere, or as water on the land. No water is added to the system, or lost from it. Therefore it is a closed system.

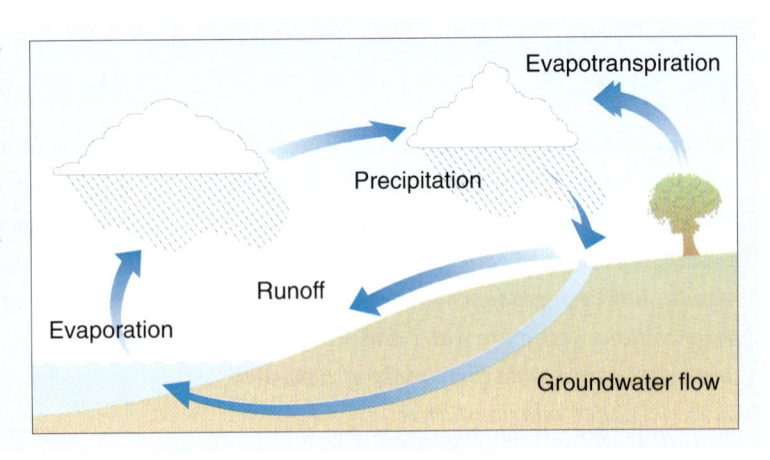

ENVIRONMENTAL THEMES • WATER

The amount of water passing a measuring point in a river channel at any given time is called the **discharge**. This is recorded in cubic metres per second (**cumecs**). The study of drainage basin discharge changes, in different weather conditions, helps predict flooding (see page 140). A **storm hydrograph**, by showing both precipitation and discharge on the same graph, allows the relationship between these two important variables to be compared.

A long delay between peak precipitation and peak discharge (the so-called **lag time**), would suggest little flood danger. A gentle increase in discharge, shown by a gently inclined **rising limb**, would confirm that the precipitation is taking a long time to soak into, and run off the land – usually because it is well vegetated. This gives the river enough time to drain the excess water.

A short lag time, and a steep rising limb, represents a serious flood risk. This can be simply caused by the main river having a great many tributaries feeding it. But steep slopes, compacted or exposed soil, and impermeable rocks have the same effect. Urban areas, with large areas of tarmac, and efficient drains leading into the river, also increase the flood risk.

The important point is that measuring and recording both aid good river and risk management.

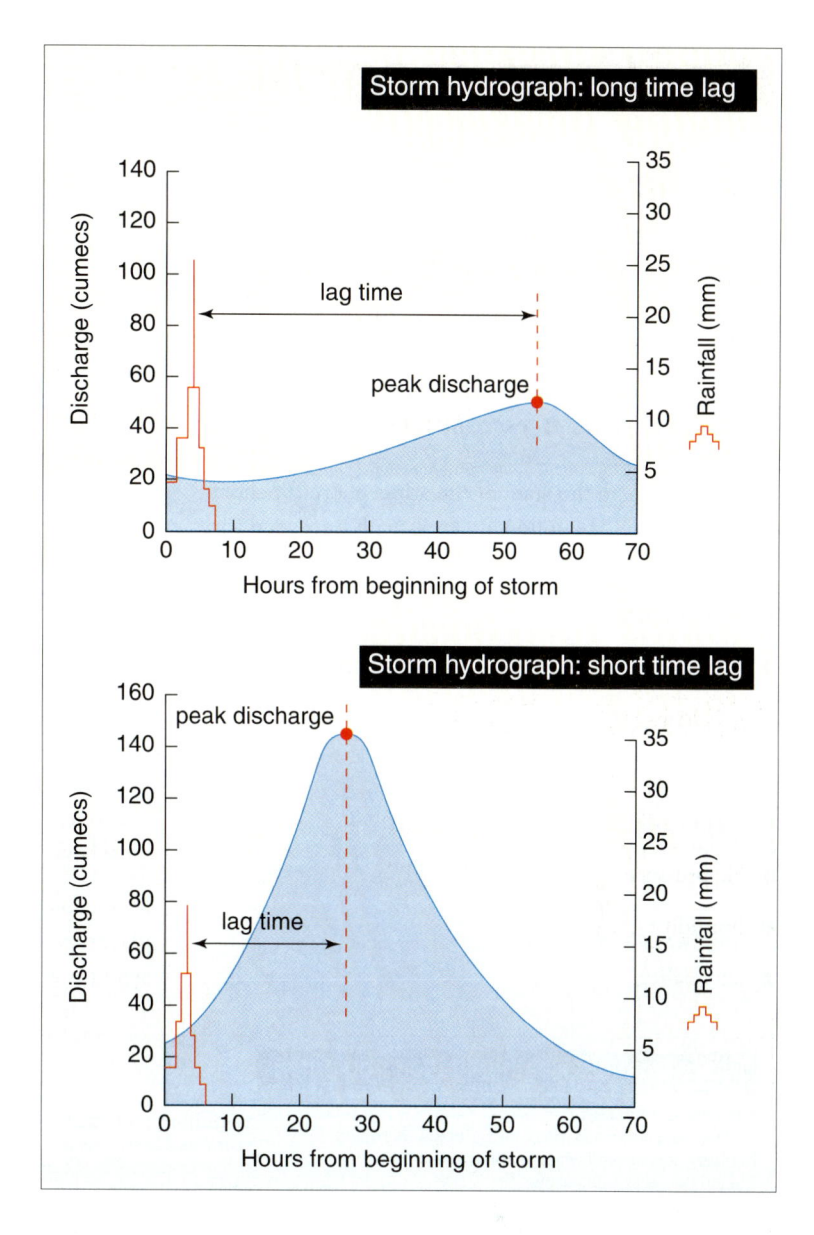

Test yourself

1. What is meant by the terms: (a) drainage basin (b) drainage divide?

2. Which of the following is not a drainage basin output?

A Evaporation.

B Transpiration.

C River carrying water to the sea.

D Water used for irrigation.

E Water in lakes.

3. What is a storm (flood) hydrograph?

Stretch yourself

Explain how vegetation prevents rapid runoff and so reduces flood danger. (You should consider the effect of leaves and branches intercepting the rain, root channels spreading deep into the soil and so on.)

ENVIRONMENTAL THEMES • WATER

Weather recording

Key points

▶ Weather refers to changing atmospheric conditions from hour to hour, day to day.

▶ Meteorologists record, measure, explain and forecast the weather.

▶ Synoptic charts show weather conditions over particular places at a specific time.

Weather refers to the state of the atmosphere for short periods of time. The following are usually recorded and measured daily:

- temperature
- precipitation (rain, snow, hail and sleet)
- sunshine
- wind
- cloud cover
- air pressure
- humidity
- air quality.

Many schools have weather stations. Some have adopted 24 hour monitoring and data logging using Geographical Information Systems (GIS) linked to their IT networks.

Most weather forecasting is done from measurements sent from land and sea recording stations to weather centres such as the Meteorological (Met) Office at Bracknell near London.

Forecasts include both long- and short-term, for the weeks and days ahead. The latter are now very accurate. This is due to high quality remote sensing radar and satellite information, and computer modelling programs based on past weather systems.

Everyone benefits from accurate forecasting – farmers rounding up livestock ahead of snow, ship captains avoiding heavy seas and families planning days out.

Weather maps (synoptic charts) and symbols

Meteorologists map weather conditions at different places on synoptic charts. However, simpler pictorial symbols are often used in newspaper and TV forecasts.

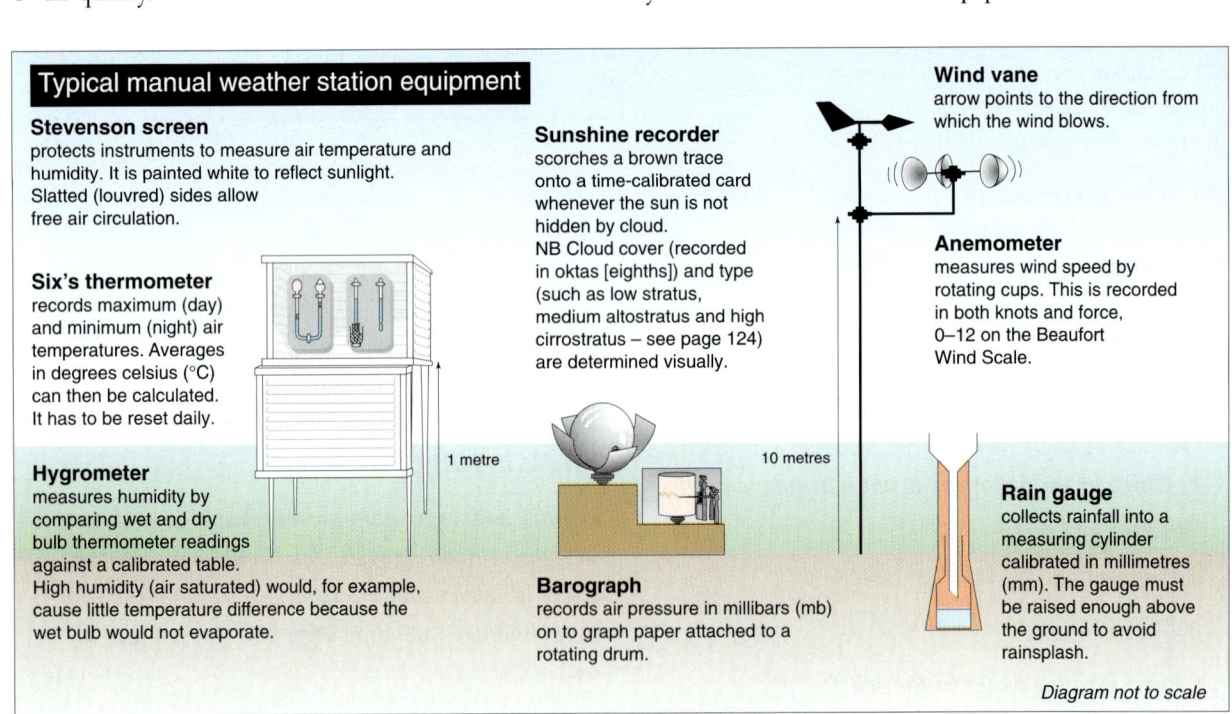

Typical manual weather station equipment

Stevenson screen
protects instruments to measure air temperature and humidity. It is painted white to reflect sunlight. Slatted (louvred) sides allow free air circulation.

Six's thermometer
records maximum (day) and minimum (night) air temperatures. Averages in degrees celsius (°C) can then be calculated. It has to be reset daily.

Hygrometer
measures humidity by comparing wet and dry bulb thermometer readings against a calibrated table. High humidity (air saturated) would, for example, cause little temperature difference because the wet bulb would not evaporate.

Sunshine recorder
scorches a brown trace onto a time-calibrated card whenever the sun is not hidden by cloud. NB Cloud cover (recorded in oktas [eighths]) and type (such as low stratus, medium altostratus and high cirrostratus – see page 124) are determined visually.

Barograph
records air pressure in millibars (mb) on to graph paper attached to a rotating drum.

Wind vane
arrow points to the direction from which the wind blows.

Anemometer
measures wind speed by rotating cups. This is recorded in both knots and force, 0–12 on the Beaufort Wind Scale.

Rain gauge
collects rainfall into a measuring cylinder calibrated in millimetres (mm). The gauge must be raised enough above the ground to avoid rainsplash.

Diagram not to scale

Synoptic chart, 07.00 hours, 19th August

Official weather symbols

Cloud cover

Symbol	Oktas	
○	0	Clear sky
◔	1	1/8 covered
◔	2	2/8 covered
◑	3	and so on
◑	4	
◕	5	
◕	6	
◕	7	
●	8	
⊗	Sky obscured	

Weather

Symbol	Weather
=	Mist
≡	Fog
,	Drizzle
•	Rain
*	Snow
△	Hail
▽	Rain shower
⊺	Thunderstorm

Wind (speed and direction)

Symbol	Speed (knots)		Beaufort force
◎	Calm		
○	1–2		0
○ with half-feather	3–7	Light air	1
	8–12		2
	13–17		3
	18–22	Moderate breeze	4

For each additional half-feather, add 5 knots

| ▶○ | 48–52 | Storm | 10 |
| ▶○ | 58+ | Hurricane | 12 |

Isobars (show air pressure in mb)
—— 1004 ——

Cold front (where a cold air mass undercuts warm air)

Warm front (where a warm air mass rises up over cold air)

Occluded front (where a cold front has caught up with a warm front, lifting the warm air completely above the cold)

Weather station summary

Temperature	Cloud cover
4°C	8 oktas
	Wind direction
	SE
Present weather	**Wind speed**
Hail	33–37 knots
	Beaufort 7

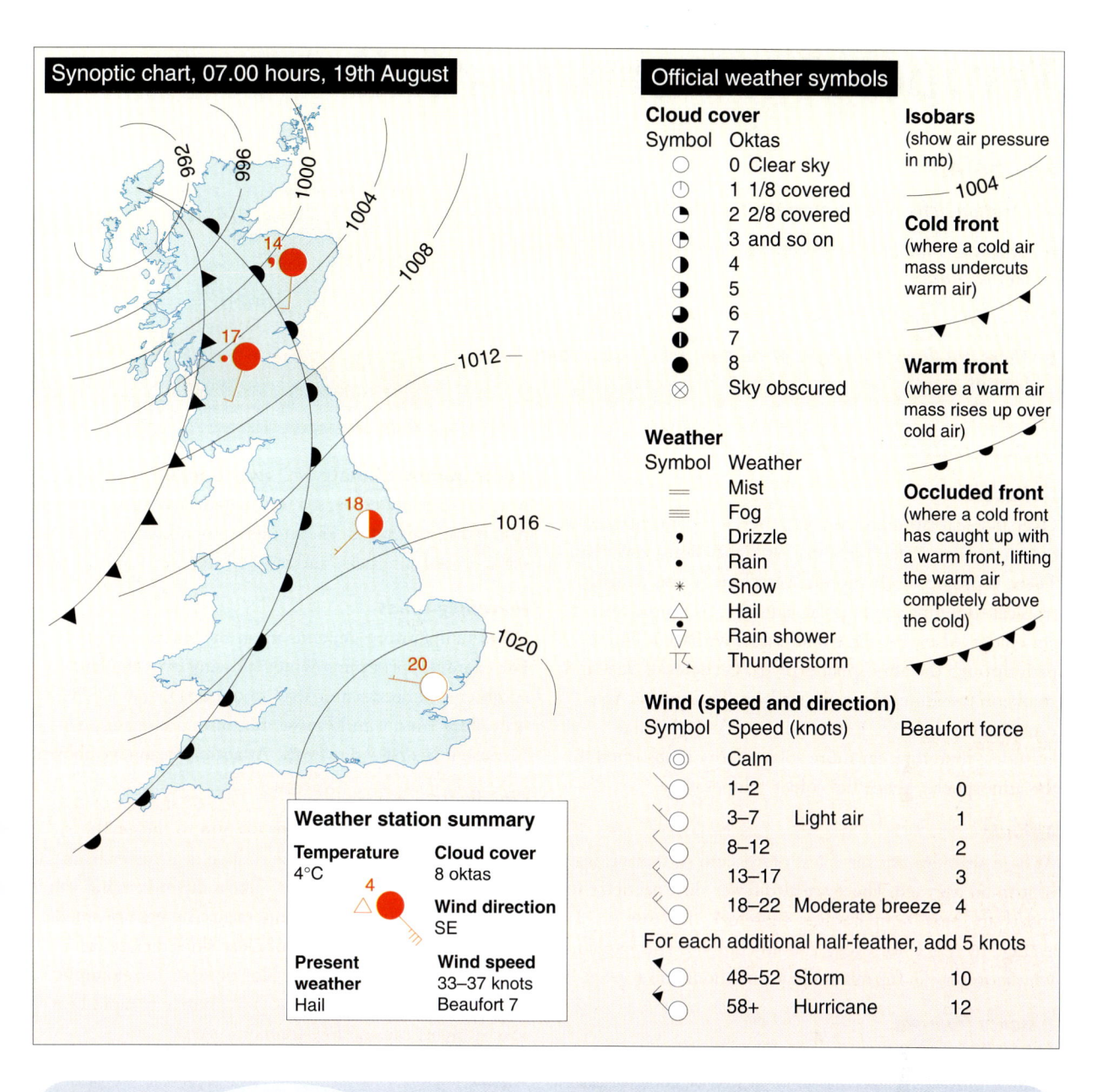

Test yourself

Study the weather station summaries on the synoptic chart above. The weather conditions in Essex would be: temperature – 20°C; clear sky; wind direction – WNW; wind speed 3-7 knots, Beaufort force 1; air pressure – 1021mb.

1. Describe the weather conditions in: (a) central Scotland (b) North Yorkshire.

2. Suggest why the weather station equipment discussed has, ideally, to be located well away from buildings and on grass rather than tarmac.

Stretch yourself

Describe and explain the difference between wet and dry bulb thermometer readings for conditions of low humidity.

ENVIRONMENTAL THEMES • WEATHER

Temperature and rainfall

Key points

▶ Location determines temperature, with seasonal changes likely.
▶ Latitude is the most important of many factors determining temperature.
▶ Rainfall is caused when warm, moist air is forced to rise and cool.
▶ There are three main types of rainfall: relief, convectional and frontal.

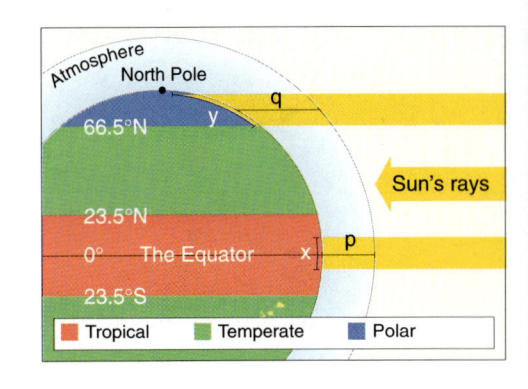

Factors influencing temperature

Latitude
Over tropical latitudes the sun's energy is concentrated onto a smaller surface area than at higher latitudes (x<y). There is progressively more area to heat as you go from tropical to temperate to polar latitudes, so temperatures get colder. Also over the tropics, the rays have a shorter path through the atmosphere (p<q). Particles of dust and smoke in the atmosphere absorb heat. The quicker the rays pass through, the less heat is lost. At high polar latitudes, therefore, far more solar energy is absorbed by the atmosphere, hence the colder temperature.

Altitude
At high altitudes, the air is less dense, and so there is less of it to be warmed. There are also fewer dust particles to absorb the heat. Temperatures, therefore, decrease on average by 6.5°C for every 1000m climbed. This explains why snow can lie for much longer on mountain tops.

Distance from sea
Land heats and cools far more quickly than the sea because only the surface has to be heated or cooled rather than a depth of water. This causes extreme temperature ranges (very hot summers and markedly cold winters) in a **continental climate** well away from the sea. Areas near, or surrounded by, sea (eg. Britain) have less extreme **maritime climates**. The moderating influence of the sea ensures cool summers, and mild winters.

Prevailing winds
Wind temperature depends upon the surface crossed. For example, prevailing winds blowing over the land in summer will be warmer than in winter. Britain's SW prevailing wind is mild in winter, but cool in summer because it has passed over the Atlantic Ocean (see above).

Cloudiness
Clouds reduce radiation from the sun to the earth during the day. At night, they reduce heat losses from the earth to the atmosphere – like a duvet keeping you warm in bed. Therefore, temperature ranges are smaller in cloudy conditions. Areas of clear skies dictate far greater temperature ranges. Hot deserts, for example, experience very high daytime heat, but very rapid heat loss at night, causing low temperatures.

Aspect
The direction in which a place faces is its aspect. This is very influential in determining local temperature variations.

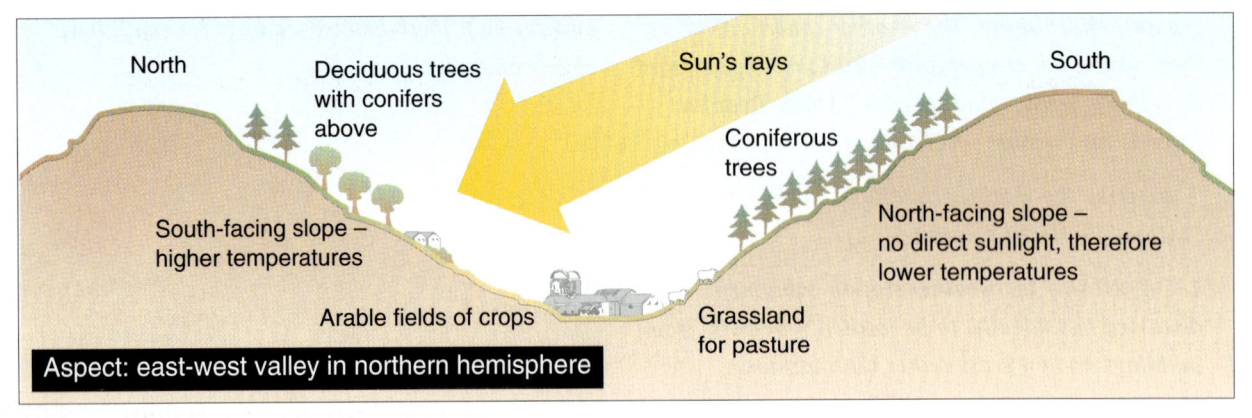

Aspect: east-west valley in northern hemisphere

Types of rainfall

There are three main types of rainfall. Each results from warm air, which can hold water vapour, rising until it cools enough to condense into cloud droplets. The altitude at which condensation starts is known as the **dew point**. These droplets mass together into clouds from which rain will fall. Other forms of precipitation, such as hail, sleet or snow, fall if the temperature is below freezing point.

Relief rainfall

This requires an upland barrier to deflect upwards a water vapour-bearing wind. For example, relief rainfall occurs over Australia's Great Dividing Range and over the Pennines, Welsh and Scottish Mountains in Britain.

Convectional rainfall

Summer heating of the land evaporates surface soil and plant water and sets up convection currents of warm, moist air. These currents rise, cool and form cloud droplets when the vapour condenses. Both showers and heavy downpours are likely. Very dramatic cloud development (with tall cumulonimbus clouds) will lead to thunder, lightning and hail.

Frontal rainfall

This results from air masses of different temperature and density meeting but not mixing. The boundary between the warm and cold **air masses** is called a **front**. The warmer, moist, less dense air is forced to rise over the colder, denser air – with cloud formation and rainfall resulting. Frontal rainfall is associated with weather systems called **depressions** (see page 124) which are particularly common in Britain in winter.

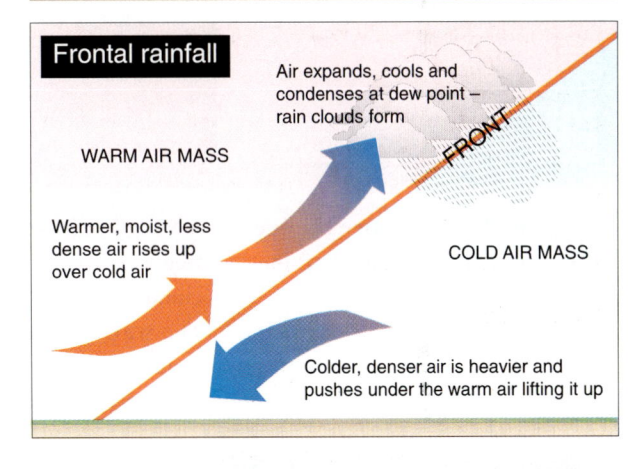

Test yourself

1. List the main factors which determine the temperature of a place.

2. Study the Aspect diagram. How is land-use affected by aspect?

3. With reference to air movements and changes in temperature, what is the common factor in all rainfall formation?

Stretch yourself

What might be the significance to polar temperatures of the colour of snow and ice?

Depressions and anticyclones

Key points

▶ Depressions are areas of low air pressure bringing cloud, rain and wind.

▶ Anticyclones are areas of high air pressure associated with settled, dry weather.

▶ Depressions dominate the British weather; anticyclones are less common.

▶ Differences in air pressure cause winds to blow.

Depressions

Depressions are areas of low air pressure which bring cloud, rain and wind. In Britain they dominate the weather, particularly in winter. They typically form over the North Atlantic Ocean where cold, dry, dense, polar air meets warmer, moist, less dense, tropical air.

The warmer air is forced to rise in upward spiralling movements generated by coriolis forces (see Wind).

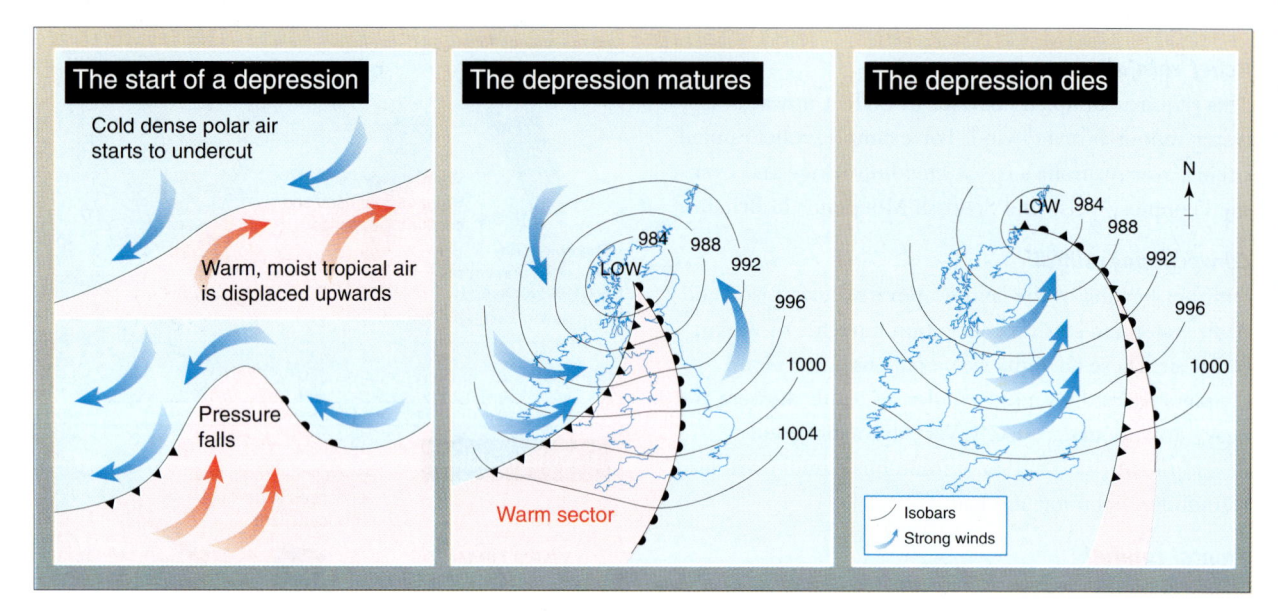

The start of a depression
Cold dense polar air starts to undercut
Warm, moist tropical air is displaced upwards
Pressure falls

The depression matures
Warm sector

The depression dies
Isobars
Strong winds

This creates **low pressure** because the weight of the air is lifted off the surface. As the system matures, stronger winds spiral anticlockwise causing the colder air to virtually surround the **warm sector**. The 'chasing' **cold front** is fastest, its steepness reflected in towering cumulonimbus rain-bearing clouds. The **warm front** ahead is of far gentler gradient. Wisps of cirrus and cirrostratus cloud extend high above low, dense, rain-bearing nimbostratus. The depression eventually decays when the cold front catches the warm front – lifting the warm air above the surface to form an **occluded front**.

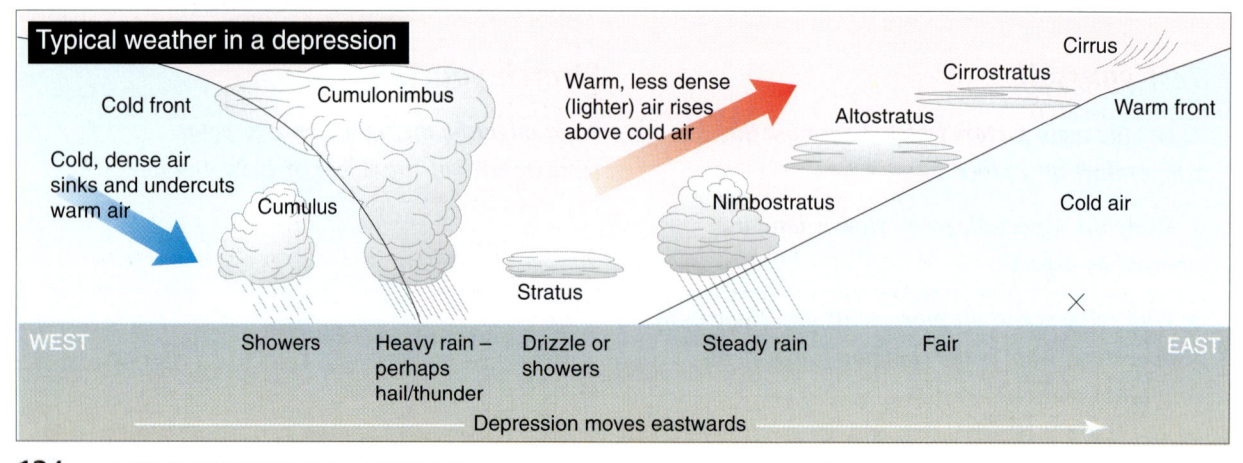

Typical weather in a depression

Cold front — Cumulonimbus
Cold, dense air sinks and undercuts warm air
Cumulus
Warm, less dense (lighter) air rises above cold air
Altostratus
Nimbostratus
Stratus
Cirrus
Cirrostratus
Warm front
Cold air

WEST — Showers — Heavy rain – perhaps hail/thunder — Drizzle or showers — Steady rain — Fair — EAST

Depression moves eastwards →

124 ENVIRONMENTAL THEMES • WEATHER

Beneath this front there is complete cloud cover and 'overcast' weather. This may shed some rain before the low pressure area fills, and the depression dies out. Depressions take at most a few days to pass over Britain. Although each depression is unique, the general characteristics are repeated – so aiding forecasting.

Anticyclones

Anticyclones are areas of high pressure where descending air 'piles up' on the surface. They are far slower moving than depressions. Although infrequent, once established they are likely to last for many days or even weeks. Descending air warms as it falls and picks up moisture. Consequently, condensation is unlikely and so clouds are rare. However, early morning dew and mist is likely in summer with frost and fog in winter. Gentle winds blow clockwise and outwards from the high pressure centre. The clear skies ensure calm, sunny weather in summer, and bright, but very cold conditions in winter.

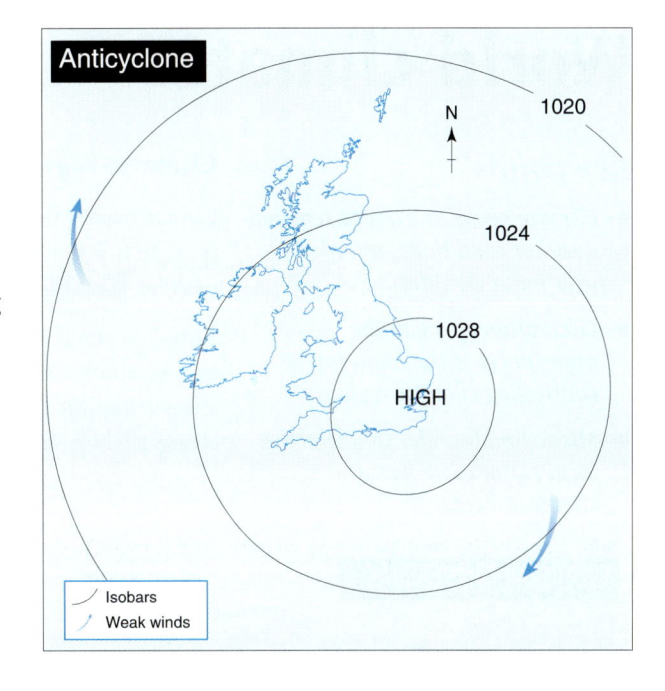

Wind

Wind is simply air moving to equalise pressure between two areas. It will blow from high to low pressure until there is no 'differential'. We talk of 'pressure gradients' – the bigger the gradient, the stronger the wind. Winds do not blow directly from high to low pressure. The earth's rotation sets up coriolis forces which deflect them.

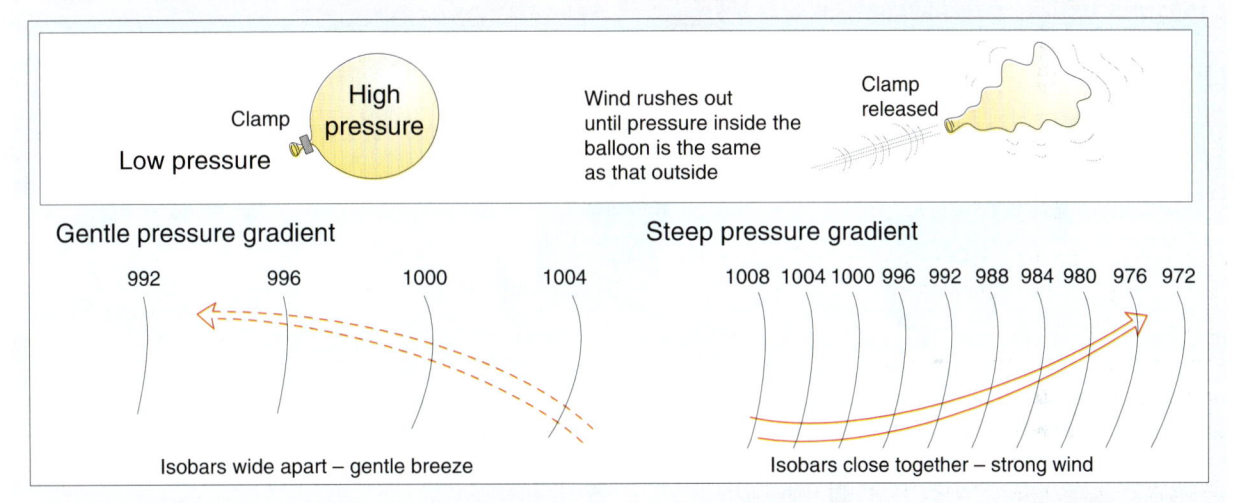

Test yourself

1. What does the isobar spacing tell you about wind speeds in: (a) a depression (b) an anticyclone?

2. BBC TV weather forecasts are ideal for testing your understanding of weather systems. Watch them carefully and try to anticipate how the forecaster will summarise the weather immediately following the synoptic charts.

Stretch yourself

Study the Typical weather in the depression cross-section diagram.

Describe the changing weather as the depression passes X.

World climates

Key points

▶ **Climate refers to average regional weather conditions, recorded over many decades.**

▶ **Circulation of air in the atmosphere is the main factor controlling climatic regions.**

▶ **Microclimates refer to distinctive local climates in special circumstances.**

Climatic regions

Climate refers to the average state of the atmosphere over long periods of time. In other words it indicates a location's normal, rather than actual, weather conditions.

Although climates vary a great deal across the globe, large areas have enough in common for **climatic regions** to be identified. Climatic region maps are always simplified. They do not show local variations or the gradual climatic changes which take place between regions.

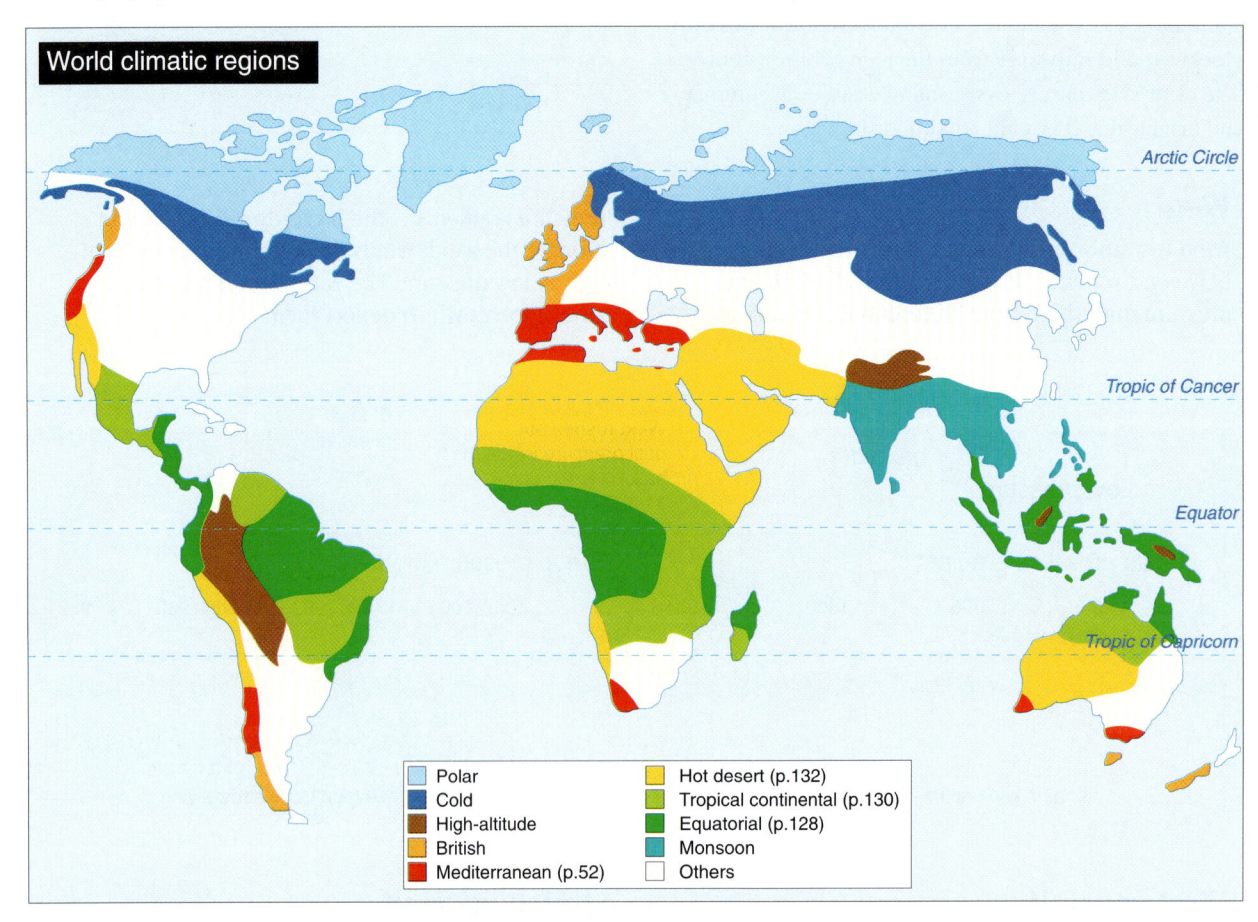

World climatic regions

☐ Polar	☐ Hot desert (p.132)
☐ Cold	☐ Tropical continental (p.130)
☐ High-altitude	☐ Equatorial (p.128)
☐ British	☐ Monsoon
☐ Mediterranean (p.52)	☐ Others

The map above makes more detailed climatic distinctions than the tropical, temperate and polar zones referred to earlier (see page 122). It is based on temperature and rainfall variations. These are explained mainly by the general circulation of air within the atmosphere.

Atmospheric circulation

Three circular movements of air in each hemisphere are called **cells**. All cells are ultimately controlled by the build-up of heat over the equator. Studying the Hadley Cell (explained on page 132) is essential to understanding all climates. It links with the Ferrell Cell, which in turn connects with the Polar Cell. The Hadley Cell helps us to explain tropical rainforest and desert climates. The links between the Ferrell and Polar Cells help explain the British climate.

Other factors which influence climates at this large scale are:

- the earth's tilt and rotation, which alters the position of the overhead sun, causing air pressures and prevailing wind directions to change
- land and sea distribution and the different temperatures of ocean currents, both of which influence the contrasts between maritime and continental climates (see page 122)
- the location of upland and lowland areas also plays a part because of the colder temperatures on higher ground (see page 122).

At the local scale unique **microclimates** can often be identified. For example, a distinctive valley microclimate in an upland area, or an urban microclimate in a built-up area.

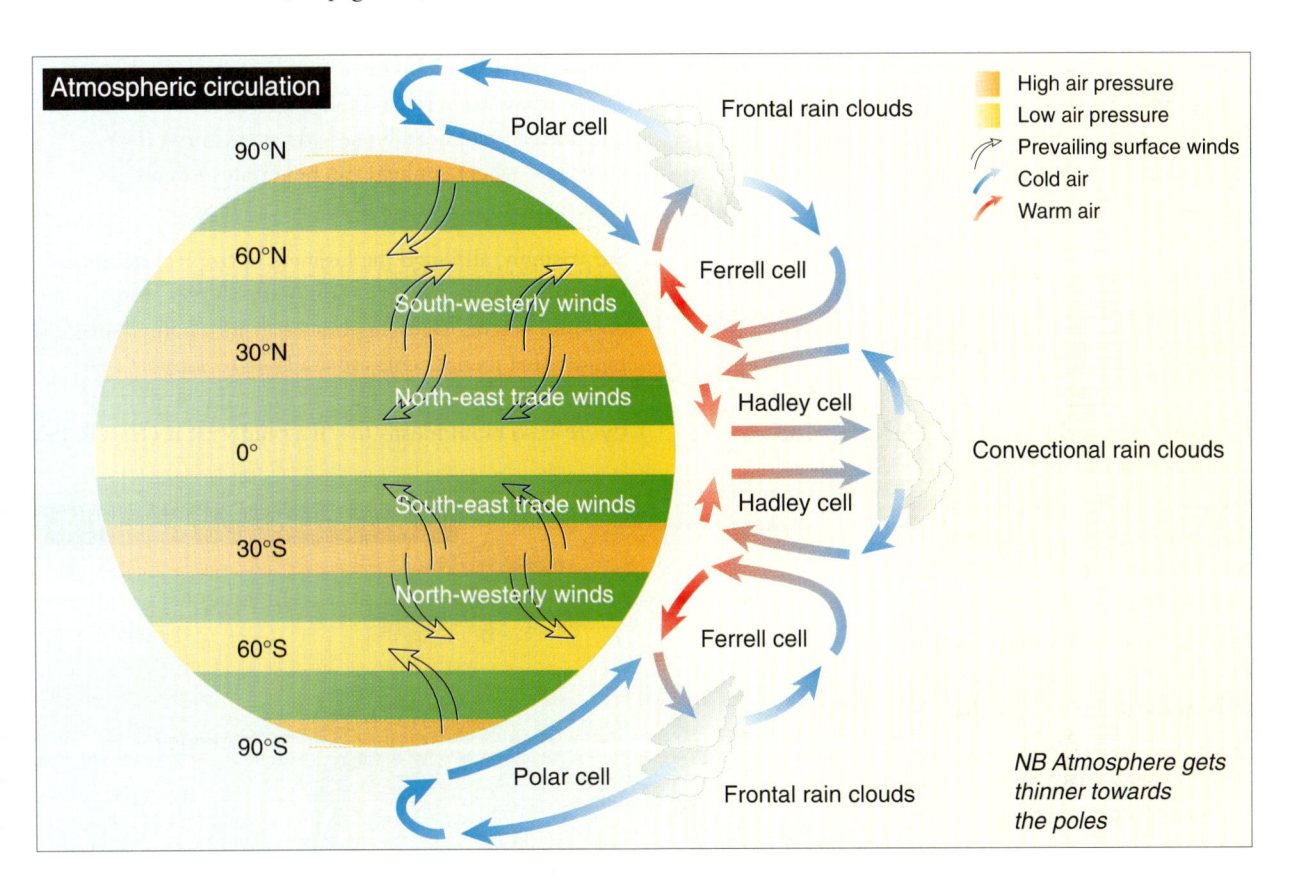

Atmospheric circulation

Key:
- High air pressure
- Low air pressure
- Prevailing surface winds
- Cold air
- Warm air

Labels: 90°N, 60°N, 30°N, 0°, 30°S, 60°S, 90°S; Polar cell, Ferrell cell, Hadley cell, Hadley cell, Ferrell cell, Polar cell; South-westerly winds, North-east trade winds, South-east trade winds, North-westerly winds; Frontal rain clouds, Convectional rain clouds, Frontal rain clouds.

NB Atmosphere gets thinner towards the poles

Test yourself

The British climate could be summarised as cool summers, mild winters and steady reliable rainfall throughout the year.

1. Using the page references on the World climatic regions map, summarise the following climates: (a) Mediterranean (b) Hot desert (c) Tropical continental (d) Equatorial.

Stretch yourself

With reference to Desertification (page 158) and Global warming: the greenhouse effect (page 160) outline the significance of human activities to climatic change.

ENVIRONMENTAL THEMES • CLIMATE

Tropical rainforests

Key points

▶ The equatorial latitude dictates high temperatures, humidity and rainfall all year.

▶ Over one-third of the world's trees grow here, in a continuous growing season.

▶ The rainforest is without comparison in its biodiversity of biota (plants and animals).

▶ Sustainable rainforest development can only be achieved by international agreement.

The equatorial zone lies between 5° north and south of the equator. At these low latitudes the sun is always at a very high angle in the sky so, during the day, temperatures are hot. This means high evaporation rates and excessive humidity. As a result, heavy convectional rain falls in thunderstorms on most afternoons. This cycle completes the world's most predictable climate: hot, wet, humid, and without seasons — until you move a few more degrees away from the equator.

These are perfect growing conditions for the most luxuriant vegetation on earth. Thousands of species of deciduous hardwood trees, creepers, shrubs, ferns, and herbs can grow in perfect harmony — not just with each other, but with 90% of the world's known animal species too! The tropical rainforest provides the ultimate example of a large-scale **ecosystem** — a closely interactive system of plants and animals coexisting with each other within a distinctive environment.

The ways in which the various plants and animals have adapted to the equatorial climate are astonishing. Five distinctive layers of vegetation can be defined, with the tallest **(emergent)** trees, over 40m high. These trees break through a **canopy** of almost continuous forest cover, in their quest for sunlight. Competition and adaptation is the key to understanding this extraordinary ecosystem.

The discontinuous **under canopy** of shorter trees may seem less successful than their taller neighbours, but they are also adapted to the environment. They too have straight, branchless trunks, with large buttress roots to support them, and a dense top foliage (crown) of dark leathery leaves, with 'drip tips' to shed water.

Each tree layer will support its own distinctive wildlife of parasites, birds, and animals — from flying squirrels living in the canopy, to baboons in the trunks! Not surprisingly the **shrub layer** beneath is limited through lack of light. The forest floor is so dark and damp, that the so-called **field layer** of ferns and herbs is very sparse. Only bacteria and fungi thrive, to rapidly rot fallen leaves and dead biota — yet next to rivers or clearings, where sunlight can penetrate, a dense undergrowth of ferns and shrubs can develop.

Surprisingly, although the lushness of tropical rainforest vegetation implies that the soil is very fertile, the opposite is true. Decaying biota rots into humus so rapidly that its nutrients are available to support new growth very quickly. But the fact that this **nutrient cycle** is so rapid means that if a rainforest is cleared, the

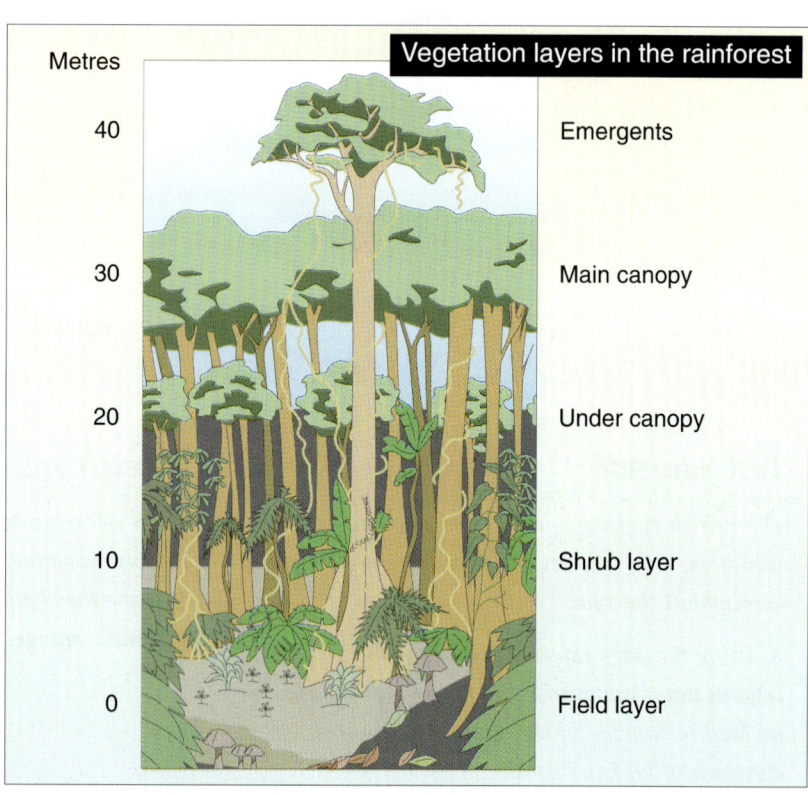

Vegetation layers in the rainforest

Metres	Layer
40	Emergents
30	Main canopy
20	Under canopy
10	Shrub layer
0	Field layer

ready supply of new humus is halted and the soil becomes quickly drained of stored nutrients. It then becomes exposed to leaching of nutrients, and to erosion by gullying during the heavy rainfalls.

For generations humans have lived in harmony within rainforests (see page 43), but recent decades have seen deforestation on a massive scale, by felling, bulldozing and burning. Reasons are cited such as the need for hardwood timbers, or for land for settlement, ranching, cash cropping and plantations, or the need for access for mineral extraction.

Population growth and economic development are putting pressures on natural resources, but there are many reasons why rainforests should be preserved:

Rainforest destruction, Brazil.

- 40% of all known drugs have been derived from rainforest species
- plant species and animal habitats are under threat
- numerous plants and animals are yet to be discovered in the rainforests
- burning rainforests adds greenhouse gases to the atmosphere and increases global warming
- over half the world's oxygen comes from the photosynthesis of rainforest trees; each tree lost is one less to convert the pollutant CO_2 to the oxygen we breathe
- indigenous tribes are losing their homelands. Soil erosion, desertification and climatic change also emphasise the need for sustainable rainforest management, on an international level.

Test yourself

1. What is meant by the terms: (a) biota (b) ecosystem (c) habitat (d) humus?

2. Tropical rainforest destruction contributes to major environmental problems such as soil erosion, desertification and climatic change. State four specific losses associated with this deforestation.

Stretch yourself

Governments, such as Brazil's, view the rainforest as a great resource to exploit for economic development through, for example, mining, HEP schemes, commercial farming and logging. Forest Indians and conservationists are unlikely to view the resulting deforestation from the same positive perspective. Clearly it is important to understand each point of view if a balance between economic development of rainforest areas and sufficient conservation is to be achieved.

What measures would you suggest are critical if sustainable development is to be achieved?

ENVIRONMENTAL THEMES • ENVIRONMENTS

Savanna grasslands

Key points

▶ Savanna grassland vegetation is associated with areas of tropical continental climate.
▶ The tropical continental climate is warm, with alternating wet and dry seasons.
▶ Some argue that savanna grasslands are not a natural vegetation, but caused by fires.
▶ Xerophytic plants, such as the baobab tree, are drought resistant.
▶ Savanna grassland in semi-desert regions is prone to overgrazing and desertification.

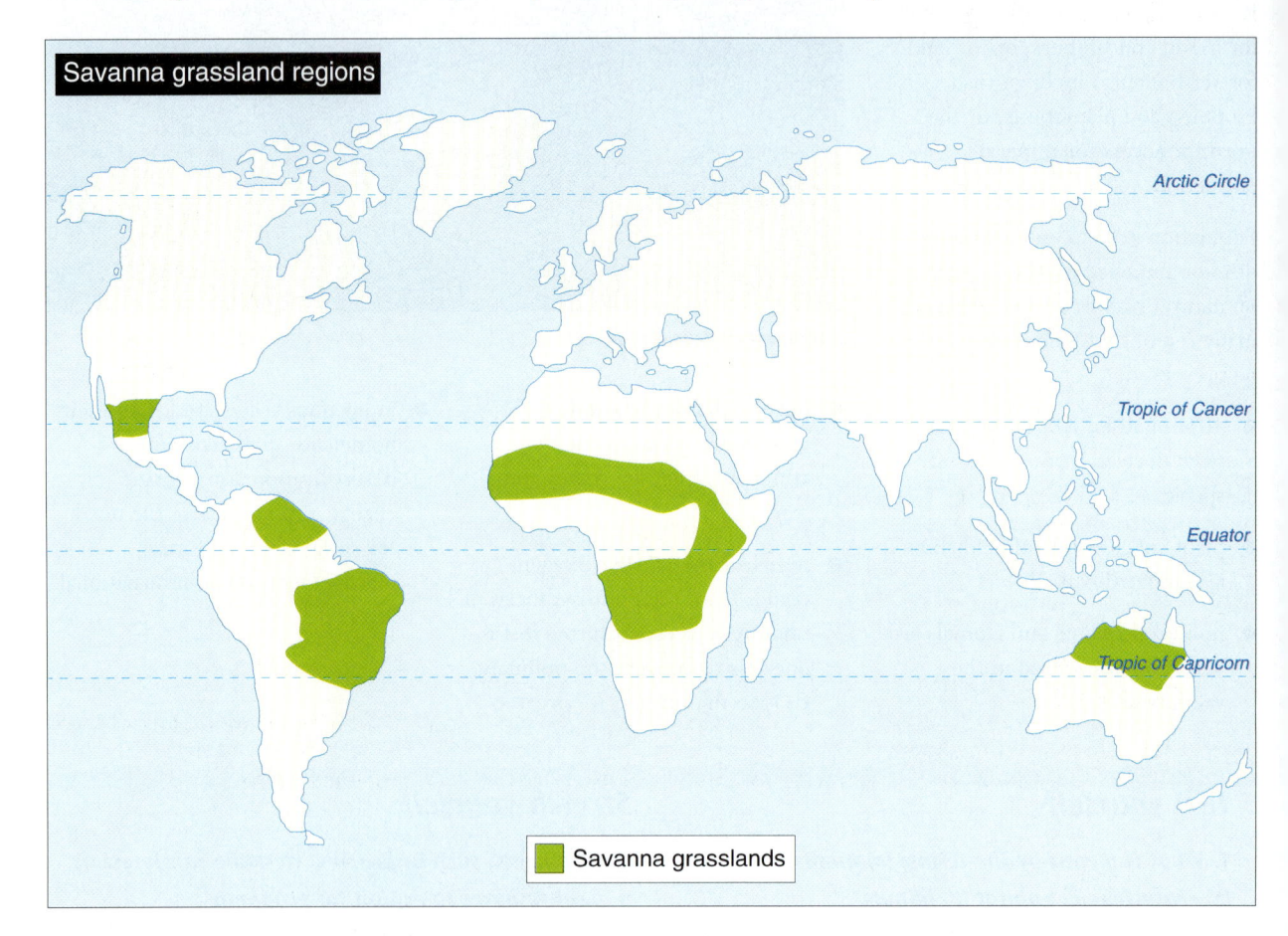

Savanna grassland regions

Savanna grasslands

Further north and south of the equatorial rainforest belt, climates become drier, with seasonal rainfall. The rainforests 'thin out' to become **parkland** – dense clumps of trees mixed with patches of tall grass. As the rainfall becomes even more unreliable, the grassland begins to dominate. This vegetation is known as savanna grassland, which usually includes scattered trees.

Savanna grassland is the natural vegetation of tropical continental climates. The tropical continental climate is warm overall, with a dry, slightly cooler season, followed by a hot, wet season. The savanna extends into the 'scrub' vegetation of its semi-desert margins.

As with tropical rainforests, the vegetation is perfectly adapted to its environment. **Grass** seeds can cope with long periods of drought before germinating as soon as the rains fall. But it is the scattered **acacia**, **baobab** and **euphorbia trees** which are amazing. They are xerophytic (drought resistant) with very long roots to tap groundwater from deep below the surface. The baobab tree can also store water in its trunk, which has very thick bark to protect it against fires.

130 ENVIRONMENTAL THEMES • ENVIRONMENTS

FIRE!

Some geographers suggest that savanna grassland vegetation is not the natural vegetation of tropical continental climates. They say that the grassland and scattered xerophytic trees are the result of fires.

These fires could have been started deliberately by nomadic cattle herders burning off the old grass during the cooler dry season in order to encourage healthier new growth as soon as the hot wet season rains come.

An alternative hypothesis is that the fires are started by lightning strikes associated with convectional thunderstorms during the hot wet season.

Baobab: a xerophytic tree.

The euphorbia tree on the front cover of this book is another example of a drought-resistant tree.

Test yourself

1. Complete the vegetation sequence north or south of the equator:

Rainforest _____ _____ _____ Desert.

2. What is a xerophytic plant?

Stretch yourself

Savanna grassland ecosystems are being changed both naturally, and by human activities. Large wildlife herds of giraffe, zebra and wildebeest, for example, can overgraze areas subjected to prolonged drought and/or fire. But it is pressure on the land from nomadic herders, such as the Fulani of West Africa, that affect the environment more.

With reference to desertification (page 158) and your own studies outline the changes to savanna grasslands resulting from human activities.

Deserts

Key points

▶ More than one-third of the earth's land surface is desert.

▶ Deserts are the driest environments on earth, but never completely rainless.

▶ Deserts are subject to extremes of temperature, especially between night and day.

▶ Deserts are not always sandy, like the Sahara; some are stony and some have areas of bare rock.

Deserts are areas of the earth's surface receiving less than 250mm of rain per annum (each year). Most, but not all, deserts are hot: the Gobi Desert in winter is one of the coldest places on earth!

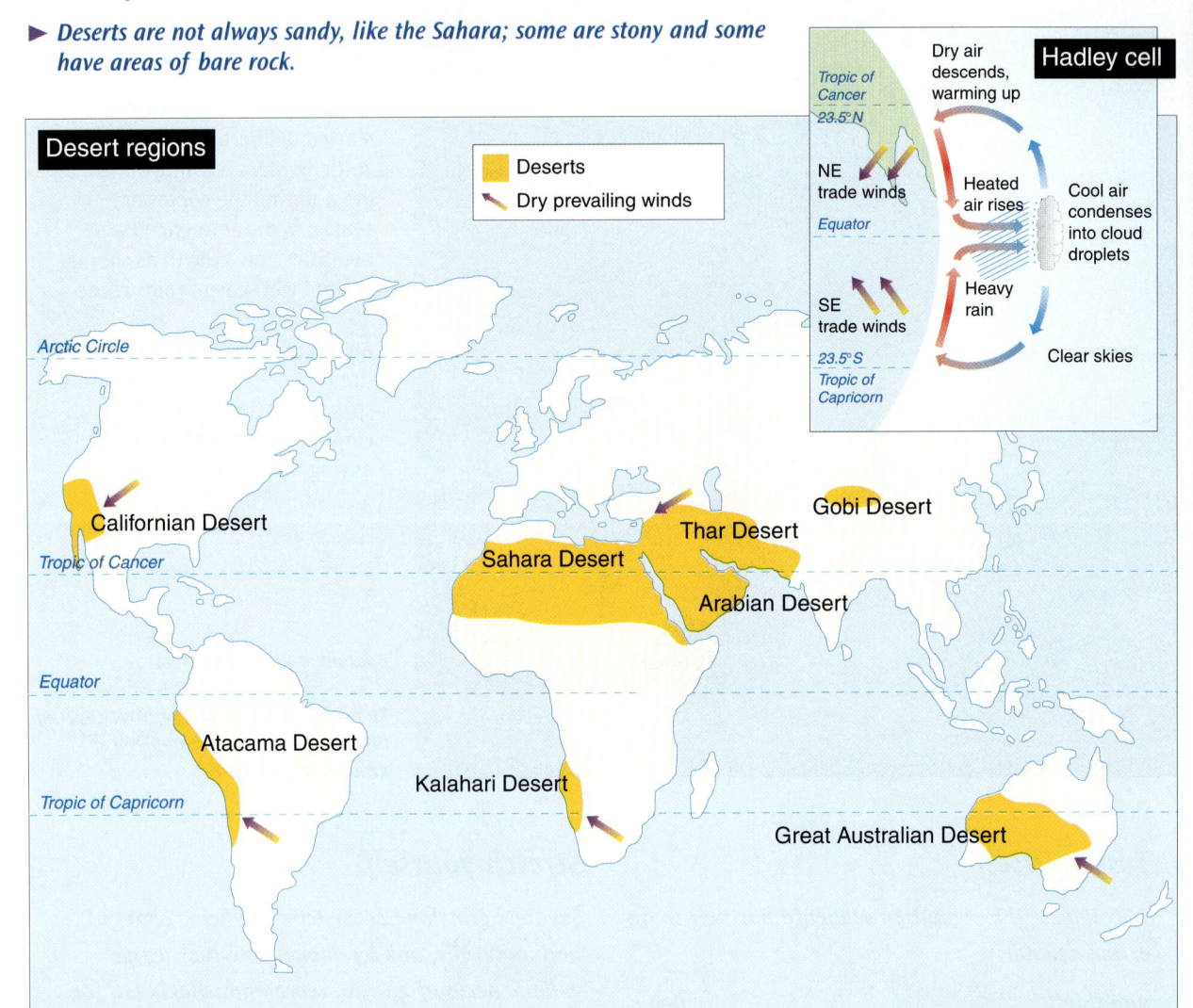

Most of the world's deserts have a tropical latitude. Although the role of prevailing winds from dry land, and the presence of 'rain shadow' areas is important, it is latitude which best explains the desert climate.

Temperatures are highest over the equator. Warm air masses, laden with evaporated water vapour, rise through the atmosphere to very high altitudes. Here they cool and condense, to give the heavy daily rainfall typical of equatorial rainforest areas. But at this high altitude the cold air masses spread north and south before descending, due to their greater density, over the Tropics of Cancer and Capricorn. Here the descending air warms up and retains water as vapour. As a result, the skies over the tropics are normally cloudless.

Characteristics of the world's great deserts are:

- rare clouds
- little rain
- very hot days
- extremely cold nights.

The air masses complete the cycle by returning to the equator as reliable trade winds (see Tropical revolving storms, page 136).

Desert vegetation has to be exceptionally specialised and very tough, in order to survive these extreme conditions.

Seeds can lie dormant for years before germinating rapidly in response to a rain shower. This can produce a desert 'bloom', which lasts only a few weeks as the 'ephemeral' flowering plants go through their entire life-cycle.

Another result of desert specialism is the way cacti have developed deep roots to tap groundwater, plus thick waxy water-storing stems, and thin spiky leaves – tactics to reduce transpiration and deter grazing!

The vegetation, insects, reptiles and small mammals found in deserts can best be described as scant.

Conditions are so hostile that few people attempt to live in them unless there is good reason, such as valuable mineral deposits.

At desert margins, where desert merges into **semi-desert** scrub, conditions are just capable of supporting people. But these semi-desert areas are probably the most fragile environments on earth.

Cacti flourish in the Sonora Desert, Mexico.

Sparse vegetation in the Californian Desert.

Test yourself

1. Copy and complete the following sentences selecting from the alternatives given:

Favourable/Hostile desert conditions ensure that only fragile/tough plants can survive. Special qualities are necessary/irrelevant in this wet/dry environment. Cacti, for example have waxy skins to increase/reduce transpiration and some have deep/shallow roots to tap groundwater.

Stretch yourself

Why can deserts be so hot during the day, yet bitterly cold at night?

Natural hazards and disasters

Key points

▶ *Natural hazards are associated with climate, weather and geology and they affect all biota.*

▶ *A hazard becomes a disaster according to the severity of its effect.*

▶ *Due to world population growth, more and more people are becoming vulnerable to natural hazards.*

▶ *Hazard perception, and responses, vary according to the event, location and people.*

Natural hazards are sudden, severe events which make the natural environment difficult, if not impossible to manage, and disrupt human life. When natural hazards cause very high levels of death and damage to property, the term **disaster** becomes valid. Most natural disasters are related to **four** hazards, all concerning the physical, rather than biological environment:

- **floods** are the most common, most lethal, and damage the most property
- **tropical revolving storms** are the next most frequent, and almost as dangerous (they are better known as cyclones, hurricanes and typhoons, depending upon where they occur)
- **earthquakes**
- **droughts**.

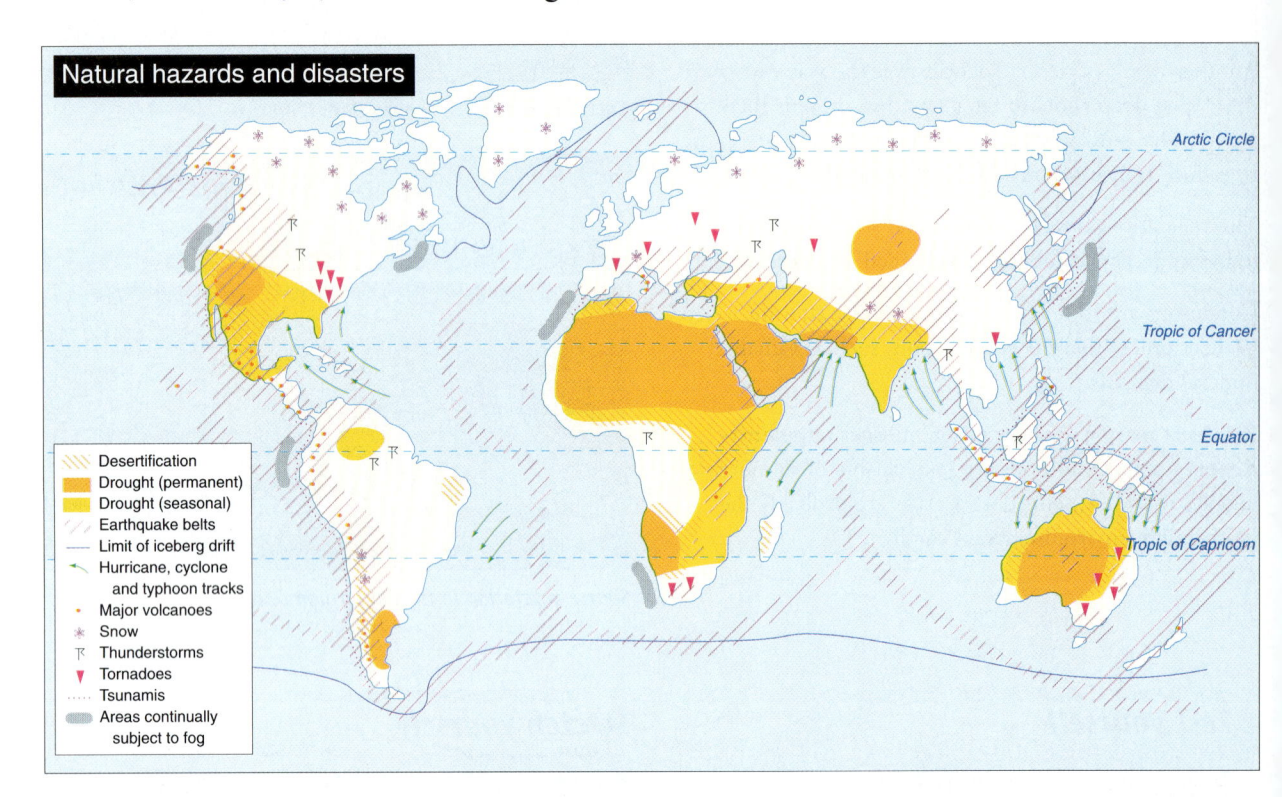

Natural hazards and disasters

Legend:
- Desertification
- Drought (permanent)
- Drought (seasonal)
- Earthquake belts
- Limit of iceberg drift
- Hurricane, cyclone and typhoon tracks
- Major volcanoes
- Snow
- Thunderstorms
- Tornadoes
- Tsunamis
- Areas continually subject to fog

Other environmental hazards account for relatively few disasters by comparison.

These include:

- **blizzards, tornadoes, willy-willies** and other very strong winds
- heavy snowstorms
- avalanches
- drifting icebergs
- fog
- thunderstorms
- landslides
- volcanic eruptions
- tsunamis (see page 143)
- bush and forest fires
- pests (such as infestation by tsetse fly, locust and grasshopper).

134 ENVIRONMENTAL THEMES • HAZARDS

As world population rises and urbanisation increases, more and more people live in places which are vulnerable to natural hazards; the number of people killed, and the amount of property lost, rises faster than the number of disasters. In many places little can be done to stop the destruction but awareness of a hazard does enable people to prepare for it.

Some hazards can be **prevented**: snow can be stabilised in avalanche zones, and river bank levées can be built up in areas prone to flooding.

With sufficient money and technology, some hazards can be **modified**, for example, Hawaiian and Italian lava flows have been diverted.

People can move away (**migrate**) but for this they need advance warning, and the means to escape. Sadly most do not have such defences and choices.

Natural hazards may affect the whole world but it is invariably the poor that suffer most. For many, particularly the poor of ELDCs, help after the event from family, friends, or emergency aid agencies, may be their only hope.

Assisting an earthquake survivor, Russia, May 1995.

Test yourself

1. What is the difference between a natural hazard and a disaster?

2. Which of the hazards mentioned on page 134 could be classified as: (a) meteorological (weather/climate) (b) geological (c) biological?

Stretch yourself

People's perception of natural hazards and their responses to them, may range from the assumption that their fate is 'in the lap of the gods' to considerable investment in practical and thorough contingency planning.

For at least two contrasting examples which you have studied, summarise the main controlling factors dictating measures taken to lessen the risks and the reasons for each approach.

ENVIRONMENTAL THEMES • HAZARDS

Tropical revolving storms

Key points

▶ Tropical revolving storms depend upon warm (tropical) sea evaporation to sustain them.

▶ Satellite remote sensing allows developing storm systems to be tracked and reported.

▶ Contingency planning, including evacuation measures and the building of safer structures, is now widespread.

Tropical revolving storms are legendary for their destructive powers. They are often known by their local names:

- **hurricanes** (in the Caribbean)
- **cyclones** (off the Indian sub-continent)
- **typhoons** (in the China seas).

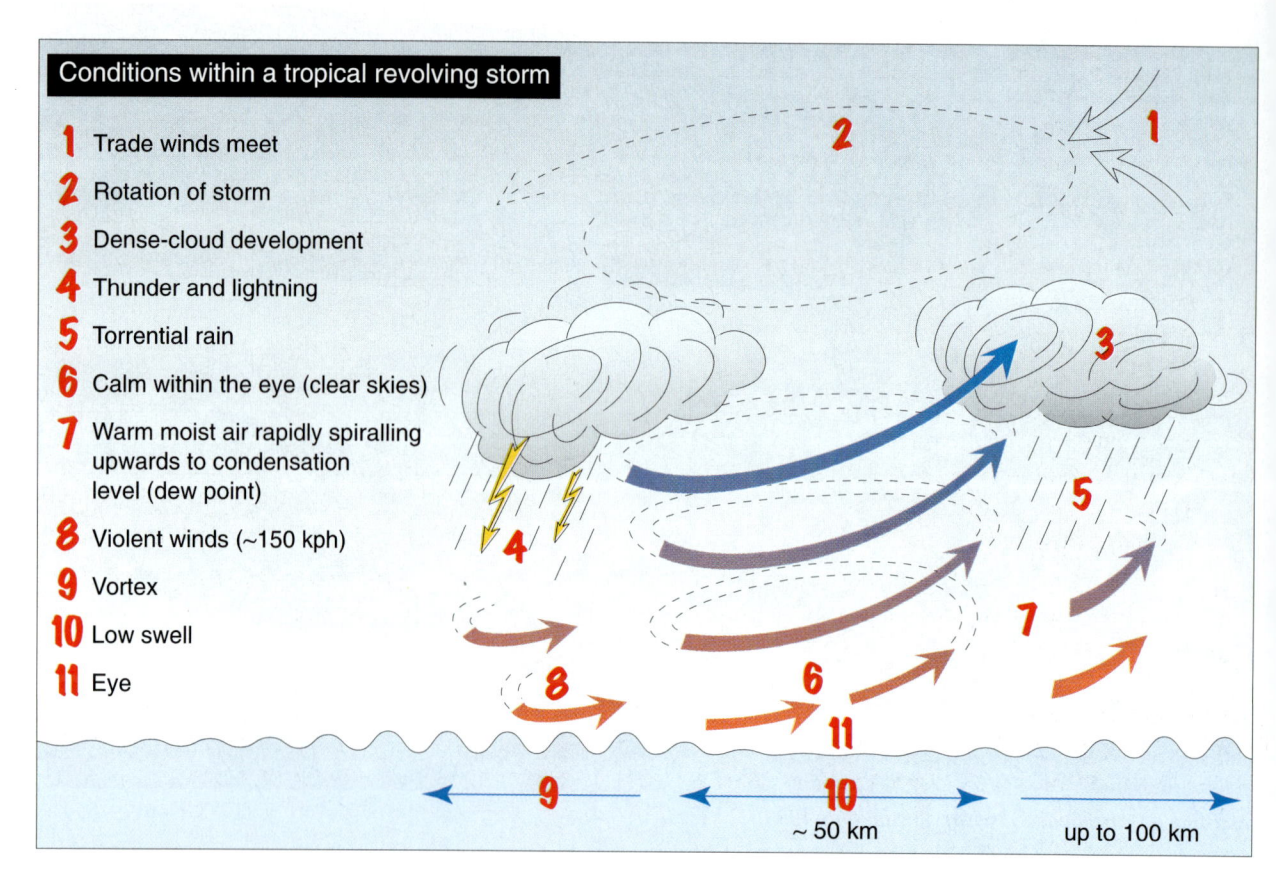

Conditions within a tropical revolving storm

1. Trade winds meet
2. Rotation of storm
3. Dense-cloud development
4. Thunder and lightning
5. Torrential rain
6. Calm within the eye (clear skies)
7. Warm moist air rapidly spiralling upwards to condensation level (dew point)
8. Violent winds (~150 kph)
9. Vortex
10. Low swell
11. Eye

~ 50 km   up to 100 km

Their origin was not understood fully until **remote sensing** from satellites had developed to the enormous sophistication we take for granted today. The **tropical location** is the key to this phenomenon. At these latitudes, ocean surface temperatures rise towards the end of summer to more than 27°C. These areas of normally very still waters (known by sailors as the **doldrums**) evaporate vast masses of water vapour. Humid updraughts result, **reducing air pressure** over the sea, and so allowing air from all around to rush in. This evaporates more water vapour, creating self-perpetuating updraughts.

High in the atmosphere, temperatures are cool enough for the water vapour to condense into cloud droplets, and so allow convectional rainfall. But in **late summer** and **early autumn** the **trade winds** meet at a similar altitude, and it is thought that they can 'kick-start' rotating storms. This is because at these latitudes the deflecting effect of the earth's rotation (known as the **coriolis force**) is particularly strong. The resulting tropical revolving storm is **funnel shaped** with warm, moist air on the outside rising rapidly. The coriolis effect causes this air to spin – anticlockwise in the northern hemisphere, and clockwise south of the equator.

The winds within this rotating **vortex** build to incredible violence, and are mixed with driving rain. Inside the funnel, cooler air descends in relatively calm conditions and this is known as the **eye of the storm**.

Heat and evaporation from the warm oceans is needed to sustain these storms, which drift like a spinning-top over the water surface. When they pass over land they very soon die out, but the frictional drag of the coastal land surface causes the winds to spiral inwards more rapidly and rotate more quickly – just as a spinning skater increases the speed of rotation by drawing in the arms to the body. This means that tropical revolving storms are at their most dangerous immediately after coming ashore.

Disaster prevention and mitigation

Once a storm has started, satellite remote sensing allows us to monitor cloud patterns and forecast its development and progression. Such **accurate forecasting**, aided by data from weather stations, ships and aeroplanes, informs the public and allows them to prepare.

▶ The USA's National Weather Service gives names to approaching hurricanes, and uses every form of media available to warn coastal states likely to be affected.

▶ Australia's Bureau of Meteorology runs a Tropical Cyclone Warning System, broadcasting *Tropical Advisories* to inform the public. A *Cyclone Warning* is repeated on TV, radio, and in newspapers when a storm is approaching.

Tornado over USA.

The USA and Australia are also expert in the construction of **storm-proof buildings**. They have developed new designs for firmer foundations, with house frames secured to the ground and bolted-on roofs in areas at risk from tornadoes (USA) and Willy Willies (Australia).

Contingency planning for storms is of key significance. **Evacuation plans** for coastal regions are well established in the USA and Australia. Even in Bangladesh, one of the poorest countries in the world, cyclone forecasting and radio warning systems have been developed. Contingency plans now exist to evacuate people in the paths of approaching cyclones to concrete shelters. Also, large banks of earth are being constructed as part of a wide-ranging *Flood Action Plan* to stop **tidal storm surges** washing inland (see page 143).

Test yourself

1. State three requirements for tropical revolving storm development.

2. What is meant by the term: contingency planning?

Stretch yourself

Never underestimate the value of analogy to understanding natural phenomena!

Pull the plug on a filled, settled bath in order to witness the spinning forces described above in action. The nature of the storm's eye can also be appreciated in the contrast between the central calm and the spiralling surrounding water's violent vortex.

Hurricane Gilbert

Hurricane Gilbert (September 1988) is of great significance because it was the most powerful storm, in its day, recorded in the western hemisphere. The following year Caribbean records were broken again by *Hurricane Hugo*. This fuelled speculation that climatic change, related to global warming (see page 160), was a factor in their severity. Since then the hurricane season has been studied with renewed interest, and in 1995 there were more tropical storms in this area than ever previously recorded!

Hurricane Gilbert is also of interest because of the contrasts it highlighted between 'affluent' North America and its 'poorer' neighbours. *Gilbert's* development, and catastrophic progress from the eastern Caribbean, was monitored carefully. Only in its final stages did it depart from the path predicted, with tragic consequences for the Mexican city of Monterrey, but to the enormous relief of the southern states of the USA.

Predicted and actual track of Hurricane Gilbert

Hurricane Gilbert, September 1988. The edge of Hurricane Gilbert can be seen touching the coast of Jamaica in this satellite photo received at the Hurricane Centre in Miami shortly after 16.00 hours GMT, 11 September.

138 ENVIRONMENTAL THEMES • HAZARDS

The contrasts highlighted by *Gilbert* could not have been more dramatic. Texas, for instance, is one of the richest of the southern American states. It was clear that, if Gilbert had reached its coast, billions of dollars-worth of damage would be done. So the people of Texas prepared thoroughly:

- *newspapers ran a Hurricane Preparation Check List, covering the necessity and availability of everything from waterproof matches to water purification tablets*
- *every window for nearly 800km² of the coast was boarded up*
- *inland hotels ran special 'hurricane rates'*
- *emergency laws were passed to allow the evacuating thousands to drive inland on both sides of the freeways (motorways), and minimise traffic congestion.*

By contrast, poorer Caribbean islands like Jamaica could make few preparations – and where do you run to on an island? 500,000 subsequently lost their homes on Jamaica alone. Mexico suffered even more because *Gilbert* effectively struck twice. On crossing the Yucatan Peninsula water and electricity supplies, and communications were cut. 100,000 were forced to flee the 190km/h winds. But *Gilbert* did not then swing north to oil-rich Texas as predicted. Mexico's northern provinces caught the full blast, with frail wooden coastal houses smashed and vehicles swept aside 'like discarded toys'. The cruellest fate awaited those who had fled westwards to the city of Monterrey. *Gilbert* broke all the rules by reaching this far inland. Flash floods engulfed roads, vehicles and buildings, and over 200 people died.

So contrasts and ironies are illustrated by *Hurricane Gilbert*. Whilst no-one would wish such a storm on any area, it is undoubted that the well-prepared Texans would have survived, and through insurance and government aid recovered any losses. But the Mexicans, 'poor neighbours' to the south, illustrated a tragic law of natural hazards – that those with least often suffer the most.

Surveying the damage, Cancun, Mexico.

Floods

Key points

▶ **Flooding is the world's most common, damaging and lethal natural hazard.**

▶ **Floods are caused by extreme weather conditions, and by human mismanagement.**

▶ **Flood warning systems, levées, canalisation, dams and afforestation are defences.**

Flooding is the world's most common natural disaster. River floods and tidal storm surges (often associated with cyclones) regularly kill thousands, and make hundreds of thousands homeless. Floods are so frequent in some areas, like Bangladesh, that disasters of epic scale attract relatively little attention from the Western media. Floods affecting our own region, where they are much less frequent, tend to command our greater attention.

Normal rainfall evaporates from, but mostly runs off and soaks into, the ground. River and groundwater levels fluctuate according to how much rain has fallen in the preceding hours (see page 119).

Prolonged, heavy rainfall increases river volumes (discharge). This can cause overflowing of banks, leading to flooding. Raised groundwater levels can have the same effect.

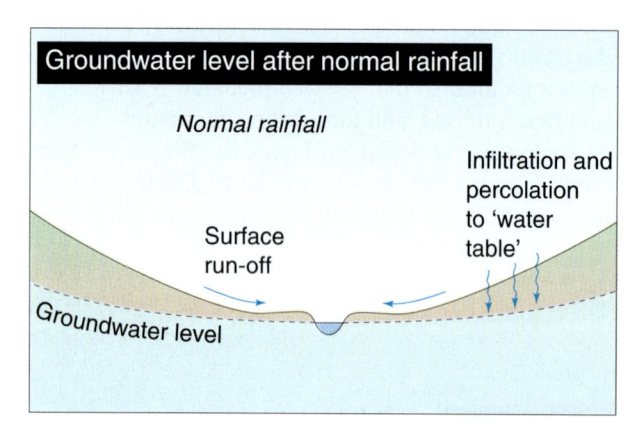

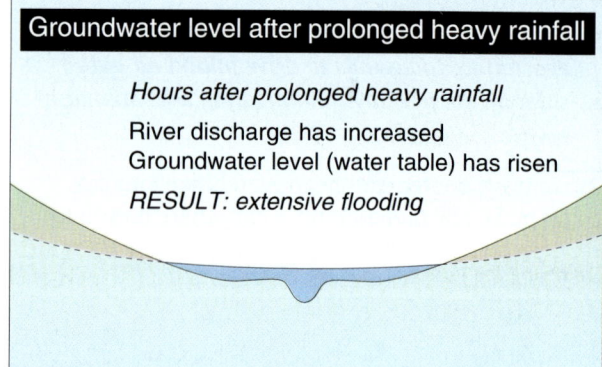

Groundwater level after normal rainfall

Normal rainfall

Surface run-off

Infiltration and percolation to 'water table'

Groundwater level

Groundwater level after prolonged heavy rainfall

Hours after prolonged heavy rainfall

River discharge has increased
Groundwater level (water table) has risen

RESULT: extensive flooding

Some **human activities** increase the chances of flooding.

Deforestation reduces the amount of water that can soak naturally into the ground, encouraging rapid surface runoff, which adds to river discharges.

Urban development can interfere with natural drainage patterns.

- Tarmac and concrete is **impermeable**, so water must be channelled through gutters and drains.
- Channelled water reaches rivers and streams more quickly than it would as groundwater.
- Streams are occasionally blocked, or more often have been diverted, culverted, and canalised to allow for building.
- Canalised channels have less friction, allowing more efficient discharge.

The cumulative result can be fluctuations of river flow with increased danger of flooding.

Flood defences

In EMDCs when regular flooding threatens inhabited areas the resources and knowledge exist to introduce flood-control strategies.

For example, the Vale of York is very prone to flooding following long periods of heavy rain, or rapid winter snow melt, putting the city of York at risk. To protect property and people, the River Ouse, through York, has had its levées (flood banks) raised and reinforced, and flood gates now protect adjacent streets.

Benefits of floods

It should be remembered that in certain cases flooding can bring benefits. For example, regular flooding of the Nile Valley in Egypt has laid fertile alluvial silt which forms the foundation of highly productive irrigated agriculture.

Queuing for food during floods in Bangladesh, 1994.

Test yourself

1. Which of the following combinations is most likely to lead to a flood?

A Low precipitation/low infiltration rates.

B Low precipitation/high evapotranspiration rates.

C Heavy precipitation/high infiltration rates.

D Heavy precipitation/high evapotranspiration rates.

E Heavy precipitation/saturated ground.

2. Copy and complete the following sentences selecting from the alternatives given:
Possible solutions to the problems of flooding along a river include raising/removing levées, narrowing/straightening the course of the channel and cutting down/planting trees to increase/reduce surface runoff.

Stretch yourself

Why do so many people, in both EMDCs and ELDCs, live in flood-prone areas?

Flooding in Bangladesh

Key points

▶ Bangladesh is one of the poorest and most densely populated countries on earth.

▶ Bangladesh consists of 80% low-lying flood plain and delta, and is very prone to flooding.

▶ Both river flooding, and tidal storm surges related to cyclones, occur in late summer.

▶ A massive Flood Action Plan, financed by the World Bank, is currently being implemented.

Bangladesh is one of the poorest and most densely populated countries in the world. Over 120 million people occupy an area equivalent to England and Wales!

Bangladesh consists of 80% low-lying flat, fertile flood plain, and delta land of alluvial silt deposited by the Rivers Ganges and Brahmaputra (Jumana). Much of the delta is made up of low, marshy islands, such as the densely populated Bhola and South Hatia.

Flood plain and delta land are perfect for intensive rice cultivation – a staple crop ideally suited to the monsoon climate. But the area is prone to potentially disastrous flooding, from rivers and from tidal storm surges caused by tropical cyclones.

Taking refuge on the roof, Bangladesh, 1995.

River flooding is most likely in late summer following the heavy monsoon rains and snowmelt in the Himalayas. Deforestation in the foothills of the Himalayas (in Nepal) has increased surface runoff into the rivers – further increasing Bangladesh's flood danger.

Tropical cyclones are also most likely to occur in late summer and early autumn (see page 136). They are funnelled northwards up the Bay of Bengal. Because the Bay gets narrower and shallower (due to silt deposition) **tidal storm surges** similar to **tsunamis** (see next page) sweep over the islands of the delta destroying property, crops, livestock and people. One storm, in 1991, killed 150,000 people.

Bangladesh: location

142 ENVIRONMENTAL THEMES • HAZARDS

The flood action plan

Bangladesh may be very poor, but it is not helpless. A massive scheme of coastal and river flood banks, funded by the World Bank, is currently being constructed. These embankments, along with concrete cyclone shelters and improved early warning systems, offer the people of Bangladesh greater hope for the future. This is particularly important given the ever increasing risks associated with global warming raising sea levels further.

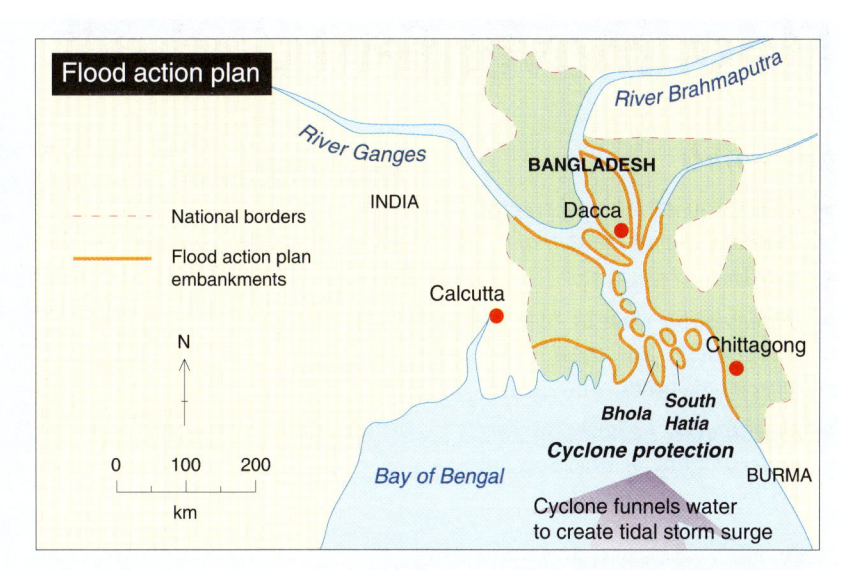

Flood action plan

- National borders
- Flood action plan embankments

Cyclone protection — Cyclone funnels water to create tidal storm surge

Tsunamis

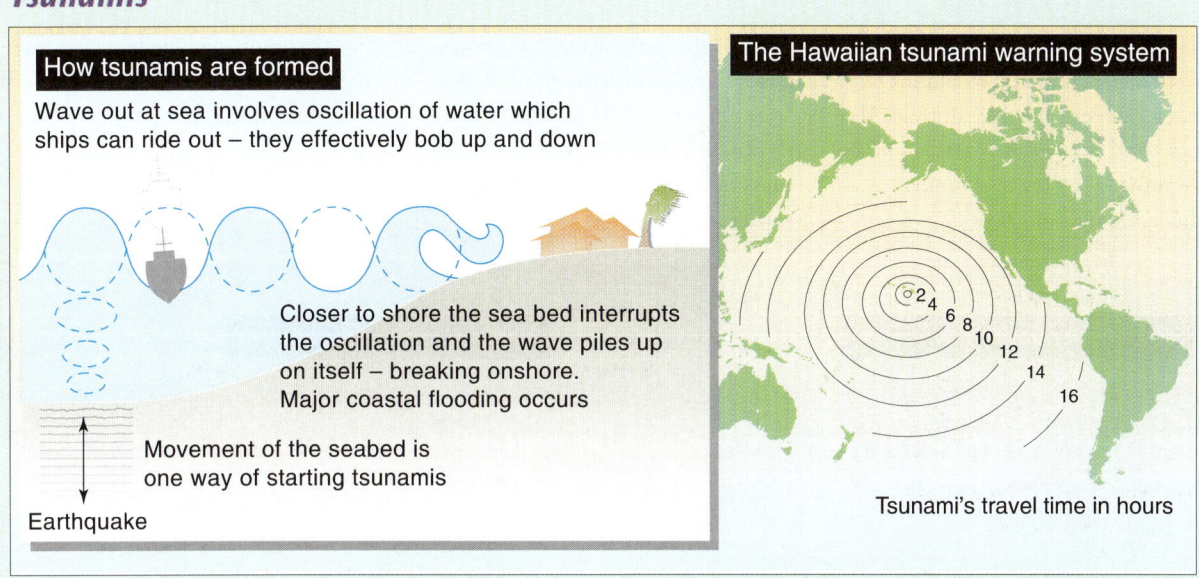

How tsunamis are formed

Wave out at sea involves oscillation of water which ships can ride out – they effectively bob up and down

Closer to shore the sea bed interrupts the oscillation and the wave piles up on itself – breaking onshore. Major coastal flooding occurs

Movement of the seabed is one way of starting tsunamis

Earthquake

The Hawaiian tsunami warning system

Tsunami's travel time in hours

Tsunamis are rare hazards misleadingly called tidal waves. Normally associated with the Pacific Ocean but not Bangladesh, they are a series of massive, highly destructive waves following at intervals of up to an hour. They are caused by tremors transmitted from ocean floor earthquakes, landslides and volcanic eruptions. On approaching the coast, especially if funnelled into an inlet, they will slow down and pile up as a massive wall of water before breaking.

Test yourself

1. Give one additional reason (to the tidal storm surges described) why flood danger increases during a cyclone.

2. Why are early warnings broadcasted by radio proving far more effective than newspapers or television?

Stretch yourself

What understandable human reaction invariably leads to a tsunami disaster being worse than it might have been?

ENVIRONMENTAL THEMES • HAZARDS

Mass movements

Key points

▶ All slope material is inherently unstable, due to the pull of gravity.

▶ Imperceptibly slow, or devastatingly fast, mass movements result.

▶ As with other hazards, an understanding of processes has led to defensive measures.

Frost shattering

Water enters cracks in the rock during the day, then freezes and expands at night, enlarging the cracks. More water enters the next day, and the cycle continues until the rock breaks.

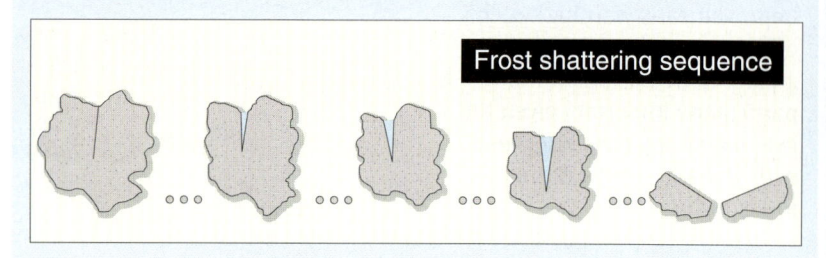

Frost shattering sequence

Landslides and avalanches are particularly dramatic examples of **mass movements**. At all times the rocks and soils of the earth's surface are moving, or trying to move, under the pull of gravity.

Any resulting movement is known as a mass movement which may range from imperceptible **soil creep** to devastating **landslides**. We classify mass movements as either **flows** or **slides**.

Flows can on average be very slow (eg. soil creep), moderate (eg. earth flow) or rapid (eg. lahar).

Slides are invariably sudden and rapid.

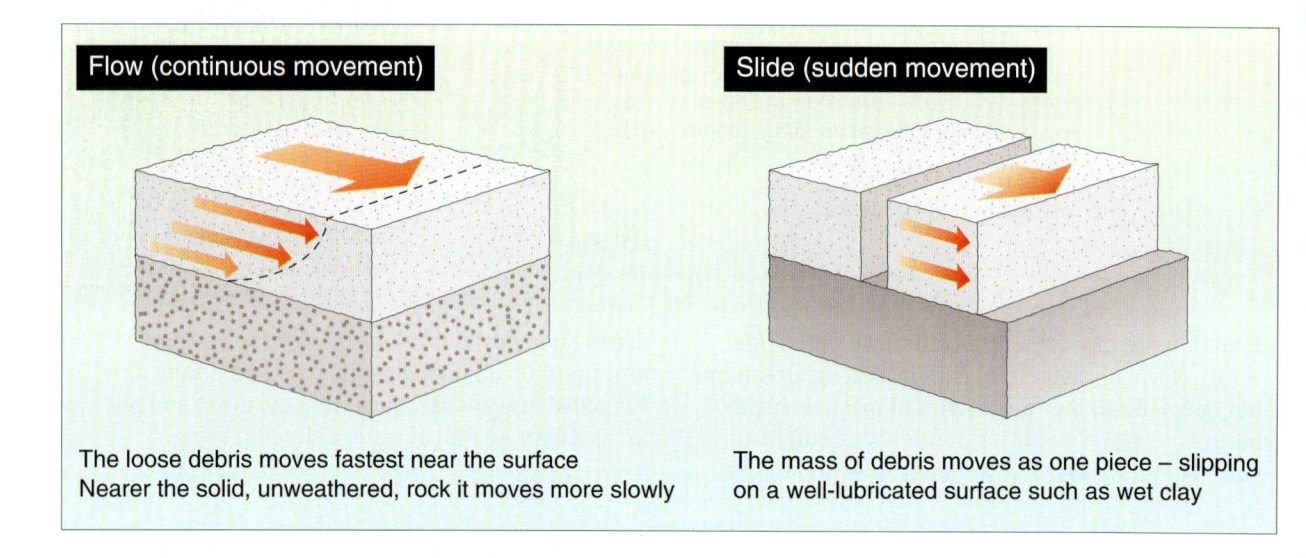

Flow (continuous movement)

The loose debris moves fastest near the surface
Nearer the solid, unweathered, rock it moves more slowly

Slide (sudden movement)

The mass of debris moves as one piece – slipping on a well-lubricated surface such as wet clay

Factors likely to lead to mass movements

Although most slopes look stable they are actually changing all the time. The changes may eventually destabilise the slope, making it susceptible to mass movement.

- **Chemical** and **mechanical weathering** break down material into smaller, collectively less stable pieces.

- **Heavy rainfall** or **snowfall** increase the weight of material on a slope.

- **Water seeping** (infiltrating and percolating) into the ground may lubricate material and allow it to flow or slide more easily.

- **Earthquakes** and **fault movements** trigger landslides in tectonically active areas (see page 148).

These mainly natural processes are often aggravated by human activities.

- **Removal of vegetation** (as in deforestation) withdraws the ground's natural protection, upsetting the amount of water in the soil and reducing root binding.
- **Undercutting** slopes at their base (as in motorway construction) steepens the slope angle, increasing instability.

Disasters and their prevention

Examples of the destructive power of landslides are all too frequent. Occasionally, they appal even the most hardened observers.

In 1963 the *Vaiont Dam*, which had been constructed on a site in northern Italy with slopes known to be unstable, was engulfed by a massive **rock slide**. This sent a 70m high **mudflow** careering down the valley, killing 2600 people.

In 1966 a primary school in *Aberfan*, South Wales was buried when a saturated coal waste tip collapsed. 116 children and 28 adults died under the **earthflow**.

In 1985 the volcanic eruption of *Nevado del Ruiz* in Columbia caused rainstorms – typical after volcanic eruptions. But the heavy rain became combined with melted summit snow and glacier ice. This in turn mixed with ash from the slopes, to cause a vast, fast-moving mudflow (**lahar**). This mudflow buried the town of Armero, killing 21,000 inhabitants.

Although it is almost impossible to prevent large natural landslides from occurring, growth in understanding is helping engineers to reduce the number of smaller landslides.

- Since the disaster in *Aberfan*, the size of mining waste tips has been regulated, and suitable drainage and vegetation cover advised.
- Careful research can now identify areas where landslide hazards exist, so that maps can be made showing areas unsuitable for building.
- Unstable material can be removed or retained behind suitable barriers.
- Rock-bolting into stable strata, and cementing of loose debris is now practised.
- Monitoring the angle of slopes in cuttings and embankments, and providing drainage and protective layers of vegetation is becoming commonplace.

Tragedy in Aberfan.

Test yourself

1. What is the essential difference between a flow and a slide?

2. What is likely to distinguish between a mudflow and an earthflow?

Stretch yourself

Much of the engineering necessary to reduce the risk of landslides involves compromises and a combination of measures, for both economic and environmental reasons.

Study any cutting, for example, in a new by-pass or motorway development near your home. Consider the factors, such as land availability, cost and visual impact likely to have led to the final engineering decisions regarding slope angle, vegetation, reinforcement, drainage and noise nuisance.

Avalanches

Avalanches are the most rapidly moving type of mass movement. They occur in high mountain areas with heavy snowfall and open slopes. **Ground avalanches** (of wet snow, ice slabs, rock debris, soil and vegetation) sliding over the ground often push a **powder avalanche** of dry snow ahead of them.

The destructiveness of avalanches often depends on whether they fall freely from open slopes or are confined within inhabited valleys. Disasters, of varying magnitude, have been recorded in most upland areas of the world, resulting in:

- *death*
- *loss of property*
- *forest damage*
- *blocked roads and railway lines, and*
- *flooding by avalanche-dammed rivers.*

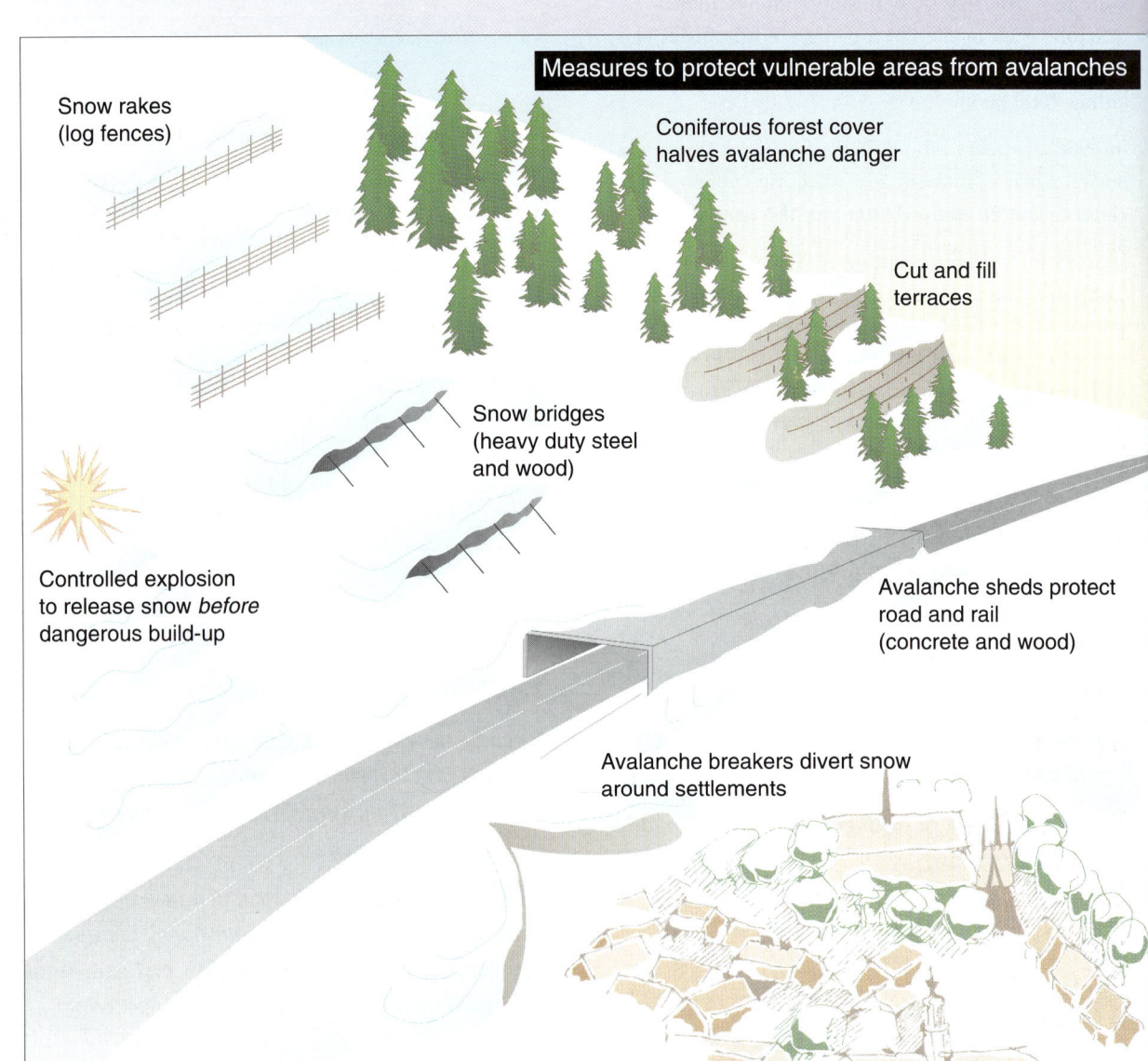

Measures to protect vulnerable areas from avalanches

- Snow rakes (log fences)
- Coniferous forest cover halves avalanche danger
- Cut and fill terraces
- Snow bridges (heavy duty steel and wood)
- Controlled explosion to release snow *before* dangerous build-up
- Avalanche sheds protect road and rail (concrete and wood)
- Avalanche breakers divert snow around settlements

ENVIRONMENTAL THEMES • HAZARDS

Research is improving the predictability of these dramatic mass movements, but they remain a particular hazard for **ski resorts** where nature's best protection, coniferous trees, have been cleared to create pistes.

Avalanche aggravators

- *increase in the snow's weight on steep slopes, following heavy snowfall or spring rainfall*
- *a sudden rise in temperature, which melts and lubricates previously bonded ice and snow*
- *pollution – in the Alps, acid rain is killing trees*
- *changes in agricultural practice (for example, so-called 'ski-rich' farmers are grazing fewer cattle on upland summer pastures; this results in longer grass which ferments and 'lubricates' the undersurface of the snow).*

Regardless of the conditions, vibration is needed to start the event. Rock falls, falling trees, passing vehicles, even skiers and snow-boarders, are capable of starting a flow which rapidly builds to a major avalanche.

An avalanche gains speed on an open mountainside.

Protection from avalanches

Although complete prevention of avalanches is probably impossible, protection from its worst effects can be achieved. Stabilising the snow is by far the most effective protection.

Avalanche damage reduction measures include:

- *forest cover, which can nearly halve avalanche damage*
- *shelters, known as avalanche sheds, built over roads (for example, through the Gotthard, Simplon and Grand St Bernard passes in the Alps)*
- *snow bridges and rakes*
- *cut and fill terraces*
- *diversionary 'breakers', up-slope of villages.*

Small explosions can also be detonated to trigger 'controlled' falls in order to prevent larger, more destructive avalanches. Careful monitoring of snow accumulation by specialist organisations (such as the Avalanche Research Centre at Davos in Switzerland) aids prediction and planning for evacuation and rescue in vulnerable areas.

The unstable earth: plate tectonics

Key points

▶ If the earth was the size of an egg, the outer crust would be thinner than the shell!

▶ The earth's rocky crust is fractured into sections 'floating' on the mantle beneath.

▶ Each irregularly shaped section can and does move, and is known as a tectonic plate.

▶ Plate boundaries are associated with most volcanoes, earthquakes and fold mountains.

The **crust** of the earth can be thought of as a raft, because it floats upon the mantle. Although the **mantle** is dense rock it can flow like 'potty putty' when, due to high temperatures, it becomes semi-molten.

The crust is divided into several huge rigid **tectonic plates** that fit together like a vast jigsaw. Despite their immense size, these plates move slowly across the mantle with the continents and oceans on top. They are driven by huge **convection currents** within the upper mantle. If its rocky structure was slightly less dense, the upper mantle could be likened to a vast pan of soup with crustal croutons floating on top!

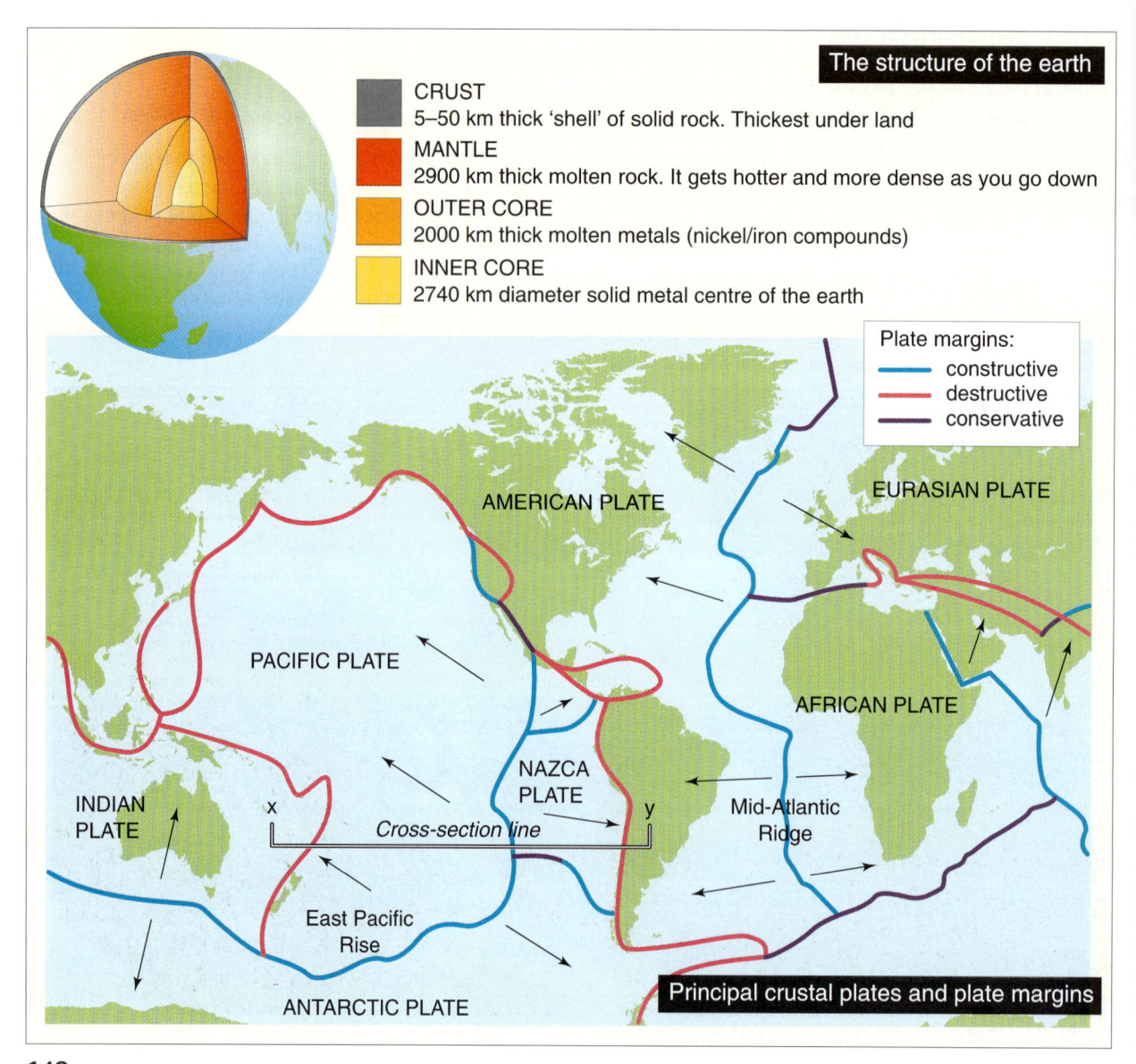

The structure of the earth

CRUST
5–50 km thick 'shell' of solid rock. Thickest under land

MANTLE
2900 km thick molten rock. It gets hotter and more dense as you go down

OUTER CORE
2000 km thick molten metals (nickel/iron compounds)

INNER CORE
2740 km diameter solid metal centre of the earth

Principal crustal plates and plate margins

Plate margins:
— constructive
— destructive
— conservative

- AMERICAN PLATE
- EURASIAN PLATE
- PACIFIC PLATE
- AFRICAN PLATE
- NAZCA PLATE
- INDIAN PLATE
- Mid-Atlantic Ridge
- East Pacific Rise
- ANTARCTIC PLATE

x — Cross-section line — y

148 ENVIRONMENTAL THEMES • HAZARDS

Over millions of years the plates have been simultaneously created and destroyed – just as they continue to be today. New crustal material is formed at spreading plate margins under some oceans, and destroyed by melting where plates collide. It is where the plates meet that most of the world's volcanoes and earthquakes occur. Major fold mountain ranges are also associated with tectonic plate margins.

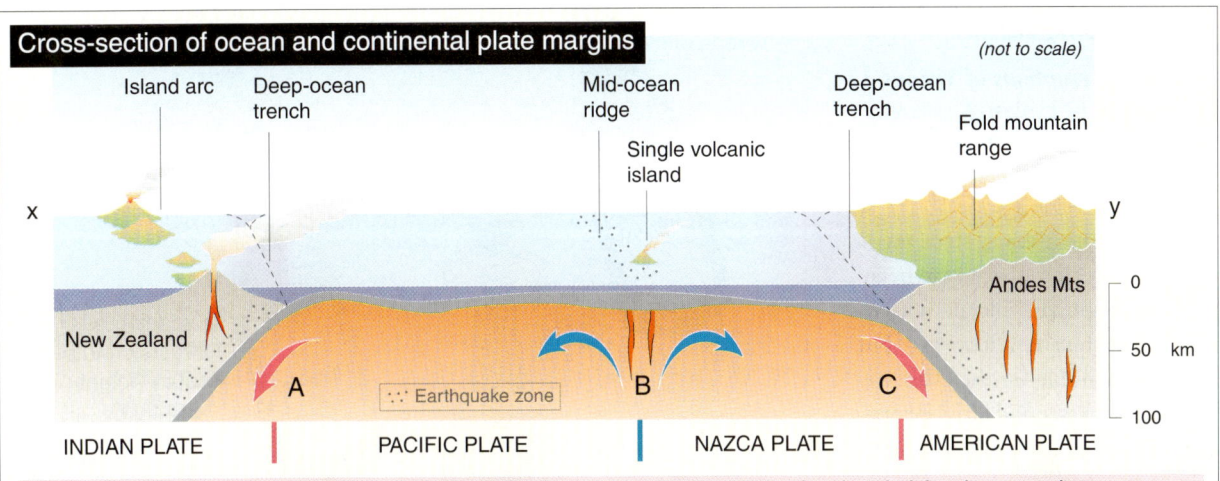

Cross-section of ocean and continental plate margins (not to scale)

A Ocean crust is forced to sink and melt at this destructive plate margin. A volcanic island arc results.

B Molten rock (magma) rises along the mid-ocean ridge creating new crust at this constructive plate margin. Some mid-ocean volcanoes break the surface to form volcanic islands.

C Ocean crust is forced to sink and melt under the edge of the continental plate. Volcanic eruptions and earthquakes occur at this destructive plate margin as the continental crust buckles into fold mountains.

Remember, there are **three types** of plate margins: **destructive**, **constructive** and **conservative**

A and C are both examples of destructive 'collisions'. Deep earthquakes, rising magma (forming volcanoes) and fold mountain building are typical features.

B is a constructive plate margin. As the plates move apart, new rock is added to the sea floor rather like toothpaste being spread along the line of the mid-ocean ridge.

Finally, conservative (transform) plate margins occur where one plate moves horizontally in relation to another.

NB Cross-section is marked (x–y) on world map on page 148.

Test yourself

1. What is meant by the following terms: (a) crust (b) mantle (c) tectonic plate?

2. Which two continents best illustrate the jigsaw-like fit of tectonic plates?

Stretch yourself

Tectonic plate movement can be modelled in a large, deep frying pan! Condensed tomato soup, heated slowly over a single heat source, should allow convection currents to circulate (as in the mantle). These carry (crustal) croutons, which both float by and collide with each other. Be warned – boiling the soup may prove memorable – but exceptionally messy!

ENVIRONMENTAL THEMES • HAZARDS

Volcanoes

Key points

▶ **Volcanoes are found along tectonic plate margins, or where the earth's crust is very thin.**

▶ **Volcanic activity is hazardous, but can bring benefits.**

▶ **Volcanic eruptions of viscous lava can be explosive, whereas fluid lava erupts mildly.**

For 4600 million years, since the earth was created, there have been volcanic eruptions. Volcanic activity is linked with natural hazards – but is also responsible for the crust we live on, the water and atmosphere essential to life, and the most fertile soils in the world.

There are many kinds of volcano depending on the nature of the volcanic activity.

Molten rock (**magma**) at very high temperature, rises under enormous pressure from the upper mantle. The magma exploits weaknesses in the crust in order to force its way to the surface. This is common along tectonic plate margins, but can also occur where the crust is very thin, such as under Hawaii.

Very thick but gaseous magma is associated with violently explosive eruptions, which hurl lava fragments, ash and dust high into the sky (rather like the cork and contents of a shaken champagne bottle).

Very fluid magma can erupt so sedately that the whole affair becomes a visually inspiring tourist attraction, as seen repeatedly on Hawaii.

Volcanic eruption analogy

Gas bubbles pressing hard against the wired cork

Wire released – cork explodes out

Escaping gas thrusts champagne out in violent 'eruption'

'Eruption' ends when the pressure is the same inside the bottle as it is outside

The volcanic cone is usually built up from layers of lava and ash debris, becoming progressively thinner away from the vent. As a general rule, the more fluid the lava, the further it flows, and so the gentler the slopes of the cone.

Volcanic eruptions are awesome:

- **lava** flows burn and bury everything in their path

- **hot ash**, dust and other debris can burn vegetation, pollute water supplies and affect people's breathing and health

- **dust** and ash from an eruption can 'seed' heavy rainstorms, creating vast dangerous **lahars**, such as the mudflow that buried Armero (see page 145).

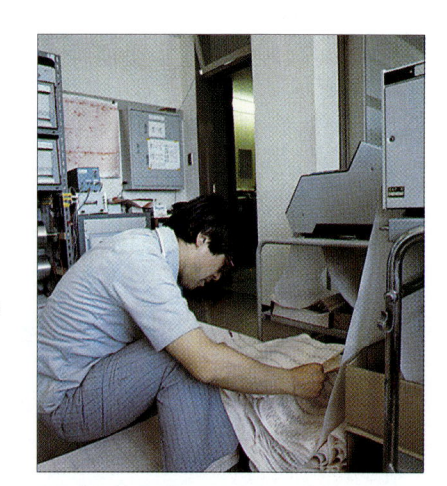

Monitoring microquakes at the Japanese Volcano Observatory.

150 ENVIRONMENTAL THEMES • HAZARDS

But volcanic activity also brings benefits:

- lava flows near the sea can create **new land**, as on Hawaii
- ash acts as a **fertiliser** to exhausted soils
- valuable **mineral deposits** (such as sulphur) are created
- **hot springs** can be harnessed for heating and to generate geothermal electricity, as in Iceland, Lardarello in Italy, and California, USA
- there is often great potential for developing tourism at volcanic sites, as in Hawaii and on Mount Etna in Sicily.

As with earthquakes, prediction of volcanic eruptions is an uncertain business – despite ground bulging and preliminary microquakes.

The effects of an eruption can be altered, however, as illustrated by recent eruptions of Mount Etna.

Mount Etna

Mount Etna has a long history of frequent eruptions, yet over one million people live on its slopes. This is because of fertile soils, rich orchards, vineyards and orange groves. There is also a thriving tourist industry, including skiing, which is a source of employment for many inhabitants.

Eruptions from the main crater are more rare than those from secondary cones and fissures. A much publicised eruption in 1983 proved the potential for lava diversion, using techniques developed on Hawaii.

Water bombing (to cool and slow the lava), diversionary walls, and canals cut by explosives and bulldozers, were considered in order to protect two towns in the lava's path. The latter proved partially successful.

In 1992 similar techniques were adopted to save Zafferana, a village of 7000 inhabitants on the volcano's eastern slope. 'Cable bombs' below the crater, created holes big enough to soak up the lava, and dams of blocks of lava and concrete were used to spread the flow. As a result the lava cooled and solidified more rapidly and Zafferana was saved.

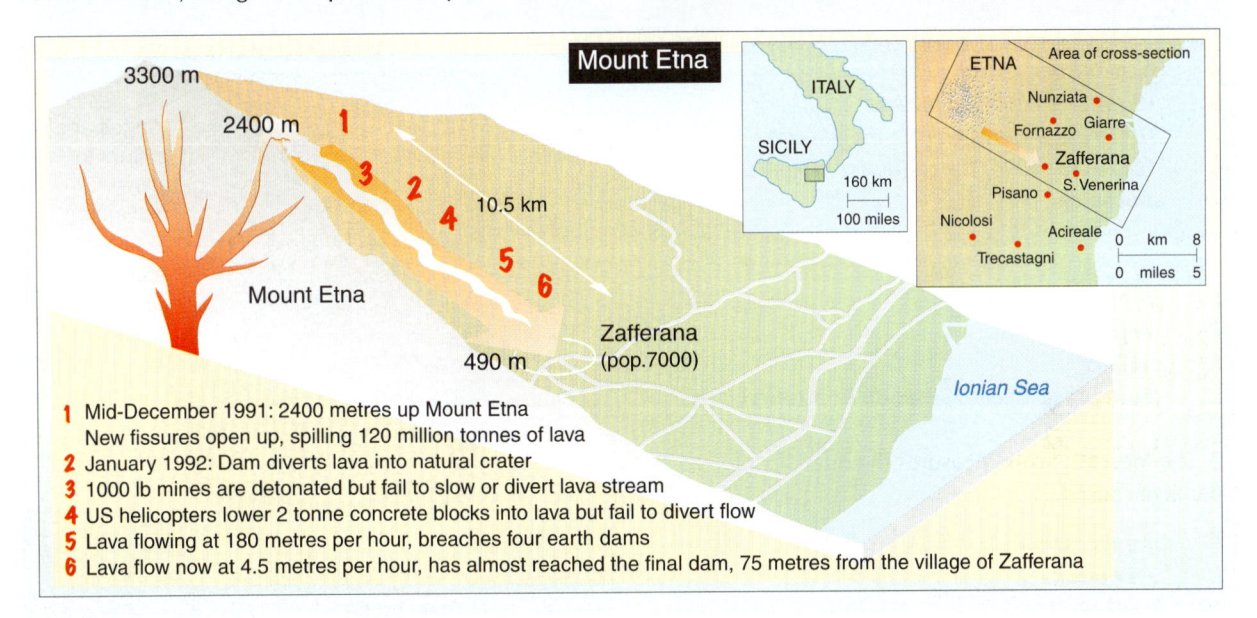

1. Mid-December 1991: 2400 metres up Mount Etna New fissures open up, spilling 120 million tonnes of lava
2. January 1992: Dam diverts lava into natural crater
3. 1000 lb mines are detonated but fail to slow or divert lava stream
4. US helicopters lower 2 tonne concrete blocks into lava but fail to divert flow
5. Lava flowing at 180 metres per hour, breaches four earth dams
6. Lava flow now at 4.5 metres per hour, has almost reached the final dam, 75 metres from the village of Zafferana

Test yourself

1. What is the difference between magma and lava?
2. Writing no more than two short paragraphs summarise the disadvantages and advantages of volcanic activity.

Stretch yourself

Appreciation of these hazards, but also volcanic benefits too, may depend much upon your time-scale.

For Etna, or any other volcano or volcanic area studied, classify both dangers and benefits as short- or long-term.

Earthquakes

Key points

▶ *Frictional forces at plate boundaries can build up, and be released violently as earthquakes.*

▶ *'When stress overcomes strength, the earthquake occurs.'*

▶ *Earthquakes and their aftershocks cannot, as yet, be predicted accurately.*

▶ *The USA (California) and Japan lead the world in earthquake preparedness.*

Tectonic plates, trying to move by or under each other, are subject to vast frictional forces. They can get locked together for years, building up enormous stresses. When at 'breaking point', this stress overcomes the strength of the rocks and the tensions are released explosively.

An **earthquake** marks this sudden jolting movement, with **shockwaves** radiating outwards from the point of fracture within the crust, known as the hypocentre (**focus**). Directly above, at the surface **epicentre**, ground shaking is strongest, with progressively less damage caused further from this point.

Measuring 'quakes

Crustal vibration of any degree is measured by **seismometer**. All earthquakes are recorded and two scales of measurement are commonly used.

1. The **Richter Scale** measures the magnitude of the 'quake.

0	Weakest perceptible
1	10 times greater magnitude
2	10x10 (100) times greater magnitude
3	10x10x10 (1000) times greater magnitude and so on
.	
.	
6+	Important
7+	Major
8+	Serious
.	(Scale, theoretically, goes on to infinity)

2. The **Mercalli Scale** measures the intensity of damage caused.

I	Imperceptible
II	Very weak
III	Weak
IV	Moderate
V	Fairly strong
VI	Strong
VII	Very strong
VIII	Destructive
IX	Very destructive
X	Devastating
XI	Catastrophic
XII	Major catastrophe

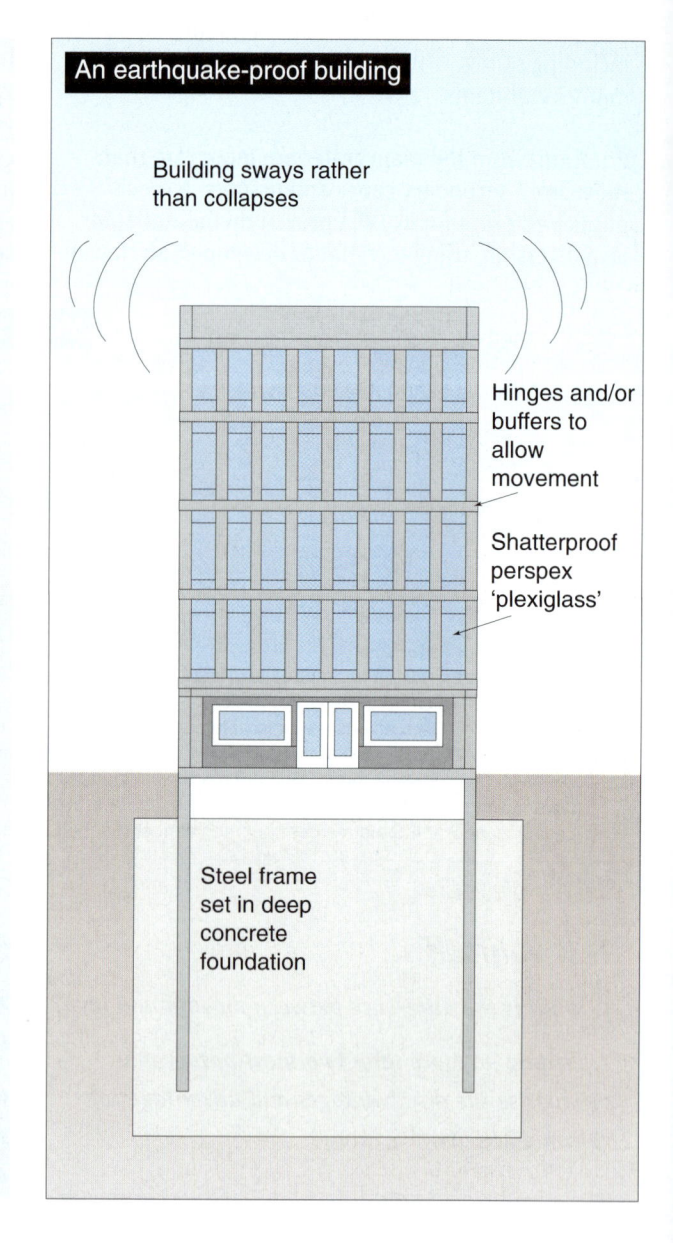

An earthquake-proof building

- Building sways rather than collapses
- Hinges and/or buffers to allow movement
- Shatterproof perspex 'plexiglass'
- Steel frame set in deep concrete foundation

Seismograph trace

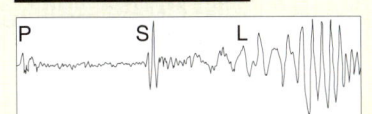

F   Focus (hypocentre)
E   Epicentre
--- P and S shockwaves
→   Surface (L) waves radiate outwards from the epicentre

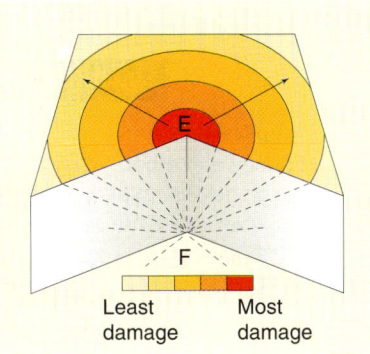

Least damage — Most damage

Seismometers are very sensitive instruments, capable of detecting and recording (on a paper trace) earthquake vibrations from thousands of kilometres away. P (**Primary**) waves arrive first, then S (**Shear**) waves followed by L (**Love**) waves which do the damage.

Earthquakes are a major natural hazard, causing high levels of death and destruction – especially in urban areas, where numerous people are buried by collapsing buildings. Many more die in the chaos and confusion which follows, as smaller, crust-settling **aftershocks** destroy already weakened structures.

Prediction and control of earthquakes

In many parts of the world, people do not accept that earthquakes represent a real danger, so they continue to build in hazardous areas. Others take a fatalistic attitude – that their fate is 'in the lap of the gods'.

Effective earthquake prediction, or even control, would be a desirable aim to help reduce suffering. Geologists have noted certain events before many 'quakes which could be read as warnings. These include:

- microquakes, before the main tremor
- bulging of the ground
- electrical changes within the rocks
- increased argon gas content in the soil.

These signs do not always occur before an earthquake, and they do not indicate a reliable time lapse before the main event.

It follows that to base evacuation of urban areas on these preliminary events would risk 'crying wolf'. Warnings might cause widespread civic panic and chaos, resulting in more harm than good. Discrete emergency service preparation is the most sensible option, given present levels of earthquake prediction.

Careful design of new buildings in urban areas can reduce the danger of collapse in earthquake zones. For example, in California (USA) and Japan, steel-framed high rise buildings are now designed to sway during a 'quake.

Contingency planning is the key. In California, highly trained relief teams have fully equipped, prefabricated emergency field hospitals in store. These are ready for rapid construction wherever needed, following a major earthquake.

Future control of some earthquakes is likely, following successful experiments on lubricating faults. Drilling 'mud' is pumped deep into the fault allowing slippage, rather than a massive build up of stress.

Test yourself

1. Name the three types of tectonic plate boundary where earthquakes occur.

2. What is the difference between the focus and the epicentre of an earthquake?

3. Why are less powerful earthquake aftershocks particularly harmful?

Stretch yourself

For any recent earthquake you have studied, prepare a key points summary using the following headings: 'Quake timing, nature and severity (eg. physical damage); Human consequences (immediate and longer term); Relief efforts (organisation and effectiveness); Lessons to be learned.

The Kobe earthquake, Japan

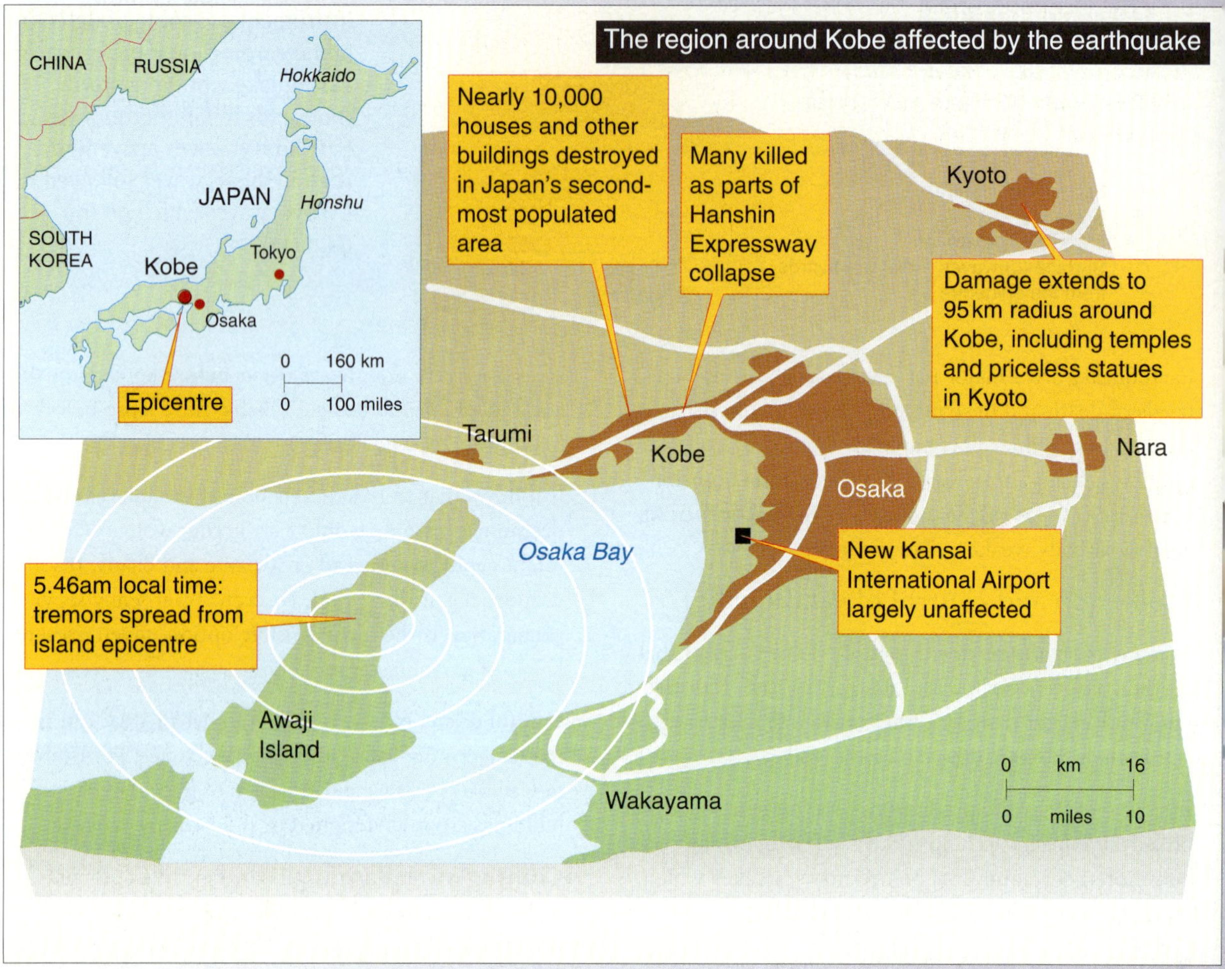
The region around Kobe affected by the earthquake
CHINA
RUSSIA
Hokkaido
JAPAN
Honshu
SOUTH KOREA
Kobe
Tokyo
Osaka
0 160 km
0 100 miles
Epicentre
Nearly 10,000 houses and other buildings destroyed in Japan's second-most populated area
Many killed as parts of Hanshin Expressway collapse
Kyoto
Damage extends to 95km radius around Kobe, including temples and priceless statues in Kyoto
Tarumi
Kobe
Nara
Osaka
Osaka Bay
New Kansai International Airport largely unaffected
5.46am local time: tremors spread from island epicentre
Awaji Island
Wakayama
0 km 16
0 miles 10

Timing	***5.46am, Tuesday January 17th, 1995***
Epicentre	***Awaji Island, Osaka Bay, Honshu***
Magnitude	***The 'quake measured 7.2 on the Richter Scale, and was Japan's worst for 50 years. The focus (hypocentre) was shallow, resulting in particularly strong shaking of the ground***
Consequences	***5000 deaths; 15,000 injuries; damage totalling £56 billion***

Japan is arguably the world's most vulnerable, yet best prepared country, regarding earthquakes. This is because it is situated on tectonically unstable ground and is densely populated, but also has great wealth. Preparedness for earthquakes is taken very seriously.

- ***All Japanese schools must, by law, have two fire and two earthquake drills each year.***
- ***Contingency plans for orderly evacuation in the event of a disaster are regularly updated.***
- ***Earthquake kits, including bottled water, emergency food, torch, first-aid kit, and protective fireproof head gear, are always on sale in shops throughout Japan.***

The historic port city of Kobe (population 1.5 million) near Osaka is an important commercial and tourist centre. Prosperous and elegant Kobe (unlike Tokyo and Yokohama) had experienced no natural disasters until this 'quake. Gracious old buildings, many made traditionally of wood, including temples, were especially vulnerable to this event.

During the 'quake and the aftershocks that followed, 12,000 buildings were damaged, along with road and rail links. Gas and water supplies were cut off, and telecommunication links paralysed. This hampered immediate relief efforts, with fire engines and ambulances having difficulty reaching the worst affected areas. Many buildings and elevated roads collapsed, despite having been built with, supposedly, sophisticated earthquake engineering. The Hanshin Expressway, for example, collapsed despite having been built to withstand 'quakes of magnitude 8.3.

Numerous fires proved hard to extinguish because water ran short. Despite public awareness and training, panic and chaos were reported. Most deaths occurred in the older residential areas, where buildings were made to less exacting standards than those expected today. Some modern steel-framed buildings that should have swayed, also collapsed. The government was criticised for poor damage prevention, and for slow, uncoordinated and inadequately equipped relief efforts.

This catastrophic event dented Japan's reputation as the world's most organised, disciplined and disaster-prepared country, and proved the necessity for ongoing review of construction design criteria and contingency planning.

Commuting and clear-up coexist along the Hanshin Expressway.

Drought

Key points

▶ Droughts are climatic hazards, associated with areas of unreliable rainfall.

▶ Droughts in the Sahel region of Africa have been associated with major famines.

▶ Australia accepts and adapts to regular drought hazard.

A **drought** is a period of continuous dry weather, and is a climatic hazard.

England and Wales occasionally suffer bad droughts – the summers of 1976 and 1995 being of particular note. Months without rain increase the demand for water, as farmers are forced to irrigate crops and gardeners endeavour to save their lawns, flowers and vegetables. During a drought, reservoir and groundwater supplies fall rapidly. Restrictions on water supply always follow, because there is no national water grid to allow efficient transfer of water from upland regions in the north and west, to areas of deficit to the south and east. Restrictions on the use of water vary from hosepipe bans to rationing. In 1995 rationing was avoided in parts of West Yorkshire only because of 24-hour road tanker convoys topping up depleted reservoirs!

Droughts in England assume very humble proportions when considered alongside those of Africa.

In recent decades the **climatic change** and rainfall uncertainty of the Sahel region (south of the Sahara Desert) has resulted in increasingly variable rainfall and a general trend of decline. From the 1920s to the 1960s the rains extended well into the southern Sahara. This encouraged people to move into the area. But in the early 1970s a series of droughts occurred along 3800km of the Sahel through Ethiopia, Sudan, Chad, Niger, Mali and Mauritania. Four years of subnormal rainfall created the worst drought for sixty years, forcing millions of pastoral nomads to migrate southwards with their animals, leaving behind barren desert.

The 1980s saw a repeat of these drought-provoked migrations, particularly in Ethiopia and Sudan. This stimulated generous charitable and governmental aid from EMDCs, but civil war and poor transport left donated grain rotting in ports. Fortunately, some of the aid was aimed at appropriate long-term agricultural improvement. This has generated hope during the 1990s.

Australia: coping with drought

Even drier countries, such as Australia, can cope with the threat of drought given sufficient planning and investment. Much of Australia is arid or semi-arid, having less than 500mm of rain per annum. But it is the variability of the rainfall that is the real problem.

On average, drought occurs once in every three years somewhere in the continent. With half of Australia's exports being commercial farm products, and one million people dependent on farming in dry areas, the effects of drought can be serious. Crop failures, livestock deaths and the financing of irrigation schemes, (as in the Snowy Mountains) are an expensive drain on the economy.

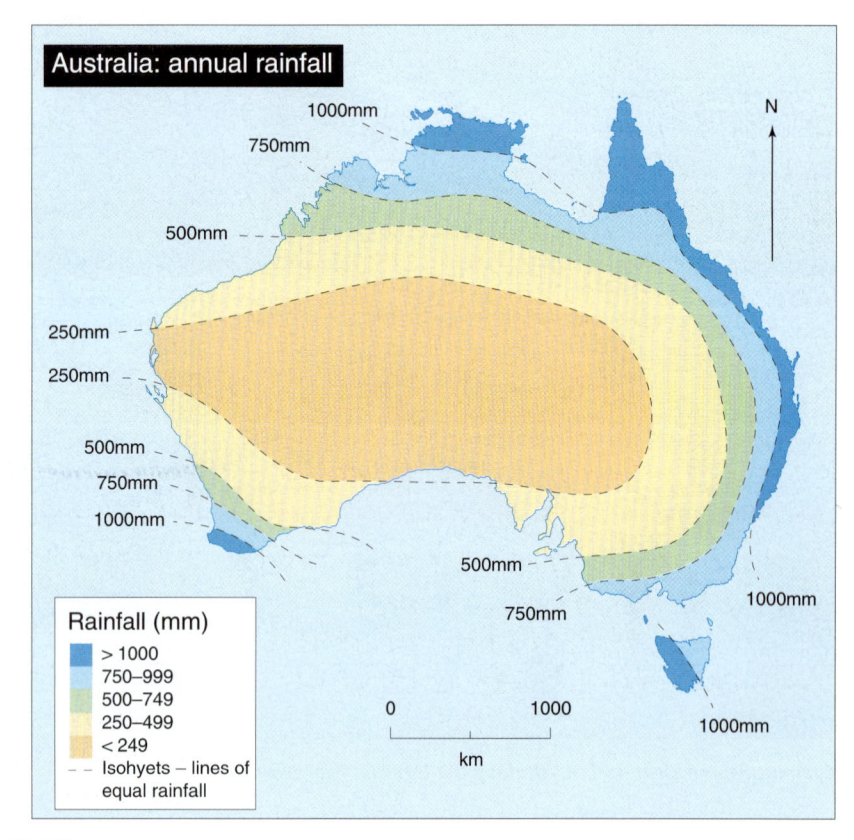

Australia: annual rainfall

Rainfall (mm)
- > 1000
- 750–999
- 500–749
- 250–499
- < 249
- Isohyets – lines of equal rainfall

As a result, Australia adopts a very realistic (pragmatic) approach of acceptance and adaptation to the hazard:

- water tanker fleets are available for emergency situations
- troops are trained to aid full-time firefighters when dry grass, scrub and trees catch fire
- crop and livestock prices increase in unaffected areas, allowing farmers to save money to cover losses when their area is (inevitably) affected
- farmers are experienced in drought management, always keeping some land fallow to conserve moisture and allow for cultivation when rains fail
- seed wastage is reduced by rapid machine planting as soon as the rains fall
- irrigation is common and co-ordinated, harnessing the tremendous reservoir potential of Australia's Great Dividing Range.

Drought in New South Wales, Australia.

A dried up lake bed, Western Australia.

Test yourself

1. Copy and complete the following sentences selecting from the alternatives given:

A drought is a period of continuous hot/dry weather. It is a geological/climatic hazard particularly common in areas with unreliable/low rainfall such as the Sahara/Sahel region of Asia/Africa.

Stretch yourself

Media coverage of major famines associated with droughts, such as those experienced in sub-Saharan Africa, tend to prompt great public pressure on EMDC governments with food surpluses, such as those within the EU, to send sufficient excess grain in order to feed everyone and so 'solve the problem'.

Consider critically this as a 'solution' by anticipating the effects on, for example, farmers in the region receiving aid.

Desertification

Key points

▶ *Desertification, the process of desert spread, represents semi-arid land degradation.*

▶ *Desertification results from human mismanagement as well as climatic change.*

Desertification is the process of desert spread, and is causing increasing concern in the areas in which it occurs. **Climatic change** and consequent lowering of rainfall may be a cause (as with the Sahel droughts, see page 156). More often it is **human mismanagement** of a fragile environment which causes desertification.

Increasing populations demand more food. Some farmers cannot afford to leave land fallow to replenish nutrients. This results in rapid exhaustion of the soil, leaving the land less able to support future crops. Increasingly poor plant cover makes the soil less able to hold water and more susceptible to wind erosion.

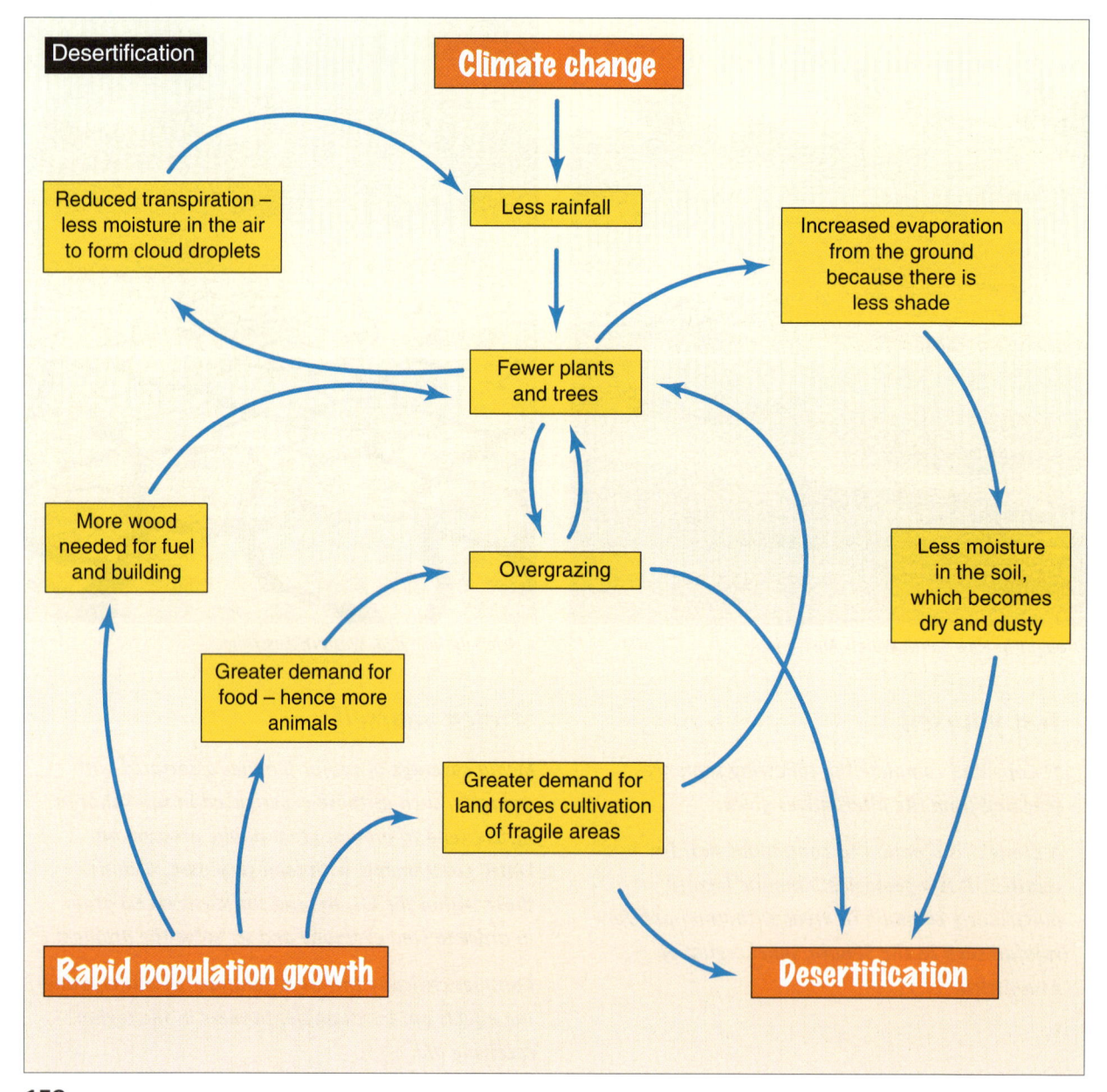

Desertification

- Climate change
- Less rainfall
- Reduced transpiration – less moisture in the air to form cloud droplets
- Increased evaporation from the ground because there is less shade
- Fewer plants and trees
- More wood needed for fuel and building
- Overgrazing
- Less moisture in the soil, which becomes dry and dusty
- Greater demand for food – hence more animals
- Greater demand for land forces cultivation of fragile areas
- Rapid population growth
- Desertification

158 ENVIRONMENTAL THEMES • HAZARDS

As **population pressure** increases, herdsmen have less space to graze cattle and goats, so animals return to graze before vegetation has had time to regrow. Overgrazing and trampling add to **soil deterioration** and create further danger of **wind erosion**. Loss of vegetation and spreading desert sands also lead to more rapid rainfall runoff. Less water retained in the soil makes future vegetation growth even more unlikely. This gradually worsening chain of events is repeated in a **vicious circle**.

The continent of Africa, with its ancient and fragile soils and uncertain rainfall, has suffered most from desertification. In the Sahel region 7 million km^2 (twice the area of India) could be at risk. As illustrated above, **land mismanagement** is a key problem. This takes four forms:

1. *Deforestation*

    The clearing of forest (for farmland and fuel) not only removes the soil's protection from sun, wind and rain, but also contributes to the decline in rainfall. This is because growing trees diffuse water, drawn through their roots, back into the atmosphere through their leaves, in a process called **transpiration**.

2. *Overgrazing*

    In the Sahel, over 20 million people are **pastoral nomads** (herdsmen), rearing cattle, goats and camels (see page 42). Reduced pasture is itself cause for concern. Too often, overgrazing is exacerbated, because large herds indicate wealth and status.

3. *Overcultivation*

    If government does not invest in agriculture to improve yields when population increases, more land is needed. Even the most marginal land, on steep slopes with thin soils, may be cultivated. Ever-shorter fallow periods, and cash-crop planting on the best land (to meet foreign debts), is intensifying the pressure on fragile land.

4. *Poor irrigation*

    Badly planned or abused irrigation schemes can be disastrous. Unlike rainwater, surface waters and some soils contain traces of salt. Continuous application of irrigation water to poorly drained schemes can cause **salinisation**. This excessive build up of salt eventually kills the crops.

Out of balance with the environment: nomadic farmers in Niger.

Test yourself

1. What is the correct sequence of factors leading to the formation of a desert? A Bare soil. B Less rain. C Desert. D Climatic change. E Vegetation dies.

2. Which one of the following is most likely to slow down the process of desertification?

    A Clearing of vegetation for more grazing land.
    B Encouraging nomads to keep more livestock.
    C Increasing the use of agrochemicals.
    D Limiting livestock numbers to stop overgrazing.
    E Cutting down more trees to provide fuel and building materials.

Stretch yourself

It is of note that satellite remote sensing of the Sahel over recent years has shown both expansion and contraction of the Sahara's margins, rather than the remorseless advance feared by many.

What environmental and human factors are likely to determine advance one year, yet retreat the next?

Global warming: the greenhouse effect

Key points

▶ CO_2 and other greenhouse gases insulate the earth.

▶ Air pollution, related to burning fossil fuels and tropical rainforests, adds to these gases.

▶ The natural greenhouse effect is now imbalanced and the earth is getting warmer.

▶ Global climatic change and rising sea levels will affect all nations and people.

▶ International cooperation and agreements on reducing greenhouse gas emissions are essential.

The **greenhouse effect** describes abnormal heating of the earth's atmosphere. An accelerating accumulation of so-called **greenhouse gases**, principally carbon dioxide (CO_2), trap heat that would otherwise escape into space. The gases act just like a glass greenhouse. They allow the short-wave radiation from the sun through to the earth, but then trap some of the longer wavelength radiation that would otherwise be emitted from the earth into the atmosphere. This means that the earth is getting warmer. Global warming is one of the most pressing environmental issues of our time, and the consequences of this huge dilemma will affect all humanity.

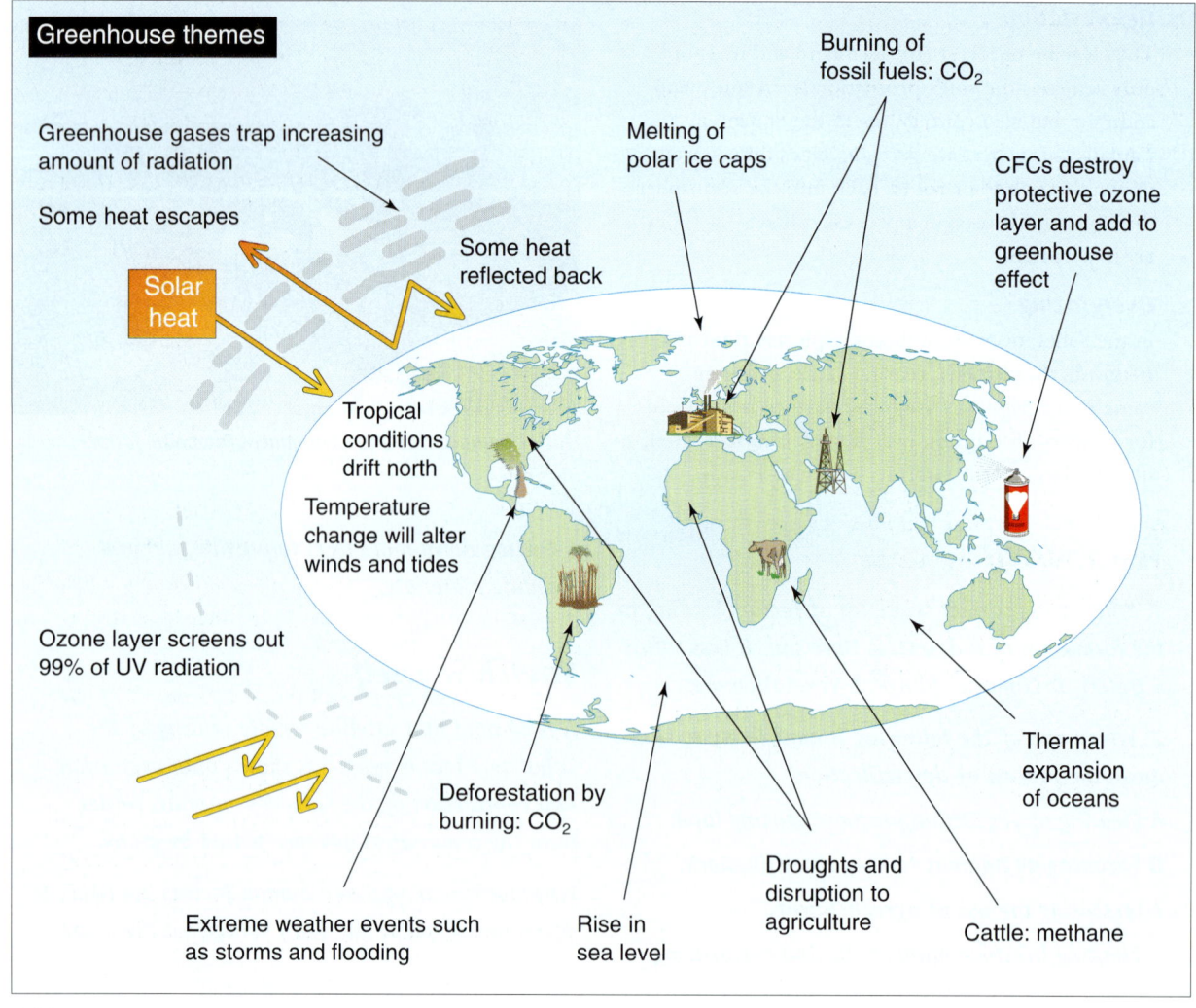

Greenhouse themes

- Greenhouse gases trap increasing amount of radiation
- Some heat escapes
- Solar heat
- Some heat reflected back
- Melting of polar ice caps
- Burning of fossil fuels: CO_2
- CFCs destroy protective ozone layer and add to greenhouse effect
- Tropical conditions drift north
- Temperature change will alter winds and tides
- Ozone layer screens out 99% of UV radiation
- Deforestation by burning: CO_2
- Extreme weather events such as storms and flooding
- Rise in sea level
- Droughts and disruption to agriculture
- Cattle: methane
- Thermal expansion of oceans

ENVIRONMENTAL THEMES • HAZARDS

The world's population is growing rapidly and as the ELDCs of the South become industrialised they burn fossil fuels at an increasing rate. CO_2 levels could easily double within the next century, thickening the 'chemical blanket' and changing rainfall patterns and sea levels, with potentially disastrous consequences.

Greenhouse gases

CO_2 accounts for about 50% of global warming. Most has come from the burning of fossil fuels, which began during the Industrial Revolution. The burning of tropical rainforests, at an average rate of over 40 hectares a minute, is another major source. (Remember – trees take CO_2 from the air, and lock up the carbon as they grow.)

Chlorofluorocarbon (CFC) gases are 10,000 times more efficient in trapping heat than CO_2.

Methane and other greenhouse gases are also important. Methane is growing even faster than CO_2; most is 'ejected' by ever-increasing numbers of cattle. Microbe activity in (rice) padi fields, the burning of industrial waste, emissions from coal mines and natural gas pipelines – all add methane to the atmosphere.

Nitrogen oxides are steadily increasing too. These are associated with the burning of fossil fuels, but also given off by fertilisers.

The last century has seen global warming of more than 0.5°C. Predictions to the 2030s range from another 1.5°C to 4.5°C. If present trends continue the world could be 8°C warmer in less than a century. These figures may seem very small (and they are predicted averages which mask variations), but in geological terms they assume enormous significance: the average temperature difference between the last Ice Age and today was only 4°C! Worldwide research into this and related issues (such as the destruction of the ozone layer), is slowly being coordinated. It is now acknowledged that unprecedented levels of international cooperation between scientists, governments, environmental pressure groups and individual citizens will be required if the effects are to be combated.

Test yourself

1. State the four main greenhouse gases and their sources.

2. Copy and complete the following sentences selecting from the alternatives given:
Global warming is a biological/climatic hazard affecting EMDCs/the whole world. Only international cooperation to limit future/past emissions of greenhouse gases will address the problems some countries/we all face relating to climatic change and sea level rise/fall.

Stretch yourself

Deterioration of the ozone layer is related to the greenhouse effect by the influence of CFCs. These are used in aerosols, foam blown plastics (often used for food cartons), computers, air conditioners and refrigerators. They drift up to attack the earth's protective ozone layer and have already caused a huge hole over the Antarctic with another developing over the Arctic. Increasing skin cancers may result.

How aware are you of 'ozone friendly' products? What individual actions and personal decisions are you already adopting to be more 'environmentally friendly'? Are there benefits of mass individual awareness about global warming and the reasons for it?

Answers to test yourself and stretch yourself exercises

P.2-3 World population distribution
1. Population distribution maps show where people are located. Population density maps show how many people live in certain areas – whether crowded, moderately or sparsely populated. 2. Population density is shown by choropleth mapping. This technique uses progressively darker shades to indicate increasing population density.

P.4-5 World population growth
1. The population explosion refers to the accelerating rate of world population growth during the 20th century. It is mainly, however, a feature of ELDCs. 2. For population to increase, there must be more births than deaths. The bigger the difference between birth and death rates, the greater the rate of population increase.

SY Long-term population forecasting is inevitably speculative. However, population growth rates in few, if any societies nowadays are determined solely by nature. As economies develop, so do educational and female career opportunities. Family planning choices will be available to more people, therefore progressively reducing the rate of growth. (However, see *Reasons for population change* below.)

P.6-7 Population distribution and growth: Egypt
1. The areas of densest population follow the River Nile. Most people, therefore, are clustered within a long but narrow region – hence linear population distribution. 2. Primary health care was devised by the World Health Organisation (WHO) to improve the health of poor people, especially children, in ELDCs. It involves schemes to improve water supply and sanitation, health education, medical services and diet. 3. Overpopulation describes a situation where an area has more people than the available resources and technology can support.

SY Family planning is, inevitably, a sensitive issue. Egypt's revised approach appreciates religious and cultural sensitivities in a cost-effective programme. It integrates family planning into primary health care schemes that use local skills to the benefit of all.

P.8-9 Reasons for population change
1.(a) A high rate of population growth is more than 2.5%. (b) A low rate is less than 1%. 2.(a) Debilitating diseases, such as bilharzia, make people unwell enough to prevent them working efficiently. However, they are not necessarily fatal. (b) Diseases of affluence include heart disease, stroke and cancer. They are associated with over-indulgence and stress in EMDCs.

SY The experience of most EMDCs would suggest that economic advancement leads to smaller families, due to improved health and lower mortality, the spread of education and new economic expectations. However, many ELDCs, such as Kenya, find that economic development can lead to faster population growth rates as improvements in diet and health care lower infant mortality rates.

P.10-11 Population structure
1. A population pyramid is a mirror bar graph showing age-sex structure. 2. A dependency ratio expresses the number of dependent children and aged supported by working adults. 3. Population problems in ELDCs could be summarised as too many children and rapid growth. In EMDCs, however, the problem is usually an ageing population.

SY In ELDCs, high birth rates result in a large proportion of the population being under 15 years old. Within a few years these 'juveniles' become fertile young adults producing children of their own. Even with reductions in family size due to family planning programmes, the absolute population numbers continue to grow rapidly. Consequently, poverty, malnutrition, and so on increase also. In EMDCs, the so-called 'population time bomb' is their increasingly 'top heavy' age structures. The growing threat is that there will be insufficient tax-paying working adults to support their pension requirements.

P.12-13 Cycles of misery
1.(a) Low productivity means not enough being produced, on average, per person. (b) Lethargy refers to tiredness and a lack of energy. (c) A deficiency disease is caused by a lack of essential nutrients in the diet. (d) Anyone undernourished simply does not have enough food. (e) Anyone malnourished has an inadequately balanced diet.

SY ELDC cycles of virtue

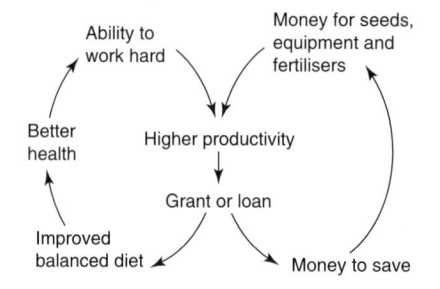

Ability to work hard → Higher productivity → Grant or loan → Money to save → Money for seeds, equipment and fertilisers → Higher productivity → Improved balanced diet → Better health → Ability to work hard

P.16-17 Types of migration
1.(a) Temporary migration – commuting. (b) Permanent migration – changing address. (c) Voluntary migration – West Indian immigration into Britain. (d) Forced migration – refugee movements. 2.(a) To commute is to travel regularly to and from work. (b) A dormitory settlement is one, such as a village, where the majority of residents are commuters living and so sleeping there. (c) Economic migrants move seeking employment and so financial opportunities. (d) Refugees are forced to move for safety – to flee war, persecution, or natural disaster. (e) Push factors force people to move. (f) Pull factors are opportunities, anticipated or actual, that attract migrants.

P.20-21 What is a settlement?

1. A conurbation is a large, sprawling urban area formed by the merging of towns and cities. 2. Site is the actual land a settlement is built on, whereas situation refers to its position relative to other places or landscape features. 3.(a) Important original settlement location factors include water and wood supply, dry, sheltered, fertile land, defensibility. (b) Water supply is still an important EMDC settlement location factor, but could be supplied by Water Companies using pipelines. Fertile land is irrelevant to urban industrial settlements, as is a wood supply for construction and fuel. 'Civil order' and agencies of the law, such as the police, remove the need to defend your own settlement.

P.22-23 Settlement hierarchy, spacing and service provision

1.(a) A hierarchy is a ranked order of importance. (b) Range represents the maximum distance someone is prepared to travel for a good or service. (c) The threshold is the minimum number of customers required to keep a business going. (d) Low order goods tend to be cheap and bought frequently. (e) High order goods and services are more expensive and obtained less frequently. (f) Hypermarkets are very large self-service superstores often found in suburban out-of-town locations. (g) Suburban retail parks often contain hypermarkets. They offer shopping facilities with easy car parking and a variety of both complementary and competing stores.

SY People's expectations have increased over recent decades with the rising incomes of many. More working and independent women, for example, reduce the time available for 'traditional' roles such as food preparation. Wealth and new technology have improved choice – hence ownership of cars, freezers, microwave ovens and so on which allow busy people to enjoy, for example, wider diets, with less effort.

P.24-25 Urbanisation and urban growth

1.(a) Urban means built-up – usually a town or city. (b) Rural refers to open land – the countryside. (c) Urbanisation reflects a population change from rural to urban locations. (d) Counter-urbanisation refers to the reverse of urbanisation – a change from urban to rural locations. 3. Asia is the world's most populated continent, and has the most millionaire cities. 4.(a) 1300 million. (b) 700 million.

SY The world's rural population has grown at an increasing rate from 900 million in 1800 to a likely 3000 million in 2000. In contrast, the world's urban population has also grown, but at a far more rapidly accelerating rate from 50 million in 1800 to a likely 3100 million in 2000.

P.26-27 Urban problems – and solutions – in ELDCs

1.(a) Shanty towns are settlements of shacks, built at very high densities, usually on the outskirts of ELDC cities. They are built by incoming migrants who often squat illegally. (b) They are neither planned, served with basic utilities, or constructed from conventional materials. 2. Site and service schemes are self-help projects, often funded by UN agencies, which provide incoming migrants with building plots laid out with basic services such as roads, water supply and sewerage. 3. The informal service sector of an ELDC economy refers to tax avoiding self-employment in services such as shoe-shining and street trading.

SY The poor in Britain could expect to qualify for subsidised housing, with power and piped water, and to receive education and health care as a right. Basic dietary needs could also be expected to be met, and television considered normal. In India, however, poverty is more likely to be abject, with the rights and expectations outlined above considered a luxury.

P.30–31 Urban land-use zones and models

1. The central business district (CBD) is likely to be found in the centre of an urban area. This is because historically the CBD has been the most accessible place for businesses to maximise their customers and so profits. Consequently shops, banks, offices and so on will have outbid all other potential land-uses to achieve a central location. 2.(a) A model in Geography is a diagram or theory used to simplify reality. A good model would be neither too generalised, nor too complicated. (b) Models help Geographers understand and explain key aspects of the complex real world.

SY Urban land-use models take no account of variations in relief, or how settlements change over time according to historical events and, latterly, planning decisions.

P.34–35 Organised urban change

1. A planner directs and monitors urban change. It is his/her job to determine, for the benefit of residents, business and visitors what needs changing, when and how. This involves consulting all interested parties before making decisions on new building and transport developments. 2.(a) Suburban sprawl represents the uncontrolled expansion of built-up areas into the surrounding countryside. (b) Green belts and wedges control this sprawl. The former are 'rings' of open countryside beyond the established urban outskirts, protected from new development by strict planning controls. (c) Green wedges are more realistic given the need for transport routes into the urban area. They can allow inner city residents easier access to open space.

SY Copenhagen's overall theme has been to allow the urban area to expand because people wanted to move out from congested and deteriorating inner city districts. However, the expansion has been in a controlled manner, in order to ensure access to open spaces and new suburban employment opportunities.

P.38–39 Transport and urban traffic management

1.(a) Transport mode refers to the means of transport – whether by road, rail or air, for example. (b) A transport network is the system of routes (links) connecting places (nodes). (c) The pedestrian/vehicle conflict expresses common city centre problems of congestion, pollution and accidents relating to too many vehicles having to share roads with pedestrian shoppers, workers and visitors.

P.40–41 Farming as a system

1. C. 2.(a) Arable farms grow crops, whereas pastoral farms rear animals. (b) Near-subsistence farming produces food mainly for the family's own consumption. Commercial farming is 'agribusiness' producing crops and/or animals for sale. (c) Intensive farming achieves high outputs through labour or capital investment in machinery and agrochemicals. Extensive farming, in contrast, invests less – with reduced outputs as a result.

P.42–43 ELDC extensive farming systems

1. Pastoral nomadism and shifting cultivation are examples. 2. They can only support very low densities of population. Consequently rapid population growth threatens these systems. Also, governments object to the tribes ignoring political borders.

SY (a) Small separated rainforest clearings are sheltered from direct rainsplash and wind erosion by the surrounding trees acting as a windbreak. (b) Cutting the trees to shoulder height does not kill them. Consequently, their living roots continue to bind the soil together and they regenerate quickly once the clearings are abandoned. (c) Only cultivating the clearings for 3 to 5 years ensures that the soil is not totally exhausted. The rainforest, consequently, can successfully restore itself. Overcultivation, however, would leave virtually bare, exhausted soil vulnerable to erosion.

P.44–45 ELDC intensive farming systems

1. Plantation agriculture and rice cultivation are examples. 2. Such systems are highly productive – producing high yields per hectare. 3. Rice is very nutritious – rich in carbohydrate, fibre and vegetable protein. It also stores well.

SY 'Native' wages may be very low and jobs insecure because plantation products are vulnerable to fluctuating demands from overseas markets. Also, much of the profit generated is likely to return to the multinational's EMDC of origin. Finally, monoculture is very susceptible to pests and diseases.

P.48–49 Farming in Britain

1.(a) Physical factors influencing farming in Britain include variations in climate, landscape (relief) and soils. (b) Human factors include transport, nearness to markets, likely profits, plus CAP influences such as guaranteed prices, intervention buying, grants, quotas and set-aside.

SY The contrast between hill sheep and arable farming illustrates this well. Hill sheep farming is associated with upland areas, such as the NW Highlands of Scotland, where steep slopes, heavy precipitation, leached soils and cool July temperatures prohibit more profitable forms of agriculture. Hardy sheep are, however, particularly suited to such relatively hostile conditions. In contrast, the flat lowlands of E Anglia and Lincolnshire, for example, with moderate precipitation, thick fertile soils and warm sunny summers allow highly profitable arable cultivation.

P.50–51 The European Union

1. Current members of the EU are France, Italy, Netherlands (Holland), Germany, Belgium, Luxembourg, UK, Irish Republic (Eire), Denmark, Greece, Spain, Portugal, Sweden, Finland, Austria. 2.(a) Intervention buying, by the CAP, guarantees farmers a set price for their produce. However, it led to overproduction and vast stockpiles – the infamous food 'mountains and lakes'. (b) Quotas, set for each farmer, now limit production. (c) Subsidies continue to support less profitable, but nonetheless important forms of agriculture, such as hill sheep farming. (d) Set-aside limits production further by reducing the arable cultivated area.

P.52–53 An EU problem region: southern Italy

1. Italy's affluent North can be contrasted to its relatively poorer South. 2. The Mezzogiorno's physical problems included rugged relief, Mediterranean climate and thin soils. (b) Human problems included overdependence on inefficient farming, absentee landlords, land fragmentation, poverty, ill health and poor infrastructure (roads, water supplies, sewerage and so on).

SY (a) Rugged relief, with restricted accessibility, poor soils and undrained marshes are not untypical of ELDCs. Likewise, difficult climates with, for example, droughts followed by severe rainfall are not uncommon. Furthermore, the human problems listed above – all 'pushing' migrants to urban industrial areas – are also typical. (b) The 'solutions' adopted in this case would be denied to most ELDCs, simply because of their high cost.

P.54–55 Farming and public awareness

1. Malnutrition and undernourishment are still common because global food production is not evenly distributed. Consequently, many ELDCs face great shortages which they cannot afford to overcome by buying from EMDCs with surpluses. 2. 'Factory farming' uses intensive methods such as stall feeding and feed additives, whereas 'organic' methods are natural – using no artificial aids.

SY To combat erosion, depending on the examples chosen, you might consider soil conservation measures such as: (a) reforestation and afforestation (b) hedge and tree windbreak planting (c) controlled grazing (d) contour ploughing and terracing (e) fallow periods, intercropping, strip cropping and crop rotation.

P.56–57 A multi-purpose river project: the Aswan High Dam, Egypt

1. Benefits include controlled river flow, so all year navigation and no flooding. Abundant HEP is available for urban industrial demands and to pump irrigation water for extra cultivation of both near-subsistence and cash crops. New fishing and, particularly, tourism opportunities have been created. Problems include the high cost of construction – with loans still not paid back. Both local people and antiquities had to be relocated. Silting of Lake Nasser will need dredging in future, yet the delta downstream, deprived of alluvial silt and flood water, is now 'out of balance' and suffering degradation. Finally, bilharzia is spreading due to the increased use of irrigation.

SY Each country sharing the Nile's water has an agreed responsibility to those downstream to control both the amount abstracted for urban industrial and irrigation uses and the pollutants released into the river. Political tensions could arise if countries abuse these responsibilities. (NB Egypt is 'at the end of the line'.)

P.58–59 Sources of energy

1. Renewable energy resources, such as hydroelectric, wind and solar power can be used over and over again. In other words they will never run out. Non-renewable resources such as coal, oil and uranium (a mineral ore used as nuclear fuel) can be used only once and so will, eventually, run out. In other words they are 'finite'.

SY The British electricity supergrid is densest in and around the main (urban) market areas. It links coal-fired power stations on the coalfields to highland HEP plants, and coastal oil and nuclear installations.

P.60–61 Coal in Britain

1. Open cast mining extracts the 'exposed' coal directly from surface quarries. Deep shaft mining, however, involves sinking shafts through overlying rocks to gain access to 'concealed' coal measures deep underground.

SY Up to the mid-1970s British electricity generation was effectively dominated by coal. Consequently, the miners exercised great power when, for example, striking in support of wage claims. Since then contraction in the coal industry has become more apparent. Cleaner fuels have been encouraged for electricity generation, industry and homes. Thousands of miners have lost their livelihoods, causing hardship in mining communities. Many argue that the decline of the British coal industry has been politically motivated – to reduce the power of the miners – and that environmental concerns have been used as a justification.

P.62–63 Oil and natural gas

1. Advantages of North Sea oil and gas include self-sufficiency which has reduced the need to obtain these relatively expensive fuels from other sources. In addition, taxation revenues have boosted the British economy further. Thousands of new jobs have been created – both directly and in support services. Disadvantages tend to be environmental. Pollution incidents, for example, regularly affect the fishing industry. However, in the long-term, the economy will have to rely less on oil and natural gas resources as they become more scarce.

SY Anti-pollution research continues into developing ever more efficient booms and dispersants. However, arguably most effective would be stricter enforcement of laws prohibiting the deliberate discharge of (oily) ballast offshore.

P.64–65 Hydroelectric power

1. Night-time electricity consumption is low, with daily peaks associated with, for example, preparing for and returning from work. Seasonal fluctuations are, to a point, predictable – but 'cold snaps' can replicate winter demands in other seasons.
2. Immediately before a popular TV programme, or following it – and certainly during a commercial break – demand surges as thousands of consumers switch on kettles, go to the toilet and so on. 3. Pumped storage schemes can 'absorb' spare electricity from conventional sources (by using it to pump water to the top reservoir). The power is, therefore, stored as potential energy which is released when electricity generating capacity is needed.

SY Advantages include the generating flexibility, minimal pollution (visual only) and low running costs once the scheme is constructed. Disadvantages include the 'drowning' of large areas of particularly useful (low) land in highland regions. Unfortunately such regions are often remote from urban areas demanding the most electricity. Consequently, much HEP potential remains unexploited.

P. 66–67 Nuclear power

1. The mineral ore uranium fuels nuclear power stations. 2. Safety and nearness to large amounts of water for cooling are the two most important location factors. A coastal location is usually viewed as easier to 'evacuate'.

P.68–69 ELDC energy: a case for alternatives?

1. HEP; biomass; biogas; solar; wind; geothermal; tidal; wave. 2. The most important reason why ELDCs should adopt renewable energy resources is because in the long-term they should prove far cheaper than non-renewables.

SY Virtually all of Britain's (economic) HEP potential is now exploited. 'Wind farms' are increasingly common in upland areas and likely to be constructed offshore in future. Wave and tidal power offers further potential – with the Severn Estuary considered a possible site for a major tidal barrage. Solar power in southern regions could become more realistic in the long-term, as global warming shifts Mediterranean climatic conditions northwards. Egypt's HEP potential is best demonstrated by the Aswan High Dam scheme. Solar power also offers great scope in this desert country – providing it could be made more cost-effective. Wind power also has potential, but turbines would be vulnerable to damage from blowing sand.

P.70–71 Energy and the environment

1.(a) Fossil fuels, such as coal, oil and gas, are the remains of plants and tiny sea creatures which lived millions of years ago. Forests were drowned when sea levels rose, and the rotting vegetation was buried under deposits of sand and mud. Compression changed these deposits into sedimentary rocks with oil and gas deposits trapped within the strata. (b) Rain is naturally acid. However, acid rain refers to particularly acidic precipitation polluted by sulphur dioxide and nitrogen oxides emitted from the burning of fossil fuels. (c) Pollution is an all-embracing term for any contamination or spoliation of the environment. (d) Conservation refers to preservation, protection and 'cleaning up' of the environment.

SY 'Green energy' is better, rather than perfect, in an environmental sense. Even renewable energy resources have some disadvantages – but they usually tend to be visually intrusive rather than ecologically damaging.

P.72–73 Employment structure

1.(a) Burundi and Ethiopia are ELDCs. Brazil and South Korea are NICs. The UK and USA are EMDCs. (b) The ELDCs are dominated by primary occupations and are therefore positioned at the apex (top) of this particular triangular graph. NICs have more balanced industrial structures and so are found in the centre of the graph. The EMDCs are dominated by tertiary occupations and are, consequently, positioned at the bottom of the graph. (c) As a country develops, it moves towards the bottom left of this graph.

SY The rate of economic development is suggested by the length of line. The longer the line, the more rapid the rate.

P.74–75 Industrial systems and location factors

1. D. 2.(a) Power, raw materials and site conditions such as firm, flat, accessible land are physical industrial location factors. (b) Labour, markets, transport, capital and government intervention through local and regional planning are human factors.

P.76–77 Industrial location at global, national and local scales

1. Modern industrial estates are usually located away from town centres because of their high land values and traffic congestion.
2. Infrastructure is an all-embracing term used to describe an area's basic framework of, for example, power and water supplies, transport networks, industrial, commercial and domestic services such as sewerage and telecommunications, and education facilities.

SY The late eighteenth to early twentieth century Industrial Revolution in Europe was mainly powered by coal-fired steam engines. Coalfield locations industrialised because coal was so bulky to transport. European nations introduced industrialisation into their colonies during this period. Indeed, it is notable, nowadays, that many former colonies, such as India, continue to industrialise using coal as an important power resource.

P.80–81 Industrial activity and pollution

1.(a) The four categories of pollution discussed are air, water, noise and visual. (b) Air and noise pollution in the Lower Swansea Valley came from coalmining and heavy industry – especially smelting. Water in the River Tawe and canals was polluted by industrial effluent. Visual pollution came from slag heaps and, latterly, derelict factories, abandoned infrastructure and wasteland.

P.82–83 The iron and steel industry: development and change

1. Likely location requirements would include: raw materials, power, water, labour, flat land, transport and accessibility. 2. Rationalisation means to improve efficiency by more effective organisation. It normally involves, therefore, reducing the workforce and reorganising those left to be more productive. Nationalisation refers to national governments taking over ownership and so control of an industry. (Many industries in Britain, such as coal and steel, were nationalised following World War II. Most have since been 'privatised' – returned to independent ownership.)

SY Recycling of scrap iron and steel is increasingly common.

P.84–85 OS map skills

1. Sandfields (74 90) is a built-up residential area. 2. A roundabout at 795 862 links junction 38 of the M4 with the A48(T). 3. The total map area shown, exceeds 120 square kilometres. 4. The nearest beacon to the one at 742 883 is 450m to the ENE. 5. At a scale of 1:100,000, each grid line on the map would be 1cm apart. 6. From 778 889 to 790 889 the slope starts very steep before becoming progressively gentler. The slope aspect is westerly overall.

SY (a) 80 93 shows upland slopes well drained by streams running in v-shaped valleys. 78 86 is flat lowland, below 10m, and drained artificially by ditches. (b) Margam (78 87) lies SE of Port Talbot. It is a linear settlement following the A48(T) and constrained to the east by the M4 and steep slopes beyond. It occupies a mainly flat site and probably serves the heavy industry (steel works) to its SW. (c) The steel works occupies a large flat, drained site. It needs the dense rail network, linked to the docks at Port Talbot, because both its raw materials (including coal) and finished products are very bulky. It has additional power from electricity, fresh water supplies for cooling (772 865) and access to a large labour force in both Margam and Port Talbot. The oil refinery (71 95) also has power, cooling water (702 954), access to labour and freight railway lines. However, it additionally has pipeline and canal transport. The most unusual feature about this site is that it is on hilly ground – presumably because Crymlyn Bog to the west could not be drained. (d) The principal routeways across this map extract, including railway, A and B roads, and the M4 motorway, are constrained by the variable relief. A common theme is that they define the lower edges of steep slopes. (e) South of northing 90, the most common hill top land-use is mixed wood.

P.86–87 The micro-electronics industry: Silicon Glen and science parks

1. A footloose industry has a relatively free choice of location. 2. Skilled workers represent the most important location factor in high tech industries. Good transport, research facilities and attractive out-of-town locations are also important. 3. A greenfield site develops open countryside for urban growth.

SY As more firms want to move into an area, so the value (and consequently cost) of land goes up. Similarly, increasing (and so competing) demand for appropriately skilled staff increases their salary demands. Rival firms may attract your expensively trained workers through better salaries and/or conditions. However, too many new firms would lead to overproduction and, consequently, failure of the least competitive. At worst, a recession could close many firms, leading to high unemployment in the area.

P.88–89 Manufacturing industry in ELDCs

1.(a) The modern sector is factory based, in major cities, and similar to industry in EMDCs. (b) The traditional sector is rural based 'cottage industry', using craft skills and appropriate technology. 2. C.

SY Limited capital, the high cost of imported fuel and raw materials, plus poorly educated and industrially unskilled workers prohibits 'modern' industrialisation in rural areas. However, ready availability of, for example, local agricultural based raw materials and abundant workers with craft skills, encourages 'traditional' approaches.

P.90–91 Multinational companies and aid

1. Multinational companies are usually run from EMDCs, have branch factories worldwide, produce the world's main brand-name goods, are massive employers and make huge profits. 3. Aid is the giving of money, technology and resources by one country, or an organisation, to another country.

P.92–93 World development characteristics

1. North: North America, Europe and Australasia. South: South America, Africa and Asia. 2. Stage 1: Amazonia. 2: Bangladesh. 3: India. 4: Portugal. 5: UK.

P.94–95 World development measures

1. There is a negative correlation between GNP per capita and infant mortality. 2. Poorer ELDCs are associated with higher infant mortality, greater numbers of patients per doctor, low rates of adult literacy, low industrial energy consumption and few newspapers sold per thousand people.

SY This last measure is a particularly sophisticated indication of development because it gives information about literacy, 'disposable' income available for a luxury (rather than a necessity) and people's desire to be informed.

P.96–97 World trade

1.(a) A commodity is a useful product. (b) Imports are commodities from abroad. (c) Exports are commodities sent abroad. (d) A deficit results from a company or country spending more than it earns. (e) A surplus is the opposite. (f) A tariff is (usually) a duty or tax on imported goods.

SY (a) Similar companies join together to form cartels. (b) This is bad for the consumer because they restrict competition and so control market prices unfairly.

P.98–99 Tourism

1.(a) Leisure is free time. (b) Recreation refers to the means people adopt to enjoy their leisure. (c) Tourism involves travelling for this recreation. 2. B.

P.102–103 National Parks

1. Honeypot locations are not just beauty spots. They include any recreational area or facility prone to overcrowding. This is because people 'swarm' to them 'like bees to a honeypot'. 2. D Workers/holiday houses.

P.106-107 Limestone landforms

1. (c) 2. (e) 3. (d) 4. (b) 5. (a). 6. (a) Permeable rock allows water to pass through it. In pervious limestone the water flows along bedding planes and down joints. In porous chalk it passes through pore spaces. (b) Impermeable rock is effectively solid – allowing no water through.

SY Water samples both from upstream of a swallow hole (sink) and immediately downstream of the area under investigation could be tested for both pH and (soluble) calcium content (calcium hydrogencarbonate). An increase in both, recorded downstream, would suggest that the river had flowed through limestone.

P.108–109 Glacial landforms of erosion

1. (i) 2. (f) 3. (g) 4. (j) 5. (b) 6. (h) 7. (a) 8. (d) 9. (c) 10. (e).

SY Glaciers are dirty because, for sufficient snow to compress into glacial ice, 20 to 30 years of accumulation is required. Consequently, frost-shattered rock debris from the slopes above will be mixed in with it. Rock debris also falls down crevasses (major cracks in the ice) and is plucked and abraded from the valley walls and floor. Alpine valley glaciers in summer, for example, once the surface snow melts, look like frozen slag heaps!

P.110–111 Glacial landforms of deposition

1.(a) 8. (b) 3. (c) 1. (d) 9. (e) 2. (f) 10. (g) 5. (h) 6. (i) 4. (j) 7.

P.112-113 Coastal landforms of erosion

1.(a) Water running up the beach from a breaking wave is called swash. (b) Water returning back down the beach is called backwash. (c) The swash from summer constructive waves is stronger than the backwash. As a result, material from the nearshore zone is transported up to build the beach.
(d) During winter storms destructive waves break more frequently. The backwash has less time to drain away and so the returning surface water drags material back down the beach.
2. Waves erode the coast by solution (corrosion), abrasion (corrasion), attrition and hydraulic action.
3. Joint – cave – arch – stack – stump.

SY As the cliff retreats, the wave cut platform expands. However, the bigger the platform gets, the more wave energy is lost, through friction, rolling over it. There must come a point, therefore, when there is not enough energy left over to continue eroding the wave cut notch. Consequently, the cliff retreat sequence stops. This point might be illustrated by the cliff foot end of the sloping wave cut platform still being exposed at high tide.

P.114-115 Coastal landforms of deposition

1.(a) Longshore drift is caused by waves and so swash running up a beach at an angle. The backwash returns, however, directly down the beach. Consequently, material is moved along the beach in zig-zag movements. (b) Groynes are breakwater fences built at regular intervals along holiday beaches to stop longshore drift removing all the material. (c) Coastal defence using rock armour (piles of granite blocks) has proved a cheap alternative to solid concrete sea walls. (d) Rebuilding beaches using sand dredged from offshore is called beach nourishment.

SY Hard engineering is the traditional, expensive approach using, for example, concrete sea walls to deflect the waves. In contrast, soft engineering, such as beach nourishment, is cheaper and makes informed use of 'nature's own defences'.

P.116-117 River landforms

1. Rivers near their source flow down steep gradients eroding V-shaped valleys. Nearer the river mouth, however, gradients are gentler. The river contains more water and sediment and meanders over a wide flood plain of deposited material called alluvium.

SY Likely river channel alterations include deepening and straightening to allow easier navigation. Banks are often reinforced to fix the channel's course, particularly in urban areas. Levées may be built higher to reduce the risk of flooding. Smaller channels may be culverted underground, to allow building above (see OS map page 85, grid square 76 90).

P.118-119 Drainage basins and storm hydrographs

1.(a) A drainage (river) basin is an area of land drained by a river and its tributaries. (b) A drainage divide (watershed) is a ridge of higher land separating one drainage basin from another. 2. E. 3. A storm (flood) hydrograph is a graph which shows how river discharge responds to a particular rainstorm. It is used to assess flood risk.

SY Rain is intercepted by foliage (leaves and branches) and some of this water is evaporated directly from it. Most, however, eventually drips through or trickles down branches and the stem before spreading along root channels deep into the soil. All these natural delays give the area time to cope with the rainstorm water – rather than running straight off a bare, compacted surface and immediately into the river system.

P.120-121 Weather recording

1.(a) 17°C; 8 oktas cloud; SSW wind 8-12 knots, Beaufort force 2; 1005mb; rain.
(b) 18°C; 4 oktas cloud; SW wind 3-7 knots, Beaufort force 1; 1015mb.
2. Weather station equipment should be located well away from buildings which may shade instruments and deflect or shelter the wind and rain. Likewise a tarmac surface could affect temperature and humidity readings by heating up in direct sunlight.

SY Low humidity would cause a large temperature difference because the water soaking the wet bulb's muslin wrapping would evaporate and so cool this thermometer.

P.122-123 Temperature and rainfall

1. Latitude, altitude, distance from sea, prevailing winds, cloudiness and aspect are the main factors which determine the temperature of a place.
2. The warm south-facing aspect is more built-up. It is warm enough to grow arable crops on the lower slopes and deciduous trees further up. Conifers on the highest ground extend much lower down into grazing on the shaded and so cooler north-facing slopes. 3. All rainfall formation involves warm, moist air being forced to rise and cool.

SY The white surface of snow and ice will reflect much of the sunlight – so reducing polar temperatures further.

P.124-125 Depressions and anticyclones

1.(a) Isobars close together indicate strong winds in a depression. (b) The widely spaced isobars in an anticyclone indicate gentle, if any, wind.

SY High cirrus clouds, falling pressure and increasing wind speeds would indicate the arrival of the depression. This would be followed by steady rain from nimbostratus clouds. A calmer period of drizzle or showers would then follow with rising temperatures (in the warm sector). Heavy rain with perhaps hail and thunder from towering cumulonimbus clouds would come next. Rising pressure, very strong winds from a different direction and falling temperatures would then indicate the arrival of the 'chasing' cold front. Finally, showers from clearing skies would complete the passing of the depression before the next weather system arrives.

P.126-127 World climates
1.(a) The Mediterranean climate has hot, dry summers and warm, wet winters. (b) The hot desert climate is dry, with high temperatures all year unless moderated by the sea. (c) The tropical continental climate is warm overall with a dry, slightly cooler season followed by a hot, wet season. (d) The equatorial climate is hot, wet and humid throughout the year.

SY Deforestation, by reducing transpiration, has been proved to be significant in contributing to climatic change in areas, such as the Sahel, now suffering desertification. Global warming is now accepted to be due to an accelerating accumulation of greenhouse gases, especially CO_2, emitted by industrialised countries. Furthermore, with ELDCs industrialising and tropical rainforests being cleared, there is potential for significant further climatic change in future.

P.128-129 Tropical rainforests
1.(a) Biota is a collective name for all plants and animals. (b) An ecosystem is an ordered and highly integrated community of plants and animals within a distinctive environment. (c) A habitat is the natural home of a plant or animal. (d) Humus is the dark-coloured, organic top layer of the soil. 2. Tribal homelands, plant species, animal habitats and medicines are lost with tropical rainforest destruction.

SY Deforestation need not be destructive. The key issue is that responsibility for rainforests needs to be taken by the relevant national governments. More National Parks and Forest Reserves would help – but they are not essential providing that mining and logging companies are controlled. The latter, for example, should only be granted licences on condition that they replant as many trees as they cut. Certainly, clearance by burning should be avoided wherever possible. Furthermore, trade restrictions could be placed on endangered hardwood species (in the same way that rare animals are protected).

P.130-131 Savanna grasslands
1. Rainforest – parkland – savanna grassland – scrub – desert. 2. A xerophytic plant is drought resistant.

SY Increasing herd sizes of domesticated animals, such as the Fulani's long-horn cattle, are making problems related to overgrazing, such as soil erosion, worse. Larger tribes also need more land to cultivate their near-subsistence crops. More trees and shrubs are cleared, therefore – for land, fuelwood and building materials. Vegetation clearance contributes to soil erosion and encourages desertification.

P.132-133 Deserts
1. Hostile desert conditions ensure that only tough plants can survive. Special qualities are necessary in this dry environment. Cacti, for example, have waxy skins to reduce transpiration and some have deep roots to tap groundwater.

SY During the day there is no cloud cover to shade the sun. Rapid and extremely effective heating of the land surface results. At night, however, the lack of clouds means that there is no insulation for the land. Consequently, the heat of the day radiates rapidly away.

P.134-135 Natural hazards and disasters
1. A natural hazard is a sudden, severe event, such as a flood or earthquake, where the natural environment becomes difficult, if not impossible to manage. Should people fail to cope with it, resulting in many deaths and much damage to property, then it would be called a disaster.
2.(a) Meteorological hazards: tropical revolving storms, tornadoes, willy-willies, blizzards, snowstorms, thunderstorms, floods, droughts, fog, fire and icebergs. (b) Geological hazards: earthquakes, volcanic eruptions, tsunamis, landslides and avalanches. (c) Biological hazards: pests.

P.136-137 Tropical revolving storms
1. For tropical revolving storms to develop the season has to be late summer early autumn (when trade winds meet at a similar altitude), ocean temperatures must be greater than 27°C and the coriolis force must be strong. 2. Contingency planning refers to all the preparations made in advance of a likely hazard. For example, it might include evacuation plans and practice drills, food, water and medical stockpiles, special building designs and flood defences.

P.140–141 Floods
1. E. 2. Possible solutions to the problems of flooding along a river include raising levées, straightening the course of the channel and planting trees to reduce surface runoff.

SY In both EMDCs and ELDCs low-lying flood plains tend to be accessible (usually nearer the sea) and to enjoy excellent soil quality. Their flat land is easy to build on.

P.142–143 Flooding in Bangladesh
1. During a cyclone torrential rain will increase the flood danger. 2. Early warnings broadcasted by radio are proving far more effective than newspapers or television because radios do not require literacy and are widely available.

SY The infrequency of tsunamis and the misleading term 'tidal wave' do not help promote an understanding that they are a sequence of waves. Coastal survivors would be desperate to return to the shore in order to help relatives, friends and other victims caught in the first wave. Yet those who return are exposed to swamping from bigger waves yet to come!

P.144–145 Mass movements
1. Flows are progressive movements where the surface layers move quicker than the material deeper down. Slides are sudden movements where the material gives way in one mass. 2. A mudflow contains up to 50% water. An earthflow, however, contains less than 20% water.

SY Cuttings may have steeper slopes (to save land) than might seem 'natural' – planted with trees and shrubs to help hold the slope material together. The vegetation not only looks attractive but screens traffic noise too. Very steep and vertical walled cuttings in urban areas have to be concreted.

P.148–149 The unstable earth: plate tectonics

1. (a) The earth's crust is its outer rocky shell. (b) The mantle is the hot, dense semi-molten rock beneath the crust. (c) A tectonic plate is a rigid crustal segment of varying size and shape that floats on the mantle beneath. 2. The east coast of South America and the west coast of Africa show the tectonic jigsaw well.

P.150–151 Volcanoes

1. Magma is the molten rock of the upper mantle. Only when this erupts from the crust, whether on land or under the sea, does it get called lava. 2. Disadvantages of volcanic activity include the death, injury and destruction caused by lava flows, hot ash, dust and lahars. Advantages, however, include new land created by coastal lava flows, soils fertilised by ash falls, tourist potential on and around the least violent active volcanoes, plus geothermal energy potential and related mineral deposits.

SY Mount Etna's eruptive history is well documented. The immediate dangers during any eruption are followed by the lasting effects of destroyed farmland and, to a lesser extent, property. But the benefits can also be both short- and long-term. Recent eruptions have become 'media circuses', much to the benefit of local hoteliers. Long-term benefits relate to the area's agriculture and tourism, as outlined above.

P.152–153 Earthquakes

1. Earthquakes occur along constructive, destructive and conservative plate boundaries. 2. The focus of a 'quake is the point within the crust that fractures when tensions relating to frictional forces are released explosively. The epicentre is the earth's surface directly above this point which suffers the greatest impact of the 'quake. 3. In the hours following a major 'quake many shocked survivors, whether physically injured or not, are unlikely to receive help from over-stretched emergency relief services. Desperate searches for relatives buried amongst the rubble are understandable – but often ill-advised. The danger of aftershocks causing further collapses is ever present. Indeed, it has been known for survivors to take refuge in a weakened building only for the structure to collapse, with fatal consequences, during an aftershock.

P.156–157 Drought

1. A drought is a period of continuous dry weather. It is a climatic hazard particularly common in areas with unreliable rainfall such as the Sahel region of Africa.

SY Emergency food aid from EMDCs to a sub-Saharan country facing a major drought could be thought of as a moral obligation – certainly an honourable and decent humanitarian gesture. However, long-term food aid is counter-productive. Very often, for example, temperate cereals are unsuited to the dietary requirements of people from tropical latitudes. But the main problem is the harm done to local agriculture. This is because the value of domestically produced farm products collapses if 'free' donated alternatives are available. Long-term aid, therefore, should be directed at promoting the recovery of local food production.

P.158–159 Desertification

1. D-B-E-A-C. 2. D

SY Rainfall variations from year to year have a marked effect on determining whether the Sahara Desert's southern margin advances or retreats. This is because grassland in the semi-desert Sahel region has proved remarkably tolerant to rapid recovery once rain falls following a drier period. The real danger comes from population pressure. This forces too many to rear animals and to cultivate this marginal land. The Sahel is fragile at best and so likely to degrade rapidly if overused.

P.160-161 Global warming: the greenhouse effect

1. The four main greenhouse gases are CO_2 and nitrogen oxides emitted from the burning of fossil fuels, CFCs from fridges and aerosols and methane from cattle and padi fields. 2. Global warming is a climatic hazard affecting the whole world. Only international cooperation to limit future emissions of greenhouse gases will address the problems we all face relating to climatic change and sea level rise.

SY More and more producers of everything from toiletries to fast food are helping us all make informed choices. Indeed, such is the growing environmental awareness of teenagers and young adults that it is proving very good business to promote 'environmentally friendly' products. Mass individual awareness, not just about global warming and the deterioration of the ozone layer, but about all environmental issues, can, therefore, change our world for the better!

INDEX

accessibility 3, 12, 43, 52, 82, 83, 100, 129
acid rain 70, 71
Afghanistan (birth/death rates) 8
aid 9, 88, 90-91, 92, 135, 156
altitude 3, 122, 127, 132
Amazonia/Amazon Basin, Brazil (farming) 12, 43
anticyclones 124-125
appropriate technology 14, 68, 88-89
arêtes 109
Aswan High Dam, Egypt (multi-purpose river project) 6, 7, 47, 56-57, 68
atmosphere 3, 118, 120, 126, 136, 150, 161
Australia (disaster prevention/drought) 137, 156-157
avalanches 100, 134, 135, 144, 146-147

Bangladesh (flooding) 137, 140, 141, 142-143
  (population density) 3
  (rice farming) 12, 45
beaches 114
birth rates 8, 9, 26, 29, 93
Brazil (biomass energy) 69
  (industry) 72, 83
  (rainforest destruction) 129
  (shifting cultivation) 43
business parks 87

Calcutta, India (millionaire city) 25, 28, 29
Caribbean (emigration) 16, 17
  (tropical revolving storms) 138-139
caves 107, 113
central business district (CBD) 22, 23, 30, 32, 39
Chernobyl, Ukraine (nuclear disaster) 66, 67
climate 2, 3, 41, 122, 126-127, 134
  British 48, 122, 127
  climatic change 42, 129, 143, 156, 158, 160-161
  equatorial 44, 128
  hot desert 132-133
  Mediterranean 52
  microclimate 126, 127
  monsoon 3, 12, 45, 142
  tropical continental 130-131
coasts 112-115
  management 115
Columbia (volcanic mudflow/lahar) 145
commuter villages 33, 77
conflicts of interest 102-103
contingency planning 136, 137, 147, 153, 154, 155
conurbations 20
Copenhagen, Denmark (urban planning) 34-35
coriolis forces 124, 125, 136
correlation 94
corries 109

death rates 8, 9, 13, 26, 93
deforestation 129, 140, 142, 145, 159
demographic transition model 8, 9
deposition 110-111, 112, 114, 116, 117
depressions 123, 124-125

desertification 42, 54, 68, 129, 130, 158-159
deserts 57, 132-133, 156
development 92-95
diets 8, 11, 13, 45, 93
disasters 16, 134, 137, 138-139, 145, 146, 154-155
discrimination 17, 19
diseases 8, 12, 13, 14, 15, 29, 57, 67, 88
drought 130, 134, 156-157
drumlins 110

earthquakes 3, 134, 143, 144, 148, 149, 151, 152-155
economic development 72, 89, 90, 92-95, 129
ecosystems 128
education 8, 9, 15, 26, 89, 92, 93, 95
Egypt (Aswan High Dam) 47, 56, 57, 68
  (disease) 13
  (population) 6, 7, 10
employment structure 72
energy 58-71
  alternative and renewable 58, 64, 68, 69, 70, 71, 72, 151
  coal 58, 60, 61, 68, 71, 75, 76, 77, 82, 83, 88, 93, 161
  electricity 58, 59, 60, 61, 65, 68, 75
  fossil fuels 58, 69, 70, 72, 75, 93, 160, 161
  hydroelectric power (HEP) 56, 64, 65, 70, 71, 88
  natural gas 61, 62, 63, 68, 71, 161
  nuclear 66-67, 68, 70, 71
  petroleum (oil) 58, 62, 63, 68, 71, 88, 93
  resources 3, 52, 67, 96
  supergrid 58, 59, 75
enterprise zones 36, 79, 81, 83
environments 128-133
erosion 108, 109, 112, 113, 115, 116, 117
  soil 129, 158, 159
erratics 110
Ethiopia (population) 4, 91
  (semi-desert) 12, 156
European Union (EU)
  Common Agricultural Policy (CAP) 48, 49, 50, 51, 53
  immigration 18, 19
  Mezzogiorno, Italy 52-53
  trade 97

farming (agriculture) 2, 3, 9, 12, 40-57
  economic development 92, 93
  ELDC 12, 42-45, 156
  environmental damage 129, 147, 159
  'Green Revolution' 46-47
  in National Parks 103, 105
  systems 40, 41
  transhumance 16
  UK 48, 49
fire 100, 131, 134, 157
floods 3, 13, 26, 61, 65, 119, 134, 139, 140-143
  flood plains 3, 20, 45, 116, 117, 142
  Nile, River 6, 56, 57
  prevention 135, 137

freeze-thaw cycles 108, 144
fronts 123, 124

General Agreement on Tariffs and Trade (GATT) 97
Geographical Information Systems (GIS) 120
Germany (Turkish immigration) 18, 19
glaciers 100, 108-111, 145
global warming 129, 138, 143, 160-161
gorges 107, 117
government intervention 75, 79, 80, 81, 86
green belts and wedges 33, 34
gross domestic/national product (GDP/GNP) 79, 92, 93, 94, 95

Hadley Cell 126, 127, 132
Hawaii (volcanoes) 135, 150, 151
hazards 134-161
honeypots 103, 104-105
Human Development Index (HDI) 94-95
hydrological (water) cycle 118

Ice Ages 107, 108, 161
India (overcrowding) 27, 28
  (rice farming) 45, 46
  (solar energy) 69
Industrial Revolution 8, 21, 24, 36, 38, 77, 78, 96
  pollution 81, 161
industry 58, 59, 72-91
  decentralisation 76
  deindustrialisation 79, 80, 81
  development 50, 53, 68, 79, 88-89, 90
  footloose 86
  high technology 86-87, 88
  informal service sector 27
  iron and steel 72, 81, 82-83
  manufacturing 27, 28, 59, 72, 81, 82, 88, 89, 92, 93, 96
  service sector 72, 92, 93, 99, 100
  systems and location factors 74, 75, 76
infrastructure 77, 87, 90, 100, 101
inner city 31, 32, 34, 35, 77
Italy (landslide disaster) 145
  (*Mount Etna, Sicily*) 151

Japan (earthquake preparedness/Kobe) 152, 153, 154-155
  (economic development) 9, 86, 97

Kenya (tourism) 101
Kingston upon Hull, UK (traffic management) 39
  (urban settlement) 21

land reform 12, 53
land-use models 30-31
landforms 106-117
landslides 100, 134, 143, 144
latitude 84, 122, 128, 132, 136
leaching 55, 70, 129
leisure and recreation 49, 51, 98, 102-105
life expectancy 11, 95
limestone 105, 106-107
London Docklands, UK (urban redevelopment) 36-37

longitude 84
longshore drift 114-115

magma 150
Malaysia (plantation farming) 44
malnutrition 13, 15, 54, 93
markets 12, 74, 75, 88
mass movements 144-147
meltwater 107, 110
Mercalli Scale 152
Mexico (Hurricane Gilbert) 138-139
Mezzogiorno, Italy (EU problem region) 19, 52-53
migration 8, 16-19, 26, 29, 42, 135, 156
    guest workers 18, 19
    immigration 11, 17, 18, 19
millionaire and super cities 25, 28
moraines 105, 110
multi-cultural society 17
multinational companies 88, 90-91, 96

National Parks 80, 101, 102-105
    Lake District 111
    Peak District 102
    Snowdonia 65, 109, 111
    Yorkshire Dales 104-105, 106, 107
natural hazards 3, 26, 134-161
new towns 86
nutrient cycle 128

Ordnance Survey maps 84-85
outwash plains 110
overgrazing 42, 130, 159
ox-bow lakes 117
ozone layer 161

Pacific Rim countries (trade) 97
permeable and impermeable rocks 106, 107, 118, 119, 140
pests 3, 12, 13, 26, 42, 47, 54, 134
Philippines ('miracle rice') 46
Physical Quality of Life Index (PQLI) 95
planning 34-37
    industrial 74, 75, 79
    tourist 101, 105
    urban 23, 34-37
pollution
    atmospheric 11, 34, 38, 55, 67, 69, 70, 71, 80, 99, 147, 160
    oil 62, 63
    visual 61, 71, 80
    water 13, 14, 54, 71
population 2-15
    control 7, 9
    density 2, 33, 142, 154
    dependency ratios 10, 11, 93
    distribution 2, 6
    ELDC 4, 8, 9, 10, 11, 12, 13, 14
    EMDC 4, 8, 9, 10, 11, 13
    'explosion' 4
    growth 4, 6, 7, 8, 9, 12, 29, 46, 68, 92, 93, 129, 134, 161
    natural increase 6, 8
    optimum 7
    overpopulation 7, 43, 54

planning 8, 11, 26
problems 6, 11, 43, 159
pyramids 10
rural depopulation 100
precipitation 118, 119, 120, 122, 124, 125, 126, 128
    associated problems 132, 133, 140, 144, 147, 150, 156, 157, 158
    types 123, 136
prevailing winds 122, 127, 132
primary health care 7, 14-15
pyramidal peaks 100, 109

recreation 102-105
refugees 16, 19
relief 3, 88, 123
resources 2, 3, 7, 52, 72, 88, 90, 92, 129
ribbon lakes 110
Richter Scale 152, 154, 155
rivers 107, 109, 116-117
    flooding 140, 142
    river (drainage) basins 118-119
Rostow's model 92
Rwanda (forced migration) 16

Sahel, Africa (desertification) 156, 158-159
    (farming) 42
savanna grasslands 130-131
science parks 87
Scotland (micro-electronics) 86
    (soil erosion) 55
settlement 2, 3, 20-33, 77, 129
    hierarchy 22, 23
    services 22, 23
shanty towns 14, 16, 26, 27, 29
site and service schemes 27
site and situation 20, 21
soil
    alluvial 3, 6, 45, 56, 117, 140
    conservation 14, 47, 53, 55
    creep 144
    erosion 54, 55, 68, 101, 129, 158
    farming 41, 46, 48
    rainforest 128, 129
    volcanic 150, 151
South Wales (industrial redevelopment) 75, 80-81, 82
    (earthflow disaster) 145
    (OS map) 84-85
Spain (tourism) 98, 99
storm hydrographs 118-119
supplies 20, 52, 82, 88, 133
swallow hole 106
Switzerland (avalanches) 147
    (tourism) 100, 109
synoptic (weather) charts 120-121, 136, 137

tariffs 97
tarns 109
technology 7
tectonic plates 3, 148-149, 150, 152
temperatures 122, 126, 127
    desert 132
    frontal rainfall 123
    ocean 136

rainforest 123
tidal storm surges 137, 140, 142
tourism 98-101
    ELDC 57, 89, 101
    EMDC 100, 151
    EU 50, 52
trade 96-97
    agreements 50, 97
    ELDC 57, 88
    world 90, 93, 96-97
trade winds 133, 136
transport 38-39
    congestion 23, 29, 34, 35, 38, 75, 77, 99, 100, 102, 139
    economic growth 92, 93
    energy 58, 62
    farming 44, 48
    industrial 74, 75, 77, 82, 83, 88, 89
    management 39
    modes 31, 36, 38
tropical rainforest 3, 43, 128-129, 160, 161
tropical revolving storms 3, 134, 136-139
tsunamis 134, 142, 143

undernourishment 13, 54
unemployment 19, 26, 27, 81, 83, 99
United Kingdom (climate) 122, 123, 124, 125
    (economic development) 9, 11
    (energy) 59, 60, 61, 62, 63, 65, 66, 67
    (farming) 46, 48
    (industry) 72, 74, 75, 77, 78, 79, 82, 83, 86, 87
    (land-use) 32, 33, 34
    (migration) 16, 17, 18, 19
    (tourism) 99, 102
United Nations Organisation 13, 14, 16, 27
United States of America (energy) 66, 67, 151
    (industry) 76, 86, 87
    (natural hazards) 137, 138-139, 152, 153
urbanisation 16, 24, 26, 135
    counter-urbanisation 19, 24
    problems 26, 27, 34
    suburbanisation 19, 32, 33
urban redevelopment 32, 34-37, 39

valleys 107, 108, 109, 116
vegetation 3, 128, 130, 131, 133, 145, 159
    xerophytic 130-131
volcanoes 134, 143, 148, 149, 150-151

wars 16, 18
water 118-119
waterfalls 107, 109, 116
watersheds 118
wave cut platforms 113
waves 112, 113, 114
weather 120-125, 126, 134, 140
weathering 106, 108, 113, 144
world development 92-95
World Health Organisation 15
World Trade Organisation (WTO) 97

xerophytic vegetation 130-131, 133